# WordPress 2.8 Theme Design

Create flexible, powerful, and professional themes for your WordPress blogs and websites

**Tessa Blakeley Silver**

PUBLISHING

BIRMINGHAM - MUMBAI

# WordPress 2.8 Theme Design

Copyright © 2009 Packt Publishing

All rights reserved. No part of this book may be reproduced, stored in a retrieval system, or transmitted in any form or by any means, without the prior written permission of the publisher, except in the case of brief quotations embedded in critical articles or reviews.

Every effort has been made in the preparation of this book to ensure the accuracy of the information presented. However, the information contained in this book is sold without warranty, either express or implied. Neither the author, nor Packt Publishing, and its dealers and distributors will be held liable for any damages caused or alleged to be caused directly or indirectly by this book.

Packt Publishing has endeavored to provide trademark information about all of the companies and products mentioned in this book by the appropriate use of capitals. However, Packt Publishing cannot guarantee the accuracy of this information.

First published: November 2009

Production Reference: 1201109

Published by Packt Publishing Ltd.
32 Lincoln Road
Olton
Birmingham, B27 6PA, UK.

ISBN 978-1-849510-08-0

www.packtpub.com

Cover Image by Vinayak Chittar (vinayak.chittar@gmail.com)

# Credits

**Author**
Tessa Blakeley Silver

**Reviewer**
Grigore Ioachim Alexandru

**Acquisition Editor**
David Barnes

**Development Editor**
Ved Prakash Jha

**Technical Editors**
Gaurav Datar
Conrad Sardinha

**Indexer**
Rekha Nair

**Editorial Team Leader**
Gagandeep Singh

**Project Team Leader**
Lata Basantani

**Project Coordinator**
Poorvi Nair

**Proofreader**
Sandra Hopper

**Graphics**
Nilesh R. Mohite

**Production Coordinator**
Shantanu Zagade

**Cover Work**
Shantanu Zagade

# About the Author

**Tessa Blakeley Silver's** background is in print design and traditional illustration. She evolved over the years into web and multimedia development, where she focuses on usability and interface design.

Tessa owns a consulting and development company hyper3media (also pronounced as hyper-cube media): `http://hyper3media.com`. Prior to starting her company, Tessa was the VP of Interactive Technologies at eHigherEducation—an online learning and technology company developing compelling multimedia simulations, interactions, and games, which met online educational requirements such as 508, AICC, and SCORM. She has also worked as a consultant and freelancer for J. Walter Thompson and The Diamond Trading Company (formerly known as DeBeers) and was a Design Specialist and Senior Associate for PricewaterhouseCoopers' East Region Marketing department.

Tessa has authored a few books for Packt Publishing, including *Joomla! 1.5 Template Design* (ISBN: 7160).

I send a huge "thank you" to the Packt team who has made this title possible and whose help in getting it out into the world has been invaluable. Special thanks to Ved, Grigore, Gaurav, and Conrad for their editing work. Additional thanks goes to Poorvi for her very hard work and diligence in keeping me to a schedule. I'd also like to thank the exemplary WordPress community and all who participate and power the open source world and strive to improve the accessibility of the Web for all. Additional thanks goes out to my very patient family who spent quite a few evenings without me while I worked on this title.

# About the Reviewer

**Grigore Ioachim Alexandru** is a web developer and an SEO engineer currently working at SITECONSTRUCT Romania, a web design company in Romania. He is studying at the FEAA college in the A.I.Cuza University in Iasi, learning economical sciences.

Alex sustained about 50 Romanian projects and an SEO book within the company he works at. Currently, Alex is actively developing his own blog as well as writing quality WordPress content and articles for various online resources.

You can follow Alex on Twitter at http://twitter.com/Designstrike.

I would like to say "thank you" to the team from Packt Publishing for giving me this opportunity to be a part of this project.

# Table of Contents

# Preface

This book will take you through the ins and outs of creating sophisticated, professional themes for the WordPress personal publishing platform. It will walk you through clear, step-by-step instructions to build a custom WordPress theme. This book reviews best practices in development tools and setting up your WordPress sandbox, through design tips and suggestions, to setting up your theme's template structure, coding markup, testing and debugging, to taking it live. The last three chapters are dedicated to additional tips and tricks for adding popular site enhancements to your WordPress theme designs using third-party plugins.

The WordPress publishing platform has excellent online documentation, which can be found at `http://codex.wordpress.org`. This title does not try to replace or duplicate that documentation, but is intended as a companion to it.

My hope is to save you some time finding relevant information on how to create and modify themes in the extensive WordPress codex, help you understand how WordPress themes work, and show you how to design and build rich, in-depth WordPress themes yourself. Throughout the book, wherever applicable, I'll point you to the relevant WordPress codex documentation along with many other useful book references, online articles, and sites.

I've attempted to create a realistic WordPress theme example that anyone can take the basic concepts from and apply to a standard blog, while at the same time, show how flexible WordPress and its theme capabilities are. I hope this book's theme example shows that WordPress can be used to create unique websites that one wouldn't think of as "just another blog".

Whether you're working with a preexisting theme or creating a new one from the ground up, this title will give you the know-how to understand how themes work within the WordPress blog system, enabling you to take full control over your site's design and branding.

I'd like to thank those of you in the WordPress community who took the time to read the first edition of this book and e-mailed me your comments along with posting your book reviews. This is your book.

# What this book covers

Chapter 1: *Getting Started as a WordPress Theme Designer* introduces you to the WordPress blog system and lets you know what you need to be aware of regarding the WordPress theme project you're ready to embark on. The chapter also covers the development tools that are recommended and web skills that you'll need to begin developing a WordPress theme.

Chapter 2: *Theme Design and Approach* looks at the essential elements you need to consider when planning your WordPress theme design. It discusses the best tools and processes for making your theme design a reality. The chapter explains some "rapid design comping" techniques and gives some tips and tricks for developing color schemes and graphic styles for your WordPress theme. By the end of the chapter, you'll have a working XHTML and CSS-based "comp" or mockup of your theme design, ready to be coded up and assembled into a fully functional WordPress theme.

Chapter 3: *Coding It Up* uses the final XHTML and CSS mockup from Chapter 2 and shows you how to add WordPress PHP template tag code to it and break it down into the template pages a theme requires. Along the way, this chapter covers the essentials of what makes a WordPress theme work and how to enable your theme to take advantage of new WordPress 2.8 features such as sticky posts and threaded comments. At the end of the chapter, you'll have a basic, working WordPress theme.

Chapter 4: *Debugging and Validation* discusses the basic techniques of debugging and validation that you should employ throughout your theme's development. It covers the W3C's XHTML and CSS validation services, along with how to use the Firefox browser and some of its extensions as a development tool, and not as just another browser. This chapter also covers troubleshooting some of the most common reasons "good code goes bad", especially in IE, along with best practices for fixing those problems, giving you a great-looking theme across all browsers and platforms.

Chapter 5: *Putting Your Theme into Action* discusses how to properly set up your WordPress theme's CSS stylesheet so that it loads into WordPress installations correctly. It also discusses compressing your theme files into the ZIP file format to share with the world and running some test installations of your theme in WordPress' Administration panel so that you can share your WordPress theme with the world.

Chapter 6: *WordPress Template Tag, Function, and CSS Reference* covers key information under easy-to-look-up headers that will help you with your WordPress theme development—from the CSS class styles that WordPress itself outputs, to WordPress' PHP template tags and plugin hooks, to a breakdown of "The Loop" along with additional WordPress functions and features such as shortcodes that you can take advantage of in your theme development. Information in this chapter is listed along with key links to bookmark, in order to make your theme development as easy as possible.

Chapter 7: *Ajax/Dynamic content and Interactive Forms* continues showing you how to enhance your WordPress theme by looking at the most popular methods for leveraging AJAX techniques in WordPress using plugins and widgets. It also gives you a complete background on AJAX and when it's best to use those techniques or skip them. The chapter also reviews some cool JavaScript toolkits, libraries, and scripts you can use to simply make your WordPress theme appear "Ajaxy".

Chapter 8: *Dynamic Menus and Interactive Elements* dives into taking your working, debugged, validated, and properly packaged WordPress theme from the earlier chapters, and enhancing it with dynamic menus using the SuckerFish CSS-based method and Adobe Flash media.

Chapter 9: *Design Tips for Working with WordPress* reviews the main tips from the previous chapters and covers some key tips for easily implementing today's coolest CSS tricks into your theme, as well as a few final SEO tips that you'll probably run into once you really start putting content into your WordPress site.

# What you need for this book

Essentially, you'll need a code editor, the latest Firefox browser, and any other web browser you would like your theme to be displayed in. Most importantly, you'll need an installation of the latest, stable version of WordPress.

WordPress 2.7+ and 2.8+ require the following to be installed:

- PHP version 4.3 or greater
- MySQL version 4.0 or greater

For more information on WordPress 2.8's requirements, browse to `http://wordpress.org/about/requirements/`.

You'll also need a code editor and an image editor such as GIMP, Photoshop, Fireworks, or Corel Paint (or any graphic editor you prefer really). This book covers samples using Photoshop and some samples in GIMP.

# Who this book is for

This book can be used by WordPress users or visual designers (with no server-side scripting or programming experience) who are used to working with the common industry-standard tools such as Photoshop and Dreamweaver, or other popular graphic, HTML, and text editors.

Regardless of your web development skill set or level, you'll be walked through the clear, step-by-step instructions, but familiarity with a broad range of web development skills and WordPress know-how will allow you to gain maximum benefit from this book.

# Conventions

In this book, you will find a number of styles of text that distinguish between different kinds of information. Here are some examples of these styles, and an explanation of their meaning.

Code words in text are shown as follows: "You have to add it to your theme's header.php or files that contain the header tags "

A block of code is set as follows (Code and markup preceded and ended with ellipses "..." are extracted from the full context of code and/or a larger body of code and markup. Please reference the downloadable code packet to see the entire work.):

```
...
#container {
    font-family: "Trebuchet MS", Arial, Helvetica, sans-serif;
}
...
```

When we wish to draw your attention to a particular part of a code block, the relevant lines or items will be shown in bold:

```
<form method="get" id="searchform" action="http://yourdevurl.com/">
<div><input value="" name="s" id="s" type="text">
<input id="searchsubmit" value="Search" type="submit">
</div>
</form>
```

**New terms** and **important words** are shown in bold. Words that you see on the screen, in menus or dialog boxes for example, appear in our text like this: "The best way to proceed with the **Error Console** is to first hit **Clear** and then reload your page to be sure that you're looking only at current bugs and issues for that specific page ".

Warnings or important notes appear in a box like this.

 Tips and tricks appear like this.

# Reader feedback

Feedback from our readers is always welcome. Let us know what you think about this book—what you liked or may have disliked. Reader feedback is important for us to develop titles that you really get the most out of.

To send us general feedback, simply drop an email to feedback@packtpub.com, and mention the book title in the subject of your message.

If there is a book that you need and would like to see us publish, please send us a note in the **SUGGEST A TITLE** form on www.packtpub.com or email suggest@packtpub.com.

If there is a topic that you have expertise in and you are interested in either writing or contributing to a book, see our author guide on www.packtpub.com/authors.

# Customer support

Now that you are the proud owner of a Packt book, we have a number of things to help you to get the most from your purchase.

 **Downloading the example code for the book**
Visit http://www.packtpub.com/files/code/0080_Code.zip to directly download the example code.
The downloadable files contain instructions on how to use them.

# Errata

Although we have taken every care to ensure the accuracy of our contents, mistakes do happen. If you find a mistake in one of our books—maybe a mistake in text or code—we would be grateful if you would report this to us. By doing so, you can save other readers from frustration, and help us to improve subsequent versions of this book. If you find any errata, please report them by visiting http://www.packtpub. com/support, selecting your book, clicking on the **let us know** link, and entering the details of your errata. Once your errata are verified, your submission will be accepted and the errata added to any list of existing errata. Any existing errata can be viewed by selecting your title from http://www.packtpub.com/support.

# Piracy

Piracy of copyright material on the Internet is an ongoing problem across all media. At Packt, we take the protection of our copyright and licenses very seriously. If you come across any illegal copies of our works in any form on the Internet, please provide us with the location address or website name immediately so that we can pursue a remedy.

Please contact us at copyright@packtpub.com with a link to the suspected pirated material.

We appreciate your help in protecting our authors, and our ability to bring you valuable content.

# Questions

You can contact us at questions@packtpub.com if you are having a problem with any aspect of the book, and we will do our best to address it.

# 1
# Getting Started as a WordPress Theme Designer

Welcome to WordPress theme design! This title is intended to take you through the ins and outs of creating sophisticated professional themes for the WordPress personal publishing platform. WordPress was originally, and is foremost, a blog system. Throughout the majority of this book's chapters—for simplicity's sake—I'll be referring to it as a blog or blog system. But don't be fooled! Since its inception, WordPress has evolved way beyond mere blogging capabilities and has many standard features that are expandable with plugins and widgets, which make it comparable to a full **CMS (Content Management System)**.

In these upcoming chapters, we'll walk through all the necessary steps required to aid, enhance, and speed your WordPress theme design process. From design tips and suggestions, to packaging up the final theme, we'll review the best practices for a range of topics—designing a great theme, rapid theme development, coding markup, testing, debugging, and taking it live.

The last three chapters are dedicated to additional tips, tricks, and various "how to" recipes for adding popular site enhancements to your WordPress theme designs using third-party plugins, as well as creating your own custom plugins.

## WordPress perks

As you're interested in generating custom themes for WordPress, you'll be very happy to know (especially all you web standards evangelists) that WordPress really does separate content from design.

You may already know from painful experience that many content management and blog systems end up publishing their content pre-wrapped in (sometimes large) chunks of layout markup (sometimes using table markup), peppered with all sorts of predetermined selector id and class names.

You usually have to do a fair amount of sleuthing to figure out what these id and classes are so that you can create custom CSS rules for them. This is very time consuming.

The good news is, WordPress publishes only two things:

- The site's textual content—the text you enter into the post and the page administration panels
- Supplemental site content wrapped in list tags—<li> and </li>—which usually links to the posts and pages you've entered and the meta information for those items

That's it! The list tags don't even have an ordered or unordered defining tag around them. WordPress leaves that up to you. You decide how everything published via WordPress is styled and displayed.

The culmination of all those styling and display decisions, along with special WordPress template tags that pull your site's content into you design, are what your WordPress theme consists of.

# Does a WordPress site have to be a blog?

The answer to this question is—no. Even before the release of themes in WordPress 2.x, WordPress has been capable of managing static pages and subpages since version 1.5. Static pages are different from blog posts in that they aren't constrained by the chronology of posts. This means you can manage a wide variety of content with pages and their subpages.

WordPress also has a great community of developers supporting it with an ever-growing library of plugins. Using plugins, you can expand the capabilities of your server-installed WordPress site to include infinite possibilities such as event calendars, image galleries, sidebar widgets, and even shopping carts. For just about anything you can think of, you can probably find a WordPress plugin to help you out.

By considering how you want to manage content via WordPress, what kind of additional plugins you might employ, and how your theme displays all that content, you can easily create a site that is completely unique and original in concept as well as design.

Again, WordPress was built to be a blog system, and it has some great blog post and category tools. But if you want to use it to manage a brochure-style site, have a particular third-party plugin to be the main feature of your site, and downplay or even remove the blog, that's fine too! You'll just tweak your theme's template files to display your content the way you prefer (which is something you'll be very good at after reading this book).

# Pick a theme or design your own?

I approach theme design from two angles.

- **Simplicity**: Sometimes it suits the client and/or the site to go as bare-bones as possible. In that case, it's quick and easy to use a very basic, already built theme and modify it.

- **Unique and Beautiful**: Occasionally, the site's theme needs to be created from scratch so that everything displayed caters to the specific kind of content the site offers. This ensures that the site is something eye-catching, which no one else will have. This is often the best route when custom branding is a priority or you just want to show off your "Hey, I'm hot-stuff" design skills.

There are many benefits to using or tweaking already built themes. First, you save a lot of time getting your site up with a nice theme design. Second, you don't need to know as much about CSS, XHTML, or PHP. This means that with a little web surfing, you can have your WordPress site up and running with a stylish look in no time at all.

# Drawbacks to using an already built theme

The drawback to using an already built theme is that it may not save you as much time as you would hope for. You may realize, even with the new header text and graphic, several other sites may have downloaded and/or purchased it for themselves and you don't stand apart enough.

Perhaps your site needs a special third-party plugin for a specific type of content; it might not look quite right without a lot of tweaking. And while we're discussing tweaking, I find that every CSS designer is different and sets up their theme's template files and stylesheets accordingly. While it makes perfect sense to them, it can be confusing and time consuming to work through.

Your approach may have started out as *simplicity*, but then, for one reason or another, you find yourself having to dig deeper and deeper through the theme and pretty soon it doesn't feel like quick tweaking anymore. Sometimes you realize—for simplicity's sake (no pun intended)—it would have been a whole lot quicker to start from scratch.

Before trying to cut corners with a preexisting theme, make sure your project really is as *simple* as it claims to be. Once you find a theme, check that you are allowed to tweak and customize it (such as an open source or Creative Commons license or royalty free purchase from a template site), and that you have a look at the stylesheet and template files. Make sure the theme's assets seem logical and make sense to you.

# Using theme frameworks

Theme frameworks are wonderful in that they provide the core functionality of a theme, already started for you. The idea is they let you create child themes off the main theme, which you can then easily style to your liking.

They're particularly useful to designers who are short on time, very good with CSS, and don't want to deal with the learning curve of having to understand WordPress' **template tags, hooks**, and **template page hierarchy**.

The whole point of this book is to introduce you to the above concepts and introduce you to the basics of WordPress theme features so that you can create elegant comprehensive themes from scratch. You can then see how getting a little creative will enable you to develop any kind of site you can imagine with WordPress. You'll also be able to better take advantage of a theme framework, as you'll understand what the framework is accomplishing for you "under the hood" , and you would also be able to better customize the framework if you'd like to.

For many frameworks, there is still some amount of learning curve to getting up and running with them. But less of it will deal directly with futzing with PHP code to get WordPress to do what you want.

I'd encourage you to take a look at development with a framework and compare it to development from scratch. Having the skills this book provides you with under your belt will only help, even if you choose to go with a framework to save time.

**Popular theme frameworks to choose from:**

More and more frameworks show up every day, and each framework tries to address and handle slightly different focuses, features, and types of developers. As a bonus, some frameworks add options into the WordPress administration panel that allow the **end user** to add and remove features to/from the child theme they've selected.

You'll want to look at frameworks in terms of the options they offer that suit your development style, needs, and the overall community the framework caters to, to see if the framework is a good fit for your site's requirements.

**WPFramework** is a good general framework to start with (http://wpframework.com/). Its aim is to stay straightforward and simple, while cutting down theme development time.

If you're interested in a framework that offers a lot of child themes that can be easily tweaked with just CSS and will also add a lot of bells and whistles for the end user in the administration panel, you'll want to look at more robust frameworks such as **Carrington** (http://carringtontheme. com/), **Thematic** (http://themeshaper.com/thematic/), and **Hybrid** (http://themehybrid.com/).

These frameworks may appear a bit more complex at first, but offer a range of rich features for developing themes and, especially if you understand the essentials of creating WordPress themes (as you will after reading this book), can really aid you in speeding up your theme development.

Again, there are many theme frameworks available. A quick Google search for "WordPress Theme Frameworks" will turn up quite a plethora to choose from.

# This book's approach

The approach of this book is going to take you through the unique and beautiful route (or unique and awesome, whatever your design aesthetics call for) with the idea that once you know how to create a theme from scratch, you'll be more apt at understanding what to look for in other WordPress themes. You'll then be able to assess when it really is better or easier to use an already built theme versus building up something of your own from scratch.

# Core technology you should understand

This book is geared toward visual designers (with no server-side scripting or programming experience) who are used to working with the common industry standard tools such as Photoshop and Dreamweaver or other popular graphic, HTML, and text editors.

Regardless of your web development skillset or level, you'll be walked through clear, step-by-step instructions. But there are many web development skills and WordPress know-how that you'll need to be familiar with to gain maximum benefit from this book.

# WordPress

Most importantly, you should already be familiar with the most current stable version of WordPress. You should understand how to add content to the WordPress blog system and how its posts, categories, static pages, and subpages work. Understanding the basics of installing and using plugins will also be helpful (though we will cover that to some extent in the later chapters of the book as well).

Even if you'll be working with a more technical WordPress administrator, you should have an overview of what the WordPress site that you're designing entails, and what (if any) additional plugins or widgets will be needed for the project. If your site does require additional plugins and widgets, you'll want to have them handy and/or installed in your WordPress development installation (or **sandbox**—a place to test and play without messing up a live site). This will ensure that your design will cover all the various types of content that the site intends to provide.

What version of WordPress 2.x does this book use? This book focuses on WordPress 2.7 and 2.8. Everything covered in this book has been tested and checked in WordPress 2.8.5. You may occasionally note screenshots from version 2.7 being used, but rest assured, any key differences between 2.8, 2.7, and even 2.5 are clearly noted when applicable. While this book's case study is developed using version 2.7 and 2.8, any newer version should have the same core capabilities, enabling you to develop themes for it using these techniques. Bug fixes and new features for each new version of WordPress are documented at http://WordPress.org.

If you are new to WordPress, then I recommend you read *WordPress Complete* by April Hodge Silver.

# CSS

I'll be giving detailed explanations of the CSS rules and properties used in this book, and the "how and why" behind those decisions. You should know a bit about what CSS is, and the basics of setting up a cascading stylesheet and including it within an XHTML page. You'll find that the more comfortable you are with CSS markup and how to use it effectively with XHTML, the better will be your WordPress theme-creating experience.

# XHTML

You don't need to have every markup tag in the XHTML standard memorized. (If you really want, you can still switch to the Design view in your HTML editor to drop in those markup tags that you keep forgetting—I won't tell). However, the more XHTML basics you understand, the more comfortable you'll be working in the Code view of your HTML editor or with a plain text editor. The more you work directly with the markup, the quicker you'll be able to create well-built themes that are quick loading, semantic, expand easily to accommodate new features, and are search engine friendly.

# PHP

You definitely don't have to be a PHP programmer to get through this book, but be aware that WordPress uses liberal doses of PHP to work its magic! A lot of this PHP code will be directly visible in your theme's various template files. PHP code is needed to make your theme work with your WordPress installation, as well as make individual template files work with your theme.

If you at least understand how basic PHP syntax is structured, you'll be much less likely to make mistakes while retyping or copying and pasting code snippets of PHP and WordPress template tags into your theme's template files. You'll be able to more easily recognize the difference between your template files, XHTML, and PHP snippets so that you don't accidentally delete or overwrite anything crucial.

If you get more comfortable with PHP, you'll have the ability to change out variables and call new functions or even create new functions on your own, again infinitely expanding the possibilities of your WordPress site.

**Beef up those web skills!**

I'm a big fan of the W3Schools site. If you'd like to build up your XHTML, CSS, and PHP understanding, you can use this site to walk you through everything from basic introductions to robust uses of top web languages and technologies. All the lessons are easy, comprehensive, and free at `http://w3schools.com`.

## Other helpful technologies

If your project will be incorporating any other special technologies such as JavaScript, AJAX, or Flash content, the more you know and understand how those scripting languages and technologies work, the better it is for your theme-making experience (again W3Schools.com is a great place to start).

The more web technologies you have a general understanding of, the more likely you'll be able to intuitively make a more flexible theme that will be able to handle anything you may need to incorporate into your site in the future.

**More of a visual "see it to do it" learner?**

Lynda.com has a remarkable course selection from the top CSS, XHTML/XML, JavaScript, PHP, and Flash/ActionScript people in the world. You can subscribe and take the courses online or purchase DVD-ROMs for offline viewing. The courses might seem pricey at first, but if you're a visual learner (as most designers are), it's worth spending money and time on them. You can refer to the official site `http://lynda.com`.

## Tools of the trade

In order to get started in the next chapter, you'll need the following tools to help you out:

# HTML editor

You'll need a good HTML editor. Dreamweaver is also a good option
(http://www.adobe.com/products/dreamweaver/), although I prefer to use Coda
for Mac (http://www.panic.com/coda/). When I was on a PC, I loved the free
text/code editor HTML-kit (http://www.htmlkit.com/). Any HTML or text editor
that lets you enable the following features will work just great. (I recommend you
enable all of the following):

- **View line numbers**: This comes in very handy during the validation and
  debugging process. It can help you find specific lines in a theme file, for
  which a validation tool has returned a fix. This is also helpful for other
  theme or plugin instructions given by the author, which refer to a specific
  line of code that needs editing.

- **View syntax colors**: Any worthwhile HTML editor has this feature usually
  set as a default. The good editors let you choose your own colors. It displays
  code and other markup in a variety of colors, making it easier to distinguish
  various types of syntax. Many editors also help you identify broken XHTML
  markup, CSS styles, or PHP code.

- **View non-printing characters**: You might not want this feature turned on
  all the time. It makes it possible to see hard returns, spaces, tabs, and other
  special characters that you may or may not want in your markup and code.

- **Text wrapping**: This of course lets you wrap text within the window, so you
  won't have to scroll horizontally to edit a long line of code. It's best to learn
  what the key-command shortcut is for this feature in your editor, and/or
  set up a key-command shortcut for it. You'll find it easier to scroll through
  unwrapped, nicely-indented, markup and PHP code to quickly get a general
  overview or find your last stopping point; however, you will still want to turn
  it on quickly so that you can see and focus your attention on one long line
  of code.

**Open source HTML editors:** I've also used Nvu (`http://www.net2.com/nvu/`) and Kompozer (`http://kompozer.net/`). They're both free, open source, and available for Mac, PC, and Linux platforms. Kompozer was made from the same source as Nvu and, apparently, fixes some issues that Nvu has. (I haven't run into any major issue with Nvu myself; both editors are a bit limited for my regular use, but I do like being able to format XHTML text quickly and drag-and-drop form objects onto a page.) Both editors have a **Source** view, but you must be careful while switching between the **Normal** and the **Source** view tabs! Nvu and Kompozer are a little too helpful, and will try to rewrite your handcoded markup if you haven't set your preferences properly!

Linux users of Ubuntu and Debian (and Mac users with Fink) might also be interested in checking out Bluefish editor (`http://bluefish.openoffice.nl`). I haven't used it myself, but the site's writeup looks great.

# Graphic editor

The next piece of software you'll need is a graphic editor. While you can find plenty of CSS-only WordPress themes out there, chances are that you'll want to expand on your design a little more and add nice visual enhancements. These are best achieved by using a graphic editor such as GIMP, Photoshop, or Fireworks. Adobe owns both Photoshop and Fireworks and also offers a light and less-expensive version of Photoshop, called Photoshop Elements that will allow you to do everything I discuss in this book (`http://www.adobe.com/products/`).

While I'm an advocate of open source software and enjoy working with GIMP, in my line of work, the industry standard is Photoshop or Fireworks. I'll be using Adobe Photoshop in this title and assume that you have some familiarity with it or GIMP and working with layers. Any graphic editor you prefer is fine. One that allows you to work with layers is very helpful, especially with the design comping (or mockup) techniques I suggest in Chapter 2.

If you need a graphic editor, then you can try GIMP. If you're on a budget and in need of a good image editor, I'd recommend it. It's available for PC, Mac, and Linux. You can get it from `http://gimp.org/`.

On the other hand, if you prefer vector art, then try Inkscape, which is also available for PC, Mac, and Linux. Bitmap graphic editors are great in that they also let you enhance and edit photographs. But if you just want to create buttons or other interface elements and vector-based illustrations, Inkscape is worth trying out (`http://inkscape.org`).

# Firefox

Finally, you'll need a web browser. Here, I'm not so flexible. I strongly suggest that you use the latest stable version of the Firefox browser, available at `http://mozilla.com/firefox/`.

Now one may ask *why use Firefox?* I view this browser as a great tool for web developers. It's as essential as my HTML editor, graphics, and FTP programs. Firefox has great features that we'll be taking advantage of to help us streamline the design creation and theme development process. In addition to those built-in features such as the DOM Source Selection Viewer and adhering to CSS2 standards as specified by the W3C, Firefox also has a host of extremely useful extensions such as the Web Developer's Toolbar and Firebug, which I recommend to further enhance your workflow.

**Get the extensions:**

You can get the Web Developer's Toolbar from `https://addons.mozilla.org/en-US/firefox/addon/60` and Firebug from `https://addons.mozilla.org/en-US/firefox/addon/1843`. Be sure to visit the developers' sites to learn more about each of these extensions.

# Developing for Firefox first

Don't worry, we won't forget about all those other browsers! However, in addition to Firefox having all the helpful features and extensions, IE has a thing called **quirks mode**, which we will learn all about in Chapter 4. While Microsoft has attempted a lot of improvements and tried to become more W3C compliant with IE7 and now IE8, there are still *some* CSS rendering issues between these IE browsers and others.

Your best bet will be to design for Firefox first and then, if you notice that things don't look so great in IE6, IE7, or IE8, there are plenty of "standardized" fixes and workarounds for these three browsers because their "quirks" are just that—wonks and well documented.

As we'll learn in Chapter 4, if you design looking at only one version of IE, then find it a mess in Firefox, Opera, or Safari, or the new Google Chrome you're going to have a much harder time fixing the CSS you made for IE in a more "standards-compliant" browser.

Firefox doesn't have to become your *only* browser. You can keep using IE or any other browser you prefer. I myself prefer Opera for light and speedy web surfing, but it doesn't handle all pages perfectly. As a designer on Mac who works with and for other creative Mac-based professionals, I regularly check my work in Safari. Firefox is one of my key web development tools.

# Summary

To get going on your WordPress theme design, you'll want to understand how the WordPress blog system works, and have your head wrapped around the basics of the WordPress project you're ready to embark on. If you'll be working with a more technical WordPress administrator and/or PHP developer, make sure your development installation or sandbox will have the same WordPress plugins that the final site needs to have. You'll want to have all the recommended tools installed and ready to use, as well as brush up on those web skills, especially XHTML and CSS. Get ready to embark on designing a great theme for one of the most popular, open source blog systems available for the Web today!

# 2

# Theme Design and Approach

Welcome to this chapter on theme design and approach. My hope for this chapter is that even you design pros may discover interesting tidbits that will help you in your WordPress theme design creation. The purpose of this chapter is to help you create a working XHTML and CSS-based mockup, with a view to having it end up being a WordPress theme while staying compliant with W3C standards and table-less CSS layout techniques.

Theme design is essentially web design and, throughout the chapter, we'll be focusing a bit more on thinking about standards and compliance first. The first part of the approach will cover what we want to design for (keeping in mind it will end up in WordPress) and the second half will focus more on creating a design that is made with the content in mind.

This approach will give us a more flexible, yet solid XHTML and CSS structure. We'll then be able to enhance and embellish that structure with great visual design. The more "standard" approach most of us are familiar with makes us create a purely visual design first and then jump through hoops to create XHTML and CSS to support that design. We then attempt to fit content into the design, often causing a few more glitches along the way. This approach often creates less-than-ideal markup and the need for hacks and fixes, just to get the design to hold up across all browsers and varying types of content.

While you might find this approach a little strange at first, it's by no means set in stone as the only right way to design! Simply read through the chapter and, even if you already have a polished Photoshop or GIMP mockup, go ahead and try to set up your XHTML and CSS mockup using the steps laid out in this chapter. You may find it helps your process.

In this chapter, we're going to take a look at:

- The essential elements you need to consider when planning your theme design
- The best tools and process for making that design a reality
- An introduction to my own **rapid design comping** strategy
- Some tips and tricks to help you define your color scheme and graphic style
- Some standard techniques for slicing and extracting images for your design

By the end of this chapter, you'll have a working XHTML-and CSS-based "comp" or mockup of your WordPress theme's design, ready to be coded up and assembled into a fully functional WordPress theme.

**Already got a design? Not a designer at all?**

That's fine! This chapter covers the ins and outs of web design best practices, with a view to ending up with a unique and custom WordPress theme. It contains time honored and tested methods for approaching compliant, accessible XHTML and CSS creation. If you're a total XHTML/ CSS design wizard, you can skim this chapter for any new tips and tricks that might be of use to you and then move on to Chapter 3.

If you're not a designer at all and you just need to convert an existing XHTML/CSS template into WordPress, I'd still recommend you skim this chapter, as it may help you better understand some of the XHTML markup and CSS in your template. You can then move on to Chapter 3 to learn how to code up and dice working XHTML and CSS templates and mockups into WordPress.

# Things to consider

First up, before we start, I'll acknowledge that you probably already have a design idea in mind and would like to just start producing it. Chances are that unless you're learning theme development solely for yourself, you probably have a client or maybe a website partner who would like to have input on the design. If you have neither, congratulations! — you're your own client. Whenever you see me reference "the client", just switch your perspective from that of a "theme designer" to "website user".

At any rate, before you start working on that design idea, take a moment to start a checklist and really think about two things:

- What type of site/blog the theme is going to be applied to
- What, if any, plugins or widgets might be used within the theme

# Types of blogs

Let's take a look at the following types of blogs (regular sites fit these types as well). These are not genres. Within these types of blog sites, you can apply any genre you can think of—horseback riding, cooking, programming, and so on.

You may be designing a theme for a specific site that has a targeted genre. You may want to make a generic theme that anyone can download and use. Still, if you target your theme to fit one of the types of blogs below, you might get more downloads of it just because it's more targeted. There's a reason why Brian Gardner's Revolution WordPress Theme is one of the top-rated themes for online news and magazine sites (http://www.revolutiontheme.com/). People who want to start a magazine or news blog know that this theme will work for their type of site. There's no need for them to look through dozens or even hundreds of more generic themes, wondering if they can modify them to accommodate their site.

Just read through the following blog types and notice which one of these types your theme fits into. Knowing this will help you determine how the content should be structured and how that might affect your theme's design.

- **The professional expert site**: This is an individual who blogs in their area of expertise to increase their personal exposure and standing. The type of design that can be applied to this site is diverse, depending on the type of expertise and what people's expectations are from that genre. For example, lawyers will have more people who are just content searchers; the cleaner and more basic the design, the better. Designers need to give the user a great visual experience in addition to the content. People in media might want to create a theme design that lends itself to listening to or viewing podcasts.

- **The corporate blog**: It's a company that blogs to reach customers and encourage closer relationships, sales, and referrals. Here, the user is actually a content searcher, so you might think a site that's simpler and focuses on text would do better. They just need the specific information about products and services, and maybe would like the opportunity to post a comment to a relevant blog post by the corporation. However, the corporation that is paying you to design the theme is really hoping to further engage the user with a great site experience and immerse them in their brand.

- **Online news source/magazine**: This is a blog that provides content on a particular topic, usually funded by ads. The design for this kind of site depends on how traditional the news content is or how appropriate the content is to put into a magazine. People looking for news and the latest updates in a genre might prefer theme designs that remind them of the experience of reading a newspaper, while magazine readers — especially for fashion, travel, people, and "bleeding-edge" technology — tend to like the site for the design experience of it as well as its content. Just pick up a paper version of any current news source or magazine and you will quickly become aware of what people in that genre are expecting.

- **The Campaign Blog**: These are the non-profit blogs run by charities or "causes". The information needs to be structured for clarity and winning people over to understanding and campaigning the cause or candidate. Most users will be content searchers and, while being appreciative of a nice and clean content structure and design experience depending on the campaign or cause, users may become critical if the site is too well designed. A user may think: "This is nice, but is it where they spend the money I donate, instead of on the cause!"

Keeping the above types of sites/blogs in mind, you can now think about your design idea and assess how appropriate it is for the type of blog or site, the kind of experience you want to give to users, as well as what you might think of the user's expectation about what the content and experience should be like.

# Plugins and widgets

The second consideration you'll want to make is about plugins and widgets. Plugins are special files that make it easy to add extra functions and features to your WordPress site. Widgets are now built into WordPress 2+ and are basically things you can put into your WordPress site's sidebar, regardless of knowing any HTML or PHP.

Plugins and widgets usually place requirements on a theme. The theme should have basic **API hooks** in place so that it can take advantage of all a WordPress plugin may have to offer. Certain CSS classes may be generated and placed into the site for headers or special text areas; a template file in the theme might need some specific PHP code to accommodate a plugin.

In Chapter 3, we'll cover the most important API hooks that will make your theme play well with most WordPress plugins. However, you should find out the theme requirements of any plugin or widget that you plan to use so that you may accommodate it when you write code for your theme.

**What kinds of plugins are available?**

You can see all the types of plugins available on the WordPress.org site, identifying them by their tags (`http://wordpress.org/extend/plugins/tags/`).

**Find out more about widgets:**

You'll be able to see a sample of widgets, as well as find out the requirements for a widget compatible theme at `http://widgets.wordpress.com/`. This will walk you through "widgetizing" (we'll cover widgetizing our theme in Chapter 8).

When you begin working on your design, you'll want to compare your sketches and design comp(s) against your plugins and widgets checklist, and make sure you're accommodating them.

**Design Comp** (abbreviation used in design and print): A preliminary design or sketch is a "comp," comprehensive artwork, or composite. It is also known as comp, comprehensive, mockup, sample, or dummy.

# Getting ready to design

You may already have a design process similar to the one I detail next; if so, just skim what I have to say and skip down to the next main heading. I have a feeling, though, that many of you will find this design comping technique a bit unorthodox, but bear with me; it really works.

Here's how this process came about. Whether or not you design professionally for clients or for yourself, you can probably identify with parts of this experience.

# A common problem

Up until a couple of years ago, in order to mock up a site design, I loaded up Photoshop and began a rather time-consuming task of laying down the design's graphical elements and layout samples, which entailed managing text layers. However, this sometimes ended up being a very large amount of layers, most of which were just lots of text boxes filled with Lorem Ipsum sample text.

I'd show these mockups to the client and they'd make changes, which more often than not were just to the text in the mockup, not the overall layout or graphical interface. As my "standard design procedure" was to have the client approve the mockup before production, I'd find myself painstakingly plodding through all my Photoshop text layers, applying changes to show the mockup to the client again.

Sometimes, I would miss a small piece of text that should have been updated with other sets of text! This would confuse (or annoy) the client and they'd request another change! I guess they figured that as I had to make the change anyway, they might request a few more tweaks to the design as well, which again were usually more textual than graphical and took a bit of focus to keep track of.

The process of getting a design approved became tedious and, at times, drove me nuts. At one point, I considered dropping my design services and just focusing on programming and markup so that I wouldn't have to deal with it anymore.

Upon finally getting an approval and starting to produce the design comp into XHTML and CSS, no matter how good I got at CSS and envisioning how the CSS would work while I was mocking up the layout in Photoshop, I would inevitably include something in the layout that would turn out to be a bit harder than I thought I would reproduce with XHTML and CSS.

I was then saddled with two unappealing options—either go back to the client and get them to accept a more reasonable "reality" of the design or spend more time doing all sorts of tedious research and experimentation with the XHTML and CSS, to achieve the desired layout or other effect across all browsers and IE.

# The solution: Rapid design comping

I soon realized the problem was me hanging onto a very antiquated design concept of what the mockup was and what production was. Before late 2005, I would have never cracked open my HTML editor without a signed design approval from the client, but why?

The Web was originally made for text. Therefore, it has a very nice, robust markup system for categorizing that text (that is, HTML/XTHML). Now with browsers that all comply (more or less) to CSS standards, the options for styling and displaying those marked-up items are more robust, but there are still limitations.

Photoshop, GIMP, and image editors have no display limitations. They were made to edit and enhance digital photographs and create amazing visual designs. They can handle anything you lay out into them, be it realistic for CSS or not. They were not designed to help you effectively manage layers upon layers of text that would be best handled with global stylings!

This realization led me to the ten step process I've termed **rapid design comping**. The term is a bit of a play on the term **rapid prototyping** which, taken from the world of manufacturing and applied to web and software development, had become very popular at the time this design process emerged for me in 2004-2005. This process is indeed inspired by, and bears some similarities to, rapid prototyping (as it is used in web and software development).

# The radical, new process—is not so new or radical?

Turns out this approach, while it took me a bit to come around to it on my own, is not that new, radical or original. Many web-compliance and accessibility experts advocate a similar approach of starting with lean, optimized, semantically ordered markup created for the content and designing specifically for that content and markup, instead of "smushing" content into heavy XHTML markup and convoluted CSS styles that were created solely to handle design decisions (in some cases, poor decisions at that).

I'm often given the argument that this approach limits design creativity. However, I'd like to point out that this approach is the whole point behind the famous CSS Zen Garden site (`http://www.csszengarden.com`). Every single design on that site has been created using the exact same, clean, compliant, accessible, and semantically structured XHTML markup. There's no reason to feel limited creatively with this design process. If anything, it should push and spark your creativity.

# Overview of rapid design comping

The following is the overview; we'll go over each step in detail afterwards:

1. **Sketch it**: Napkins are great! I usually use the other side of a recycled piece of photocopied paper—the more basic the better. No fine artist skills required!

   ○ **Perk**: Using this sketch, you can not only get your graphic interface ideas down, but you can already start to think about how the user will interact with your theme design and resketch any new ideas or changes accordingly.

2. **Start with the structure**: I create an ideal, unstyled, semantically structured XHTML document and attach a bare bones CSS sheet to it.

3. **Add text and markup**: Lots of text, the more the better! A sample of actual content is best, but Lorem Ipsum is fine too. Will you be taking advantage of WordPress forms? Be sure to add in those as well.

4. **CSS typography**: Think of your typography and assign your decisions to the stylesheet. Don't like how the formatted text looks inline? Being separated into columns with fancy background graphics won't make it any better. Get your text to look nice and read well before moving on to the layout.

5. **CSS layout**: Set up the layout. This is where you'll see upfront if your layout idea from your sketch will even work. If there are any problems at this stage, you can rethink the design's layout into something more realistic (and usually more clean and elegant).

   ○ **Perk**: Your client will never see, much less become attached to, a layout that would cause you problems down the road in CSS.

6. **CSS color scheme**: Assign your color scheme basics to the CSS. We're close to needing Photoshop anyway, so you might as well open it up. I sometimes find it useful to use Photoshop to help me come up with a color scheme and get the hexadecimal numbers for the stylesheet.

7. **Take a screenshot**: Time for your image editor! Paste the screenshot of your basic layout into your Photoshop file.

8. **Visual design**: Relax and have fun in GIMP, Inkscape, Photoshop, or Illustrator (I often use a combination of a vector editor and bitmap image editor) to create the graphical interface elements that will be applied to this layout over your screenshot.

9. **Send for approval**: Export a .jpg or .png format of the layout and send it to the client.

   ○ **Perk**: If the client has text changes, just make them in your CSS (which will update your text globally—no layer hunting for all your headers or links, and so on) and resnap a screenshot to place back in the Photoshop file with the graphic elements. If they have a graphical interface change, that's what Photoshop and GIMP does best! Make the changes and resend for approval.

10. **Production**: Here's the best part; you're more than halfway there! Slice and export the images of your interface elements you've created and apply them to your XHTML mockup with background image rules in your CSS stylesheet. Because you worked directly over a screenshot of the layout, slicing the images to the correct size is much easier and you won't discover that you need to tweak the layout of the CSS as much to accommodate the graphic elements.

If you start getting really good and speedy with this process, and/or especially if you have text overlaying the complicated backgrounds, you can also just export your images to your CSS file right away and send a straight screenshot to the client from the browser for his/her approval. Play with this process and see what works best for you.

For the purposes of this title, there's actually an eleventh step of production, which of course is coding and separating up that XHTML/CSS mockup into your final WordPress theme (we'll get to that in Chapter 3).

# Getting started

After taking all of the preceding items into consideration, I've decided that the type of theme I'd like to create, and the one we'll be working on throughout this book, is going to be an "online news source/magazine" type of site. Our site's content will be geared towards using open source software. Even though this type of site usually does very well by just focusing on the content, I would like to give users the design experience of reading a more trendy paper magazine.

# Sketching It

The whole point of this step is to just get your layout down along with figuring out your graphic element scheme. You don't have to be a great artist or technical illustrator. As you'll see next, I'm clearly no DaVinci! Just put the gist of your layout down on a sheet of paper, quickly!

The best place to start is to reference your checklist from the steps I provided, which consider how the site is going to be used. Focus on your desired layout. Consider the following questions: Are you going to have columns? If so, how many? Will the columns be on the left or the right? How tall is your header? Will your footer be broken into columns? All of these things will compose the structure of your design. You can then move on to any graphic element scheme you might have in mind. This again may involve questions such as: Would you use rounded corners on the box edges or a particular icon set? Where will you use them and how often?

In the following figure, I've sketched a basic three column layout that features using the WordPress blog to manage and feature magazine-style articles on a particular subject, rather than just straight-up blog posts.

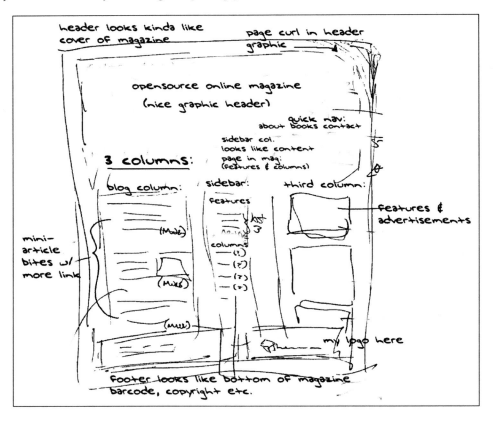

Because the design experience I want to give my site's viewers will be that of reading a paper magazine, the scheme for my graphic elements are going to focus on creating the illusion of paper edges and columned magazine-style layouts (particularly on the home page). I want the home page to feel similar to the "Table of Contents (TOC)" page in a magazine.

TOCs in magazines usually have big images and/or intro text to the featured articles to pique your interest. They then have listings of recurring columns such as "Ask the Expert" or "Rants and Raves".

Therefore, the graphical element scheme of my site that will make up the majority of the design experience, will focus on paper edges, curling up at the corners, just like a well-read, glossy, thin magazine paper tends to do. My layout is going to take advantage of the main WordPress blog, using the readily available text of the story as the intro text to pique interest. I'll use WordPress' **categorizing** feature to mimic a display of recurring columns (as in recurring articles) and the **monthly archive list** as a "Past Issues" list.

**Start small**

You may have a couple of ideas in mind; you can jot them down in quick gestures called "thumbnails". Thumbnails are a recommended and standard way to start any design mockup processes. They're a great way to be clear on the very basics of your layout before embellishing a larger (but still rough!) sketch with details.

# Considering usability

Once you've created your sketch, based on your considerations, look at it for usability. Imagine you are someone who has come to the site for the information it contains.

What do you think the user will actually do? What kind of goals might they have for coming to your site? How hard or easy will it be for them to attain those goals? How hard or easy do you want it to be for them to attain those goals?

Are you adhering to standard web conventions? If not, have you let your user know what else to expect? Web standards and conventions are more than what's laid out in a lengthy W3C document. A lot of them are just adhering to what we, as web users, expect. For example, if text has underlines in it and/or is a different color, we expect that text to be a link. If something looks like a button, we expect clicking on it to do something, like process the comment form we just filled out or add an item to our cart.

It's perfectly fine to get creative and break away from the norm and not use all the web conventions. But be sure to let your viewers know upfront what to expect, especially as most of us are simply expecting a web page to act like a web page!

Looking at your sketch, do any of the just discussed scenarios make you realize any revisions need to be made? If so, it's pretty easy to do. Make another sketch!

**Clean it up?**

This might seem to defeat the purpose of rapid design comping, but if you're working within a large design team, you may need to take an hour or so to clean your sketch up into a nicer line drawing (sometimes called a **wireframe**). This may help other developers on your team to understand your WordPress theme idea more clearly.

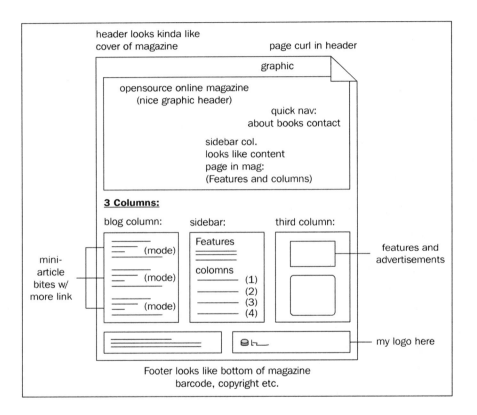

# Starting with the structure

The preceding usability scenarios deal with someone who will be looking at your content through your fully CSS-stylized WordPress theme. What if someone views this content in a mobile browser, a text-only browser, or a text-to-speech browser? Will the unstyled content still be understood? Will someone be scrolling or worse, listening and trying to tab through thirteen minutes of your sidebar blogroll or Flickr image links, before getting to the page's main content? To ensure such a scenario doesn't happen, we'll dive into our design comp by starting with the XHTML structure.

**What's semantic?**

Overall, I use the word **semantic** to refer to ensuring the unstyled order and structure of my content makes logical sense (header before main content, which comes before navigation, which comes before the footer, and so on).

Concerning strictly HTML, semantic refers to the separation of style from content by avoiding the use of presentational markup in HTML files. It also requires using the available markup to differentiate the meanings of various content in the HTML document. For instance, naturally you're familiar with headers being wrapped in header tags (`<h1>`, `<h2>`, and so on), images wrapped in `<img.../>` tags, and sections of textual content wrapped in `<p>` paragraph tags.

You can also define the content even further by taking care to place e-mail addresses inside `<address>` tags, acronyms inside `<acronym>` tags, quotes inside `<blockquotes>`, and citations inside `<cite>` tags (the list goes on). This lets anyone, as well as different processors (from browsers to other kinds of software), understand the document's content more easily.

You can learn more about semantic HTML from Wikipedia: `http://en.wikipedia.org/wiki/Semantic_HTML`.

For a comprehensive list of XHTML tags that you can define your content with, check out the W3Schools site: `http://w3schools.com/tags/default.asp`.

The HTML editors I recommended in Chapter 1 will drop these tags in for you. However, the more you understand about the XHTML tags and how to use them properly along with how they should look directly in the code view, the more solid, compliant, and accessible your markup will be.

# Creating your design

We're now ready to open our HTML editor and start producing our design mockup. Again, I understand many of you are going to have a little trouble launching your text/HTML editor without a Photoshop or GIMP comp to work from. Trust me, we'll work through the layout in XHTML and CSS using our sketch and then the final visual elements will be a breeze in Photoshop and GIMP at the end. Open your HTML or text editor and create a new, fresh `index.html` page.

# The DOCTYPE

XHTML has two common DOCTYPEs: Strict and Transitional. There's also the newer 1.1 DOCTYPE for "modularized" XHTML. The Strict and 1.1 DOCTYPE is for the truly semantic. Its requirements suggest you have absolutely no presentational markup in your XHTML. (Though in Strict 1.0, any strong, em, b, i, or other presentation tags that slip in will still technically validate on W3C's service, it's just not the recommendation for how to remain "strict".)

You can use what you like, especially if it's your WordPress site. However, if the WordPress site will not remain completely under your control, you can't control everything that other authors will add to the posts and pages. It's safest to use the Transitional 1.0 DOCTYPE, which will keep your theme valid and have more flexibility for different kinds of users and the type of content they place into the system.

For our OpenSource Magazine theme, I'll go ahead and use the 1.0 Transitional DOCTYPE:

```
<!DOCTYPE html PUBLIC "-//W3C//DTD XHTML 1.0 Transitional//EN"
"http://www.w3.org/TR/xhtml1/DTD/xhtml1-transitional.dtd">
```

You should note, while being integral to a valid template, the DOCTYPE declaration itself is not a part of the XHTML document or an XHTML element. It does not use a closing tag, even though it does look a bit like an empty tag.

**Check your editor's preferences!**

Some editors automatically place a DOCTYPE and the required html, header, title, and body tags into your document when you open up your blank file. That's great, but please go into your editor's preferences and make sure your **Markup** and **DTD** preferences are set to **XHTML** and **Transitional** (or **Strict**, if you prefer). Some editors that offer a design or WYSIWYG view will overwrite the DOCTYPE to whatever the preferences are set to, when you switch between the **Design** and **Source** (sometimes referred to as **Code**) views. Dreamweaver doesn't seem to have this problem, but you should set your DOCTYPE preferences there too, just to be safe.

# The main body

Our XHTML mockup, like all XHTML files, requires a few additional tags, which we'll now add.

## Adding the XHTML file requirements

After our DOCTYPE, we can add the other essential requirements of an XHTML file, the html tags, head tags, title tags, and body tags.

```
<html xmlns="http://www.w3.org/1999/xhtml" xml:lang="en" lang="en">
<head>
<title>My New Theme Title</title>
</head>
<body> body parts go here </body>
</html>
```

# Attaching the basic stylesheet

At this time, as we have our basic header tags created, I go ahead and attach a bare-bones stylesheet. This stylesheet just has the general items, matching div IDs and placeholders that I use for most CSS styling. But it's just the "shell". There are no display parameters for any of the rules.

## Attaching the CSS file

In your `index.html` file, add your `css` import link within the header file.

```
<head>
<title>
   OpenSource Online Magazine</title>
      <!--empty script prevents un-styled content flash in older
         browsers-->
   <script type='text/javascript' src=""></script>
   <style type='text/css' media='screen'>
   @import url("style.css");
   </style>
</head>
```

The following CSS "shell" contains empty rules for standard XHTML objects and IDs that I like to style for such as headers (h1-h4), paragraphs, anchor tags, as well as layout container IDs I'll use to hold my layout together.

Remember to apply the following CSS rules:

- XHTM objects (header, paragraph, list items, div tags, and so on) can just be listed as a CSS rule—for example, div{...} p{...}.

- ID names that are attributes and that can only be used once on a page, have a "#" hash mark in front of their CSS rule—for example, #container{...} #sidebar{...}.

- Finally, class names that are attributes and that can be applied multiple times on a page and combined with other classes, have a period (".") in front of the rule's name—for example, .floatLeft{...}.

## Creating a style.css file and including this basic shell

```
/*
    Enter WP Design & Creation Comments Here
    */
/*////////// GENERAL //////////*/
body {}
#container {}
#container2 {}
#container3 {}
/*////////// TYPEOGRAPHY //////////*/
h1 {}
h2 {}
h3 {}
h4 {}
p {}
a {}
a:hover {}
a:visited {}

/*////////// HEADERS //////////*/
#header {}
/*////////// CONTENT //////////*/
#content {}

/*////////// SIDEBARS //////////*/
#sidebarLT {}
```

```
#sidebarRT {}

/*////////// NAV //////////*/

/*////////// FORMS //////////*/

/*////////// FOOTER //////////*/
#footer {}
/*////////// IMAGES //////////*/

/*////// FUN CLASSES //////////*/
/*any little extra flares and fun design
elements you want to add can go here*/
```

# Basic semantic XHTML structure

Referring back to our sketch, we'd like our theme to have a standard header that
stretches across three columns—the left column being the main content or blog posts,
the middle column being our side bar, and a third column on the far right that will
hold our own custom feature links and/or advertisements. A footer will run across
the bottom of all three columns, naturally falling beneath the longest extending
column, no matter which of the three it is.

## Building out the body

Let's start off with some very basic code within our <body> tag to get that going.
I've included relevant id names on each div in order to keep track of them and later
to assist me with my CSS development. You'll also note, I've placed in XHTML
comments <!--//-->, which explain what each div is meant to do and where it's
closing div tag is.

```
...
<body>
<a name='top'></a><!--anchor for top-->
<div id="container"><!--container goes here-->
<div id="header">
<em>Header:</em> background image and text elements for header will go
inside this div
</div><!--//header-->
<!-- Begin #container2 this holds the content and sidebars-->
<div id="container2">
<!-- Begin #container3 keeps the left col and body positioned-->
<div id="container3">
<!-- Begin #content -->
<div id="content">
```

```
<em>Main Content:</em> Post content will go here inside this div
</div><!-- //content -->

<!-- #left sidebar -->
<div id='sidebarLT'>
<em>Left Side Bar:</em> Will contain WordPress content related links
</div><!--//sidebarLT  -->
</div><!--//container3-->

<!-- #right sidebar -->
<div id='sidebarRT'>
<em>Right Side Bar:</em> This will include additional ads,
or non-content relevant items.
</div><!--//sidebarRT -->

<div id="pushbottom"> </div><!--//this div will span across the 3 divs
above it making sure the footer stays at the bottom of the longest
column-->

</div><!--//container2-->

<div id='top_navlist'>
<em>Top Nav:</em> For reading through straight text, it's best to have
links at bottom (css will place it up top, for visual ease of use)
</div><!--//top_navlist-->

<div id="footer">
<em>Footer:</em> quick links for CSS design users who've had to scroll
to the bottom plus site information and copyright will go here
</div><!--//footer-->

</div><!--//container-->

</body>
...
```

The following screenshot is not much to look at, but it can help recognize our semantic goals for content order at work.

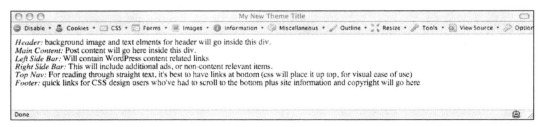

Looking at the previous screenshot, we can see that if a search engine bot or someone using a text-only browser or mobile device arrived and viewed our site. The following is the order they'd see things in:

- **Header**: Because it's good to know whose stuff you're looking at
- **Main content**: Get right to the point of what you're looking for
- **Left column content**: Under the main content, we should have the next most interesting items—features list, category (sometimes referred to as columns links), and archives (sometimes called "Past Issues" links)
- **Right column content**: It is the secondary information such as advertisements and non-content related items
- **Top page navigation**: Even though in the design this will be on the top, it's best to have it at the bottom in text-only viewing
- **Footer information**: If this was a page of real content, it's nice to see whose site we're on again, especially if we've been scrolling or crawling down for some time

**Moving navigation to the bottom:**

Some SEO experts believe that another reason to semantically push the navigation items down the page after the body of content as far as possible is that it encourages the search engine bots to crawl and index more of the page's content before wandering off down the first link it comes to. The more content the bot can index at a time, the sooner you'll be displayed with it on the search engine. Apparently, it can take months before a site is fully indexed, depending on its size. I have no idea if this is actually true, but it's inline with my semantic structure based on usability, so no harm done. You'll have to tell us at Packt Publishing if you think your content is getting better SE coverage based on this structure.

# Adding text—typography

We're now ready to make our typography considerations. Even if you're designing far into the experience side of the scale, text is the most common element of a site, so you should be prepared to put a fair amount of thought into it.

# Starting with the text

I like to add an amount of text that has a site name and description paragraph right on top in my header tags, the main body text up high in the content tags, secondary and then tertiary text below that (some of which usually ends up in a sidebar), and the navigation at the very bottom of the page in an unordered list. It's basically that "perfect page" SEO experts go on and on about—a Google bot's delight, if you will.

Minimally, I include `<h1>`, `<h2>`, `<h3>`, and `<h4>` headers along with links, strong and emphasized text, as well as a block-quote or two. If I know for sure that the site will be using the specific markup such as `<code>` or form elements such as `<textarea>` or `<input>`, I try to include examples of text wrapped in these tags as well. This will help me ensure that I create style rules for all the possible markup elements.

To help me out visually, I tweak the text a bit to fit the situation for WordPress theme designing. I put some blog posts there along with example text of features I want the blog to have, that is, "read more" links or a "how many comments" display along with samples of what kind of links the blog system will provide.

**Start with a lot of text**

Here's my secret: I use a lot of sample text. A major issue I've always noticed about design comps and reality is that we tend to create a nice mockup that's got clean, little two-word headers, followed by trim and tight, one- or two-sentence paragraphs (which are also easier to handle if you did the entire mockup in Photoshop).

In this optimally minimalist sample, the design looks beautiful. However, the client then dumps all their content into theme, which includes long, boring, two-sentence headlines and reams of unscannable text. Your beautiful theme design now seems dumpy and all of a sudden the client isn't so happy, and they are full of suggestions they want you to incorporate in order to compensate for their text-heavy site.

Just design for lots of text upfront. If the site ends up having less text than what's in your comp, that's perfectly fine; less text will always look better. Getting mounds of it to look good after the fact is what's hard.

# Choosing your fonts

When it comes to fonts on the Web, we're limited. You must design for the most common fonts that are widely available across operating systems. It doesn't mean you shouldn't spend time really considering what your options are.

I think about the type of information the site holds, what's expected along with what's in vogue right now. I then consider my fonts and mix them carefully. I usually think in terms of headers, secondary fonts, block-quotes, specialty text (like depicting code), and paragraph page text.

You can use any fonts you want as long as you think there's a really good chance that others will have the same font on their computers. Here is a list of the basic fonts I mix and match from, along with the reasons:

- **San-Serif Fonts**: These fonts don't contain "serifs", hence the name san-serif. Serifs are the little "feet" you see on the appendages of typefaces. San-Serif fonts are usually considered modern.

  ° **Verdana**: This font is common on every platform and was specifically designed for web reading at smaller web sizes. When you really want to use a san-serif font for your body text, this is your best bet. (There was a great article in *The New Yorker* in 2007 about the designer of this font.)

  ° **Arial and Helvetica**: Common on every platform, a little tame. It's great for clean headlines, but a bit hard to read at smaller font sizes.

  ° **Trebuchet**: Fairly common nowadays, and a pretty popular font on the web 2.0-styled sites. It's clean like Arial with a lot more character, it reads a little better at smaller sizes than Arial. This was originally a Microsoft font, so sometimes it doesn't appear in older Mac or Linux OSs. (Verdana is an MS font too, originally released with IE 3, but its design for screen readability got it opted quickly by other OSs.)

  ° **Century Gothic**: Fairly common, clean, and round—a nice break from the norm, although it reads terribly at small sizes. It's generally used for headings only.

  ° **Comic Sans Serif**: Another MS font, but common on all platforms. It's fun and friendly, based on traditional comic book hand lettering. I've never been able to use it in a design (I do try from time to time, and feel it's "hokey"), but I always admire when it's used well in site design (see Chapter 9 for a great example).

The following screenshot shows how the above san-serif fonts look in comparison to one another:

> **Verdana**: The quick brown fox jumps over the lazy dog.
> **Arial:** The quick brown fox jumps over the lazy dog.
> **Helvetica:** The quick brown fox jumps over the lazy dog.
> **Trebuchet MS:** The quick brown fox jumps over the lazy dog.
> **Century Gothic:** The quick brown fox jumps over the lazy dog.
> **Comic Sans:** The quick brown fox jumps over the lazy dog.

- **Serif Fonts**: These fonts are considered more traditional or "bookish," as serif fonts were designed specifically to read well in print. The serifs (those "little feet") on the appendages of the letters form subtle lines for your eyes to follow.

  ○ **Times New Roman and Times**: Very common on all platforms, one of the most common serif fonts. It comes off very traditional, professional, and/or serious.

  ○ **Georgia**: Pretty common, again predominately a Microsoft font. I feel it has a lot of character, nice serifs, and a big and fat body. Like Verdana, Georgia was specifically designed for on-screen reading for any size. It comes off professional, but not quite as serious as Times New Roman.

  ○ **Century Schoolbook**: Pretty common. It's similar to Georgia, just not as "fat."

  ○ **Courier New**: This is a mono-spaced font, based on the old typewriters and often what your HTML and text editor prefers to display (the point of mono-type is that the characters don't merge together, so it's easier to see your syntax). As a result of that association, I usually reserve this font for presenting code snippets or technical definitions within my designs.

In the following screenshot, you can see how the above serif fonts look in comparison to one another:

> **Times New Roman**: The quick brown fox jumps over the lazy dog.
>
> **Georgia:** The quick brown fox jumps over the lazy dog.
>
> **Century Schoolbook:** The quick brown fox jumps over the lazy dog.
>
> **Courier New**: The quick brown fox jumps over the lazy dog.

# Cascading fonts

When assigning font-families to your CSS rules, you can set up backup font choices. This means if someone doesn't have Century Schoolbook, then they probably have Georgia; and if they don't have Georgia either, then they definitely have Times New Roman; and if they don't have that? Well, at the very least you can rely on their browser's built-in "generic" assigned font. Just specify: `serif`, `sans-serif`, or `mono-space`.

As I want the style of my site's text to convey a friendly and modern look (similar to a magazine), my headers will be a mix of Trebuchet and Georgia, while the body content of my text will be Trebuchet as well. My font-families will look something like the following:

- For body text:

```
body {
    font-family: "Trebuchet MS", Verdana, Arial, Helvetica,
    sans-serif;
}
```

- For h1 and h4 headers:

```
h1, h4 {
    font-family: "Trebuchet MS", Arial, Helvetica, sans-serif;
}
```

- For h2 and h3 headers:

```
h2, h3{
font-family: Georgia, Times, serif;
}
```

# Font stacks

You don't have to play it safe with your font families. Today, more people are on newer computers with even more fonts available to them. Starting off with the basic "web-safe" font choices I discussed, you're free to branch out if you know that a large portion of your site's users will have a specific font you're interested in using. For instance, many users on a new Windows Vista machine will have the Cambria font, or you might feel that a lot of your viewers, being fellow designers, will have the Book Antiqua or Baskerville fonts on their Macs.

While many site users will not have special fonts installed, if the users you'd like to focus on probably do, then go ahead and design the site for them. You can then (as we'll see next) easily assign backup font choices (sometimes referred to as cascading "stacks") for all the other viewers out there. For a comprehensive article about taking full advantage of this technique, along with eight great font stacks to get started with, check out Michael Tuck's article on SitePoint: http://www.sitepoint.com/article/eight-definitive-font-stacks/.

## sIFR

There is another accessible font-replacement technique that takes advantage of the Flash player, called **sIFR** (or **Scalable Inman Flash Replacement**). I recommend this technique only for main display and/or heading text in your site. We'll look at this technique in detail in Chapter 7, when we look at ways of using the Flash player in our WordPress site.

# Font sizing

Thankfully, we seem to be out of the trend where "intsy-teensy" type is all the rage. I tend to stick with common sense. Is the body text readable? Do my eyes flow easily from header to header? Can I scan through the body text landing on emphasized or bolded keywords, links, headers, and subheaders? If so, I move on to the next step.

Determining how to size your fonts is something I can't help you with. The W3C recommends using em sizing for fonts on web pages. I, who normally treats anything the W3C recommends as scripture, actually use (gasp!) pixels to size my fonts. Or, I did until recently.

## Why pixels?

Preferring pixels is probably a hold-over from originally creating designs in Photoshop and then translating them to HTML and CSS. It was just fast and easy to see the pixel sizes in the image mockup and to pop those numbers into the CSS sheet. Plus, I generally agree with Cameron Moll of http://cameronmoll.com, that absolute sizes are very convenient to work with. Modern browsers zoom into the entire page by default and not many people know how to control font sizing separately from page zoom in their browsers anyway. Lastly, who really cares about *fully* supporting the old IE6 anymore?

I am a person who loves flexibility. After reading a recent article by Drew McLellan, I have decided to mend my wicked ways and take a stab at his method of sizing the body with a single em size and then using % (percentages) throughout the rest of the style sheet. You can read Drew's full article at http://allinthehead.com/retro/343/the-fallacy-of-page-zooming.

# Keeping it in proportion

The idea is that it's more important for your design, to have fonts stay relative and *in proportion* to one another, regardless of size. Drew's method does keep in line with my overall approach of creating my sites with locked widths, assuming vertical expansion. Resizing fonts up or down may not look wonderful, but it certainly does not break any of my designs; it just gives you bigger text to read and a little more scrolling to do.

On the whole, I can already see Drew's method potentially saving me a good bit of work here and there. While it's definitely easier to work with pixel sizes at the start, I occasionally got some feedback on a design that suggests the fonts in general just need to be "a little bigger" or "a little smaller". While I save some time up front, by not having to calculate relative em sizes, after a request like that, I certainly then have to spend a good amount of time touching every single pixel-sized font and line-height to accommodate even such a "little" request. With this method, simply bumping the original body em size up or down, sizes everything else proportionately. Plus, figuring out the percentages I want the rest of my fonts to be compared to my base body font-size, doesn't seem to make my head hurt quite like figuring out em sizes, so I've given Drew's method a go in this design.

You can set your font sizes to anything you like. I've set my overall body size to 0.8em. This is roughly equivalent to a 12px font size. The rest of my heading rules are sized up in *percentages* to sizes, that I feel look pretty good and convey how I envision the typography design to look in my original sketch:

```
body {
  font-size: 0.8em;
  line-height: 1.5em;
  font-family: "Trebuchet MS", Verdana, Arial, Helvetica, sans-serif;
}
...
h1 {
  font-size: 300%;
  line-height:100%;
}

h2 {
  font-size: 220%;
  line-height:120%;
}

h3 {
  font-size: 180%;
  line-height:100%;
```

```
}

h4 {
    font-size: 120%;
    line-height:100%;
}
...
```

**Want more info on the pros and cons of em and pixel sizing?**

A List Apart has several great articles on the subject. The two that are most relevant are How to Size Text in CSS (http://www.alistapart.com/articles/howtosizetextincss) and Setting Type on the Web to a Baseline Grid (http://www.alistapart.com/articles/settingtypeontheweb).

**Really interested in web typography?** Be sure to check out http://webtypography.net/.

# Paragraphs

No matter what sizing method you decide on, px, %, or em, be sure to give your text some extra space. With just the right amount of space between the lines, the eye can follow the text much more easily, but not too much! By setting your line-heights to a few more pixels (or em percentages) more than the "auto" line-height for the font size, you'll find the text much easier to scan online. Also, add a little extra margin-bottom spacing to your paragraph rule. This will automatically add a natural definition to each paragraph without the need for adding in hard return breaks (<br/>). You'll need to experiment with this on your own, as each font family will work with different line-height settings and font sizes.

You'll note in the previous code example, I've set my body rule to have a line-height of 1.5em. Because all other rules properties in my stylesheet will inherit from that rule, you'll note I've also set the line-height of my headers to be 100% or more, depending on the header. Now, I'll set my paragraph rule to allow a bottom margin of 5%:

```
...
p {
    margin-bottom: 5%;
}
...
```

# Default links

Many of the links in our theme are going to be custom designed, based on the `div` ID they are located in. Still, I've gone ahead and decided to adjust my basic link or `a:href` settings. I like my links to be bold and like them to stand out, but they should not have a distracting underline. However, I do feel the underline is an essential part of what people expect a link to have, so if they do decide to move the mouse over to any of the bold text, an underline will appear and they'll immediately know it's a link.

I've set the bold and underline property for my links by using the following code:

```
a {
  text-decoration: none;
  font-weight: bold;
}
a:hover {
  text-decoration: underline;
}
```

**Remember:**
If you don't like how your text looks here, then a bunch of graphics, columns, and layout adjustments really won't help. Take your time getting the text to look nice and read well now. You'll have less edits and tweaks to make later.

# The layout

Let's start making this stuff look like our sketch!

You'll notice in our XHTML markup that each of our div tags has an ID name. The div tags that are going to be our three columns are wrapped inside an outer div called container2, the main and the left columns are wrapped in a div called container3, and the entire set of divs, including the header and footer, are wrapped in a main div tag called container.

This structure is what's going to hold our content together and display WordPress semantically with the main content first. Along with this it also lets the style allow the left column to show up on the left. This structure also ensures that the footer stays at the bottom of the longest column.

In the stylesheet, I've set up my basic CSS positioning like the following:

```
body {
  margin: 0px;
  margin-top: 10px;
  font-size: 0.8em;
  line-height: 1.5em;
  font-family: "Trebuchet MS", Verdana, Arial, Helvetica, sans-serif;
  color: #666;
}
#container {
  margin: 0 auto;
  width: 930px;
  border: 1px solid #666666;
}
#container2 {
  border: 1px solid #0000ff;
}
#container3 {
  width: 670px;
  float:left;
  border: 1px solid #ff0000;
}
...
```

```
#header {
   border: 1px solid #00ff00;
   width: 930px;
   height: 300px;
}
...
#content {
 margin:0 10px;
 width: 420px;
 float:left;
 border: 1px solid #333333;
}

#sidebarLT {
  margin:0;
  width:200px;
  border: 1px solid #ff9900;
  float:right;
}
#sidebarRT {
 margin:0 10px;
 width: 200px;
 float: right;
 border: 1px solid #0000ff;
}
...
#top_navlist {
  position: absolute;
  top: 240px;
  width: 900px;
  text-align:right;
  border: 1px solid #003333;
}
...
#pushbottom{
 clear:both;
}
#footer {
 border: 1px solid #000033;
 height: 85px;
}
#footer h3{
 display:none;
}
#footerRight{
 margin: 0 10px 0 0;
 width:430px;
 float:right;
 text-align: center;
```

```
  border: 1px solid #552200;
}
#footerLeft{
 margin: 0 0 0 10px;
 width: 430px;
 float:left;
 text-align:center;
 border: 1px solid #332200;
}
```

Adding the preceding code to my stylesheet gives me a layout that looks like the following:

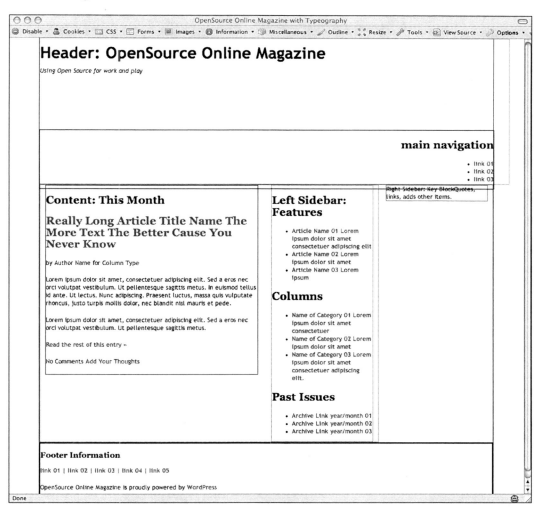

**Quick CSS layout tip:**
As you can see, I like to initially place **bright colored** borders in my CSS rules, so I can quickly check (on first glance) and see if my widths (or heights) and positioning for each of my div tags is on target. I tweak from there. As I continue to bring in all the details into each CSS rule, I remove these border elements or change them to their intended color. You can also use the **Web Developer Toolbar** to quickly see the border area of divs, as you drag your mouse over them.

# Column Layout: Floating div tags versus CSS tables

IE8 finally offers full support of CSS tables (which are actually a CSS2 standard and not a CSS3 standard). There's no doubt that CSS tables relieve a lot of frustration in dealing with column layouts in design. In this design, however, you'll note that I stick to a more traditional floating/cleared div structure that uses the pushbottom class with a clear property to make sure the footer stays at the bottom of the longest column.

The main reason behind this is to ensure that the site is easily viewed in IE6 and IE7. Plus, transitioning to CSS tables means you do lose control over your semantic "source order" of content. Whatever is in the far left column needs to come first, then the middle column, and then the right column. That would work fine for this layout, unless I ever decide to place the main content body in the middle. I would then have less important content above my main content when viewed by an SEO bot, text-only browser, or certain mobile browsers.

Despite what Rachel Andrew and Kevin Yank have to say in their book *Everything You Know about CSS is Wrong* (published by SitePoint, ISBN: 0980455227), I am not as sure as they are about the fact that source order isn't important for SEO and accessibility. So, I'm simply not ready to give up control of it.

I can't vouch for how source order truly affects SEO, so I'll give them that. However, as someone who uses her Palm Centro's browser to Google items on the go, and is then frustrated at having to scroll through piles of "junk" before getting to the page's content, and as someone who has sat in a room with a blind person using the JAWS text-to-speech web browser to test content for accessibility, I can definitely see the usability and accessibility difference when it comes to a site that does not have semantically source-ordered content.

Finding what I searched for right at the top, just under a few lines of header information, versus being buried underneath a heap of navs and blog roll links, is gratifying, yet rare, in my mobile surfing. Also, I can't begin to tell you how horrible it is to sit through and listen to a 508-compliance-tester's browser, read off 12 minutes or more of unrelated links and tertiary content, before getting to any *real* content.

You're more than welcome to not support IE6 and IE7 and go headlong into using CSS tables. I myself am going to hold off on using that technique to control layout for a bit. If you'd like more information on using CSS tables, Rachel and Kevin's book (already mentioned) is a wonderful source (for CSS tables and quite a few other CSS insights!). You can also check out A List Apart's article *Practical CSS Layout Tips, Tricks & Ideas:* `http://www.alistapart.com/articles/practicalcss`.

# Posts

Our posts are going to be handled easily by our basic XHTML object styles in our CSS sheet. Styles that we applied to our paragraphs and headers should take care of the majority of our layout's look.

## Making sure WordPress sticky posts get styled

WordPress 2.7+ does output quite a few useful classes from several different template tags. One of the newer classes enhances its new "sticky" feature. Sticky posts were introduced in WordPress 2.7. Basically, if you'd like a post to stay up at the top of the home page, you can mark it as sticky and it stays up on the front of your home page; even as newer content comes in, it will come in underneath your sticky post or posts.

WordPress outputs a simple class called `.sticky` and by simply placing this class into our `style.css` sheet, we can style it any way we want!

I'm thinking my sticky post should have a nice subtle background image to ensure it stands out (we'll get to that in a bit). For now, I'll just set the border and padding that will set my sticky posts apart.

```
...
.sticky{
    padding: 20px;
    border: 1px solid #ddd;
    background: #eee;
    margin-bottom: 10px;
}
.sticky h2{
    margin-top: 0;
}
...
```

# Forms

We'll handle some basic form fields that WordPress outputs. The reply fields and buttons are the most common output by WordPress, so we'll style for those by, again, addressing basic XHTML markup objects:

```
textarea{
 width: 430px;
 height: 200px;
 border: 1px solid #999;
}
input{
 width: 230px;
 border: 1px solid #333;
 background-color: #FFF;
}
```

WordPress also outputs some input IDs for submit buttons and the search form submit button.

```
#submit, #searchsubmit{
 width: 150px;
 border: 1px solid #333;
 background-color: #999;
 color: #FFF;
}
```

# Threaded and paginated comments

WordPress 2.7+ now offers the ability to thread or "nest" comments. This means not only can people reply to your article or post, they can reply specifically to other people's replies. At this stage in our design process, we're going to ensure that all WordPress basic features are styled and as we code up and develop our theme in the following chapters, we'll be able to easily address actual XHTML markup and CSS class names that WordPress generates.

In Chapter 3, we'll go through the ins and outs of enabling threaded and paginated comments in your theme. We'll create specific CSS rules for them at that time.

# Navigation

As we've discussed, one of the many cool things about WordPress is that it outputs all lists and links with `<li>` tags wrapping each item. This lets you specify if you want the list to be an ordered or unordered list and what ID or class you'd like to assign to it, even though by default, all lists are vertical with bullets. Using CSS, you have a wide range of options for styling your WordPress lists. You can turn them into horizontal menus and even multilevel drop-down menus! (I'll show you how to create drop-downs and more starting in Chapter 7.)

**Awesome CSS list techniques:**

**Listamatic** and **Listamatic2** from maxdesign (`http://css.maxdesign.com.au/index.htm`) are wonderful resources for referencing and learning different techniques to creatively turn list items into robust navigation devices. It's what I've used to create my Top (Page links nav), Featured, Column, and Past Issues menus in this theme. The Top menu uses **Eric Meyer's tabbed navbar** (`http://css.maxdesign.com.au/listamatic/horizontal05.htm`) and the Sidebar menus use **Eric Meyer's Simple Separators** (`http://css.maxdesign.com.au/listamatic/vertical06.htm`). I just added my own background images and/or colors to these techniques and the navigation came right together.

## Styling the main navigation

I tweaked the code from the two Listamatic sources in a few ways:

1.  I added `id="navlist"` to my **ul** inside my `top_navlist` div.

    ```
    . . .
        <div id='top_navlist">
        <h2>main navigation</h2>
        <ul id="navlist">
        <li><a href="#">link 01</a></li>
        <li><a id="current" href="#">link 02</a></li>
        <li><a href="#">link 03</a></li>
        </ul>
        </div><!--//top_navlist-->
    . . .
    ```

2. I also hid my h2 headers for the main navigation and footers that I would like people reading my site in-line unstyled to see, but is unnecessary for people viewing the styled site:

```
#top_navlist h2{
    display: none;
}
#footer h3{
    display: none;
}
```

3. I set the the height and width property of my #navlist li a so that those elements will accommodate background images that I plan to create for the interface.

4. I turned the second list into a class called tocNav, as I intend to apply it to all my blog navigation.

I now have a side bar and top page navigation that looks like the following in the style.css sheet:

```
...
#top_navlist {
  position: absolute;
  top: 260px;
  width: 897px;
  text-align:right;
}
#intTop_navlist {
  position: absolute;
  top: 173px;
  width: 897px;
  text-align:right;
}
#top_navlist h2, #intTop_navlist h2{
  display: none;
}
#navlist{
  padding: 10px 10px 8px 10px;
  margin-left: 0;
  border-bottom: 1px solid #ccc;
  font-family: Georgia, Times, serif;
  font-weight: bold;
}
#navlist li{
```

```
  list-style: none;
  margin: 0;
  display: inline;
}
#navlist li a{
  padding: 11px 30px;
  margin-left: 3px;
  border: none;
  border-left: 1px solid #ccc;
  background: #8BA8BA url(images/oo_mag_main_nav.jpg) no-repeat top
right;
  text-decoration: none;
  color: #253A59;
}
#navlist li a:hover{
  background-color: #9E9C76;
  background-position: right -37px;
  border-color: #C5BBA0;
  color: #784B2C;
  text-decoration: underline;
}
#navlist li.current_page_item a{
  border-bottom: 1px solid white;
  background-color: #fff;
  background-position: right -74px;
}
#navlist li a:visited { color: #253A59; }

...
.tocNav{
  padding-left: 0;
  margin-left: 0;
  border-bottom: 1px solid gray;
}
.tocNav li{
  list-style: none;
  margin: 0;
  padding: 0.25em;
  border-top: 1px solid gray;
}
.tocNav li a { text-decoration: none; }
.tocNav li a:hover {text-decoration: underline;}
...
```

# WordPress-specific styles for navigation

WordPress does now output several predefined CSS styles. There is a template tag that not only outputs the page links wrapped in an `<li>` tag, but adds the class attribute `page_item` to it along with several other class styles and possibilities depending on the state of the link within WordPress. For example, if the selected page link also happens to be the current page displayed, then an additional class called `current_page_item` is additionally applied.

If your WordPress theme was to take advantage of creating a robust menu for the page links, you could write individual styles for `page_item` and `current_page_item` in order to have complete control over your page links menu. This would also ensure that your menu displays whichever page is currently active.

**Multiple class styles assigned to the same XHTML object tag?**

As you can see in the DOM Source of Selection graphic, you can have as many classes as you want assigned to an XHTML object tag. Simply separate the class names with a blank space and they'll affect your XHTML object in the order that you assign them. Keep in mind that the rules of *cascading* apply, so if your second CSS rule has properties in it that match the first, the first rule properties will be overwritten by the second. There are more suggestions for this trick in Chapter 9.

This means we simply change our Listamatic CSS from an id (`#current`) within an `a:href` item, to a class within our `li` item (`current_page_item`) as follows:

```
#navlist li.current_page_item a{
  background: white;
  border-bottom: 1px solid white;
}
```

We now have a page layout that looks like the following:

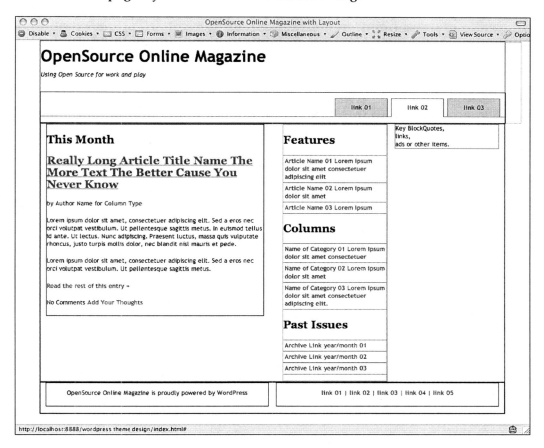

# Color schemes

Now that the general layout is hammered down, we're ready to move onto more exciting design elements.

You'll want a predefined palette of *three to ten* colors arranged in a hierarchy from most prominent to least. I like to create a simple text file that lists the colors' hex values and then add my own comments for each color and how I plan to use it in the theme. This makes it easy for me to add the colors to my CSS file, and then later to my Photoshop document as I create graphic interface elements. You can also just add these hex values and comments to your stylesheet commented out with slash-stars: `/* hex comments here*/`. For development, this can save time. Depending on how you plan to deploy your theme, you may want to remove them later, if nothing else then just to keep your CSS file size to a minimum.

**How many colors should I use?**

I've seen designers do well with a scheme of only three colors; however, six to ten colors is probably more realistic for your design. Keep in mind, WordPress will automatically generate several types of links you'll need to deal with, which will probably push your color scheme out.

Color schemes are the hardest thing to start pulling together. Designers who have years of color theory under their belt still dread coming up with the eye-catching color palettes. But the fact is, color is the first thing people will notice about your site and it's the first thing that will help them *not* notice that it is just another WordPress site (especially if you're taking the "simplicity" route and modifying an existing theme).

**Color scheme sites**

These days, color schemes are at your finger tips. You can find hundreds of thousands of great, five-color schemes on the following sites:

`http://kuler.adobe.com` and `http://www.colourlovers.com/`

# Two-minute color schemes

When it comes to color schemes, I say, don't sweat it. Mother nature, or at the very least, someone else has already created some of the best color schemes for us. Sure, you can just look at another site or blog you like and see how they handled their color scheme, but it's hard to look at someone else's design and not be influenced by more than just their color scheme.

For those intent on an original design, here's my color scheme trick. If your site will be displaying a prominent, permanent graphic or picture (most likely in the header image), then start with that. If not, go through your digital photos or peruse a stock photography site and just look for pictures that appeal to you most.

Look through the photos quickly. The smaller the thumbnails the better; content is irrelevant! Just let the photo's color hit you. Notice what you like and don't like (or what your client will like, or what suits the project best, and so on), strictly in terms of color.

# Color schemes with GIMP or Photoshop

Pick one or two images which strike you and drop them into Photoshop or GIMP. A thumbnail is fine in a pinch, but you'll probably want an image a bit bigger than the thumbnail. Don't use photos with a watermark, as the watermark will affect the palette output.

**Lose the watermark**: Most stock sites have a watermark and there's nothing you can do about that. You can create a free login on Getty Images's Photodisc (`http://Photodisc.com`). Once logged in, the watermark is removed from the comp images preview which is about 510 pixels by 330 pixels at 72 dpi, perfect for sampling a color palette.

*The watermark free image is for reference and mockups only.* We won't be using the actual images but only sampling our color palettes from them. If you do end up wanting to use one of these images in your site design or for any project, you must purchase the royalty free rights (royalty free means once you buy them, you can use them over and over wherever you want) or purchase and follow the licensing terms provided by Getty Images, Inc for rights-managed images. (Rights-managed images usually have restrictions on where you can use the image, how long it can be on a website, and/or how many prints you can make of the image.)

Once you have an image with colors you like, say, opened up in Photoshop, go to **Filter | Pixelate | Moziac** (in GIMP, just use the **Filter|Blur|Pixelize** filter) and use the filter to render the image into huge pixels. The larger the cell size, the fewer colors you have to deal with, but unfortunately, the more muted the colors become.

I find that a cell size of 50 to 100 for a 72 dpi web image is sufficient (you might need a larger cell size if your photo is of high resolution). It will give you a nice, deep color range and yet, few enough swatches to easily pick five to ten for your site's color scheme. The best part is that if you liked the image in the first place, then any of these color swatches will go together and look great! Instant color scheme!

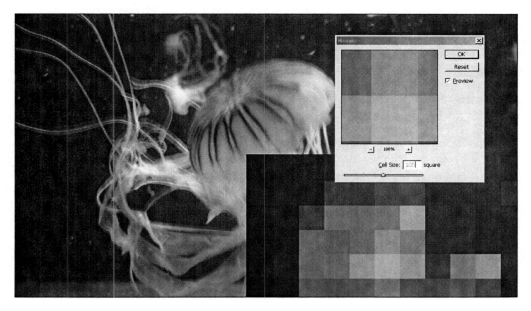

Once the image has been treated with the mosaic filter, just pick up the eyedropper to select your favorite colors. Double-clicking the foreground palette in the tool bar will open up a dialog box and you'll be able to "copy and paste" the hex number from there into your text file.

Keep track of this text file! Again, it will come in handy when you're ready to paste items into your `style.css` sheet and create graphic interface elements in Photoshop.

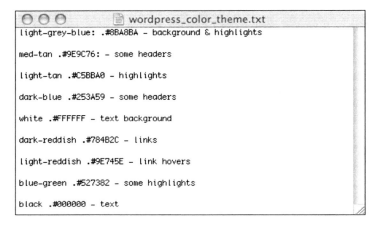

## Adding color to your CSS

After some thought, I've gone through my CSS sheet and added some color to the existing classes. I used the `color:` property to change the color of fonts. Although I'll probably be adding background images to enhance my design, I've also used the `background-color:` property to add color to the backgrounds of `div` tags in my layout which are similar to the base color of the background image I'll probably be designing.

The benefits of using the `background-color:` property, even though you intend to create images for your design are:

- In the event your images happen to load slowly (due to server performance, not because they're too big), people will see CSS color that is close to the image and the layout won't seem empty or broken.

- If you can't finish designing images for every detail, sometimes the background color is enough to take the site live and still have it look pretty good. You can always go back in and improve it later.

# Styling the special TOC headers

I've also created four new classes to handle my "TOC section headers" uniquely from regular h2 headers:

```
...
.thisMonth{
margin-top: 0;
height: 56px;
line-height: 210%;
background: #9E745E url(images/oo_mag_thisMonth_bg.gif) repeat-x top;
font-size: 320%;
font-weight: normal;
color: #ffffff;
border: 1px solid #9E745E;
}
.features, .columns, .pastIssues{
  margin-top: 0;
  height: 46px;
  line-height: 180%;
  font-size: 300%;
  font-weight: normal;
}
.features{
background: #9E9C76 url(images/oo_mag_featurs_bg.jpg) repeat-x top;
color: #ffffff;
border: 1px solid #9E9C76;
}
.columns{
background: #253A59 url(images/oo_mag_columns_bg.jpg) repeat-x top;
color: #ffffff;
border: 1px solid #253A59;
}
.pastIssues{
font-family: Georgia, Times, serif;
color: #305669;
}

...
```

Here you can see how our layout looks with some CSS color:

# Creating the graphical elements

Now, except for those multicolored borders I've put around each of my containing `div` tags (they will be removed shortly), I have an XHTML and CSS design that's not half bad. Let's polish it off!

Snap a screenshot (*Ctrl+Prt Scr* on a PC—or use Grab, the free capture program on a Mac) of your layout and paste it into a blank Photoshop document, or open it up into Photoshop.

This is where (after realizing that blocking out layout directly in CSS isn't so bad) I've had web designers argue with me about this "rapid design comping" business. All your text is now an un-editable graphic and trapped on one opaque layer. Any graphics you place on top of it will obscure the text underneath it, and any graphics you place underneath it can't be seen at all!

We're in Photoshop, the program that edits graphic images so well? Keeping in mind that images in your theme design will need to be added using CSS background-image techniques, it will probably be best to have your interface graphics set up *behind* your text layer.

Simply go to **Select | Color Range**, to select and knock out the blocks of color you want replaced with background images in your CSS. A tolerance setting of 32 is more than enough to grab the entire blocks of color. Sure, there are probably places where you plan to replace the text entirely with a graphic, in which case, you can apply the graphic over that area.

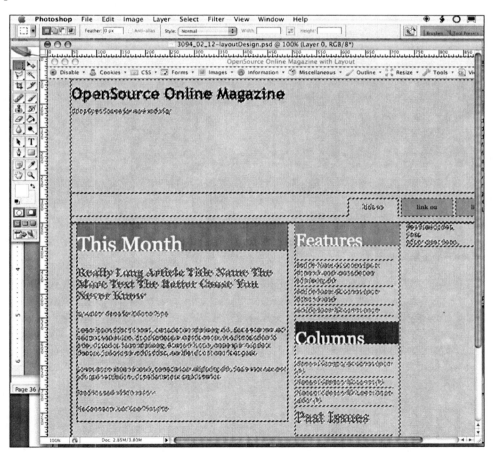

But what if your client makes a change to the text stylings? Easy! Make the requested change to your CSS file, take another screenshot of the updated index.html page in your browser and place it back inside your Photoshop file. Yes, you'll have to again knock out some of the blocks of colors so that your graphic interface elements can be seen again. Does making two mouse selections to accomplish that take more time than finding all the layers of relevant text and making the style change?

At best, it might be close. But, don't forget the real perk, your design comp is more than half way ready for production (also referred to as turning into a working WordPress theme). If the whole mockup was done in Photoshop, you'd still have all the XHTML and CSS creation to go through and then hope you can recreate what's in your Photoshop design comp across browsers.

**What about designing in a vector program?**

If you really love Illustrator or Inkscape so much, you can do one of two things. One, just design over your text image layer, and if you really must show a comp to a client, add a little text back over the areas obscured by your graphic. Or, you can open the image in Photoshop or GIMP and just as I suggested earlier, use the **Select | Color Range** tool to knock out the main block colors that will be replaced with graphics. Save as a transparent GIF or PNG, import it into your vector editor, and proceed as suggested earlier, on layers underneath the text.

# Relax and have fun designing

Now that I have my layout set up in Photoshop with the white knocked out, I can proceed with designing my graphic interface elements in the layers underneath.

As you work in your graphic editor, you may come across items that need updating in the CSS to accommodate the interface elements you're designing. I usually deal with these in two ways:

- If the CSS properties I'm dealing with need to change in size (say for instance, I wanted the top_navigation tabs to be taller, or I might decide the padding around the WordPress items inside the sidebarLT div tag needed to be taller or wider to accommodate a graphic), then, as already described, I would make the change in my CSS and take another screenshot to work with.

- If the CSS property is just being removed or handled in a way that doesn't change the size such as borders and display text, I don't take another screenshot. I just edit them out of the PSD layout and make a mental note or production to-do list item to remove the CSS property. Properties that need removing or setting to display none are pretty obvious and easy to take care of while you insert your graphic element images into CSS as background-image properties.

There are a couple of "special needs" cases in my theme design idea that I've been attempting to handle from the start. You may have noticed in my CSS layout that the header is wider at about 930 pixels than my layout at 900 pixels, and it hangs out to the left. I'm going to add a little hint of shadow and that's the amount I've allowed for it.

The border properties I've set for my main layout elements will help me lay out my graphic elements, and as the elements become finalized, I just take the eraser tool or use **Select | Color Range** again to remove them (good thing I made each `div` border property a different color!).

You can see our final result once we erase the lines and text that will be set to `display:none` or `text-indented` out of the way:

# Slicing and exporting images

When getting ready to slice your images for export, keep in mind that via the background properties in CSS you can control the top, bottom, left, or right placement, x and y repetition, as well as make the image non-repeating. You can also set the background image to "fixed", and it will not move with the rest of your page if it scrolls.

You'll need to look at your design and start thinking in terms of what will be exported as a complete image, and what will be used as a repeating background image. You'll probably find that your header image is the only thing that will be sliced as a whole. Many of your background images should be sliced so that their size is optimized for use as a repeated image.

If you notice that an image can repeat horizontally to get the same effect, then you'll only need to slice a small *vertical* area of the image. The same goes for noticing images that can repeat vertically. You'll only need to slice a small *horizontal* area of the image and set the CSS repeat rule to `repeat-x` or `repeat-y` to load in the image.

The following image details what kinds of slices should be made for tiled, `repeat-x`, `repeat-y`, and `no-repeat` background images:

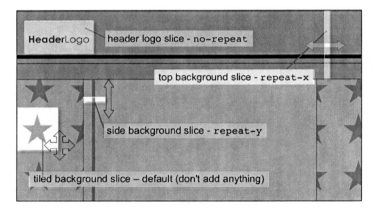

If you'd like more information on how to slice and work with background images, repeating, and non-repeating for use with CSS, check out this article from Adobe's site:

`http://www.adobe.com/devnet/dreamweaver/articles/css_bgimages.html`

Now that you've placed the slices for each of your theme image elements, export them using the smallest compression options available. Once you have each image, you can import them using the background-image, background-repeat, background-attachment, and background-position CSS properties.

Using CSS "shorthand" you can handle all of that, by adding additional property values to the background property, including the background-color property like in the following:

```
background: #fff url(img.gif) no-repeat fixed 10px 50%;
```

The first property in the above background shorthand is the hex color for the background color. If I'd like the object to also have a background image, I can do that by adding a url property after the color property that contains a path to my background image. After the url property, I can assign how I'd like the image to repeat; either it won't repeat at all: no-repeat, or it will repeat vertically: repeat-y, or horizontally: repeat-x. If I don't want the property to scroll with the page, I can assign it to be fixed. Last, I can assign it's placement. I can do general placement by specifying top left or bottom right (or any combination of those). Or, I can assign a *specific* pixel placement. When assigning a specific pixel placement, the first number will be from the top of the screen, the top being 0, and the second number will be from the left of the screen, the left being 0. If I assign a percentage, it will calculate the width of the image and position the image in the percentage of the screen (for example, half way, if the percentage is 50%) from the same percentage point inside the image (again for example, the exact middle of the image, if the percentage is 50%).

This is important to note, for instance, in my earlier example, by placing my background image at 50%, it will be centered in the middle of the screen. Using 50% is great if you want a centered image; however, if you place it 45% in, you may notice that the image seems more or less "off" from what you might expect 45% to be. This is because the browser calculated 45% in on the image and 45% in on the browser screen; just be prepared to play a bit with the CSS if you want to adjust that property with percentages.

After including our header image, I need to remove the text-header information. Rather than just deleting it from the XHTML page, I set the display for h1, h2, and p to none. That way, people who view the content un-styled will still see appropriate header information. I've also added a #date ID so that I can have the current month and year displayed under my magazine text, just like a print magazine.

Here are our #header id rules:

```
. . .
#header {
    width: 930px;
    height: 250px;
    background: url("images/oo_mag_header.jpg") no-repeat left top;
}
. . . .
```

And here are our #top_navlist ID rules, that use a single image rollover technique:

```
. . .
#top_navlist {
    position: absolute;
    top: 260px;
    width: 897px;
    text-align:right;
}
. . .
```

Wellstyled.com has an excellent tutorial on how to use a single image technique (also referred to as "CSS sprites") to handle image background rollovers with CSS:
http://wellstyled.com/css-nopreload-rollovers.html.

You can also check out CSS Tricks, and their article **CSS Sprites: What They Are, Why They're Cool, and How To Use Them** at http://css-tricks.com/css-sprites/.

To see the full and final CSS mockup style.css and index.html page, please refer to the code download section in the preface.

The final theme mockup looks like the following in our Firefox browser:

Yes, the final XHTML/CSS mockup is very similar to the Photoshop mockup. It should be almost perfect! You may still notice some slight differences. As I was putting the images into CSS, I discovered that I rather liked having each gradient section outlined using the same base color of the gradient, so I just left some border properties in the stylesheet and changed their color.

I also tested out my `top_navigation` rollover images by adding an extra link (not sure the WordPress site will have a need for a reference page, but if it ever needs it, it can have as many links as can fit across the top there!) and some plausible text to make sure the link area expands with the extra text.

# Don't forget your favicon!

You certainly don't need a favicon, but many designers view it as an indication that the site's designer didn't go that extra mile.

Favicons are those little 16 x 16 icons that appear next to the URL in the address bar of a web browser. They also show up on the tabs (if you're using a tabbed browser), in your bookmarks, as well as on shortcuts on your desktop or other folders in Windows XP and Vista.

The easiest (and quickest) way to create a favicon is to take your site's logo, or key graphic (in this case, the opened "O" in Open Source), and size it down to 16 x 16 pixels; then save it as a `.gif` or `.png` file.

Place this file in the root of your site and include it with the following tag placed in the header of your `index.html` file (in Chapter 3, we'll discuss the details of making it part of the template):

```
<link rel="icon" href="favicon.png" type="image/png">
```

This works great in all browsers except IE, and that includes IE7 and IE8 (to my disbelief!). To ensure your favicon works in all browsers, you must save it in the official Windows icon `.ico` format.

If you're using Photoshop, there's a plugin from Telegraphics you can install that will allow you to save in the Windows icon format; it is available at `http://www.telegraphics.com.au/sw/` (for Windows and Mac). Installing this plugin will allow you to save in the Windows Icon format when you select **Save As** from your **File** option.

If you're using GIMP, we'll then it's even easier. While I do most of my design work in Photoshop, when it comes to generating favicons, I gladly just switch over to GIMP. Simply choose to **Save As** in the Windows Icon `.*.ico` format instead of PNG or GIF.

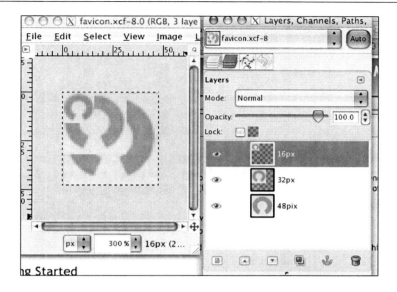

Once you have your `favicon.ico`, place the file in the root of your site's directory and place this code in the header tags:

```
<link rel="icon" href="/favicon.ico" type="image/x-icon">
```

Be sure to name your file `favicon.ico`! For some reason, even though you call the file by name in the link tag within your header tags, it just won't work if it's not named "favicon".

You may also find you need to clear your cache and reload several times before you see your new favicon. Be sure to actually clear your cache through your browser's preference panel. The keyboard shortcut *Shift+F2*(Refresh) sometimes only clears the web page cache. Some browsers cache favicons in a separate directory.

## Making your favicon high-res

A little known fact about the `.ico` format is that it can contains multiple versions of itself at different color depths and resolutions. This is how your operating system is able to display those "smooth icons" that seem to be the right resolution no matter how large or small they're displayed. You may have noticed that some favicons if saved as shortcuts to your desktop, look great and others look jaggy and terrible. The ones that look great take advantage of this feature.

The three main sizes that Windows will display a favicon in are: 16x16, 32x32, and 48x48. I've seen favicons that go all the way up to 128 x128. It's up to you; just remember, the more resolutions, color depths, and transparencies you add, the larger your favicon file is and longer it will take to load.

You'd basically use the same steps listed above to create your favicon, just starting with 48 x 48 pixels, then save it (so as to not overwrite your original file) down to 32 x 32 and last 16 x 16. I save each icon initially in PNG format, especially if I want the background to be transparent.

Again if you're using Photoshop, Telegraphics makes an additional plugin that will "bundle" all your favicon resolutions into one .ico file. It's called the IcoBundle Utility and it can be found at the same URL as the ICO Format plugin.

If you don't want to use Photoshop, GIMP can again *easily* handle this task for you. Simply open up your largest icon file and then copy and paste each additional resolution into a New Layer within that file. Then follow GIMP's **Save As** options to save it as a Windows Icon *.ico file.

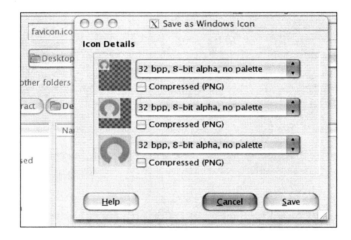

I've found Dave's article on the Egressive's site as a wonderful reference for putting a multi resolution, transparent favicon together using GIMP:

```
http://egressive.com/creating-a-multi-resolution-favicon-microsoft-
windows-icon-file-including-transparency-with-the-gimp
```

# Summary

You have now learned the key theme design considerations to make when planning a WordPress theme. We've walked through the basics of creating a great, functional XHTML/CSS mockup, complete with careful typography and color scheme considerations, tableless layout, and great graphics that we know will fit the layout because they were custom made just for XHTML and CSS. Now that we can see and even get a sense of the user experience of our mockup, let's dive right in to coding it up into a fully working WordPress theme!

# 3
# Coding It Up

We're now going to take our XHTML/CSS mockup and start working it into our WordPress theme. We'll take a look at:

- How the mockup will be broken apart into template files
- How to incorporate WordPress-specific PHP code, such as template tags and API hooks, into the template pages to create our functional theme
- We'll also cover incorporating new 2.8+ features such as sticky posts and threaded comments into your template

## Got WordPress?

First things first, you'll need an installation of WordPress to work with. As I explained in Chapter 1, I assume you're familiar with WordPress and how to use the Administration panel and have a development sandbox installation to work with.

**Sandbox**?

I recommend you use the same WordPress version, plugins, and widgets that the main project will be using, but don't use the live site's installation of WordPress. Using a development installation (also called "the sandbox") allows you to experiment and play with your theme creation freely, while the main project is free to get started using a built-in default theme to display content. Then you also don't have to worry about displaying anything "broken" or "ugly" on the live site while you're testing your theme design.

Many hosting providers offer WordPress as an easy "one-click-install." Be sure to check with them about setting up an installation of WordPress in your domain.

If you need help getting your WordPress installation up and running, or need an overview of how to use the WordPress Administration panel, I highly recommend that you read Packt Publishing's *WordPress Complete* by Hasin Hayder and April Hodge Silver (ISBN: 978-1-904811-89-3).

**Want to work locally?**

I spend a lot of time on my laptop, traveling often without a WiFi "hot spot" in sight. Having a local install (in my case, several local installations) of WordPress comes in handy for theme development. You can install local running versions of PHP5, Apache, and MySQL onto your machine, and afterwards, install WordPress.

**PC users**: WAMP Sever2 is a great way to go. Download it from `http://www.wampserver.com/en/`. You can follow Jeffro2pt0's instructions for installing WordPress in this two-part series on Weblog Tools Collection at the following web pages:

- `http://weblogtoolscollection.com/archives/2007/12/30/install-wordpress-locally-1-of-2/`
- `http://weblogtoolscollection.com/archives/2008/01/03/install-wordpress-locally-part-2-of-2/`

**Mac users**: You can install MAMP for Mac OS X. Download MAMP from `http://www.mamp.info/en/`. You can follow Michael Doig's instructions to install WordPress at `http://michaeldoig.net/4/installing-mamp-and-WordPress.htm`.

**Working with an automatically updated version of WordPress?**

If you've been keeping your WordPress installation up to date using their automatic update feature, that's great. However, you probably don't have the most recent default theme, which we'll occasionally reference. Just go to `http://wordpress.org` and download the latest installation and pull the default theme from the `wp-content/theme` directory. You don't have to upload it to your WordPress installation's theme directory; just have it handy to reference, as a few items in this book will call for it.

# Understanding the WordPress theme

Let's get familiar with the parts of a theme that your mockup will be separated into.

We'll use the default WordPress theme to review the basic parts of a theme that you'll need to think about as you convert your XHTML/CSS mockup into your theme.

Earlier, I explained that the WordPress theme is the design of the site and that WordPress generates the content. Thus, the content and the design are separate. Your theme does need to have the appropriate **WordPress PHP code** placed into it in order for that content to materialize. It helps if the theme is broken down into **template files**, which make it even easier to maintain with less confusion.

The following figure illustrates how the theme's template files contribute to the rendered WordPress page the user sees on the Web.

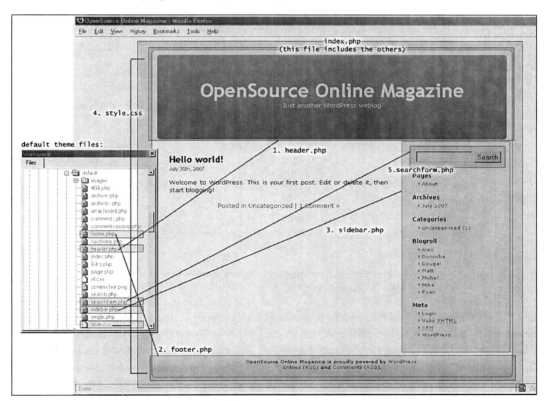

Within a theme, you'll have many individual files called template files. Template files mainly consist of XHTML and PHP code required to structure your site, its content, and functionality.

A WordPress theme's main template files consist of the main index.php file, which uses PHP code to include other template files, such as header.php, footer.php, and sidebar.php. However, as you'll learn throughout this book, you can make as many templates as you feel necessary and configure them any way you want!

Your theme also contains other types of files such as stylesheets (style.css), PHP scripts (such as searchform.php and functions.php), JavaScript, and images. All of these elements, together with your template files, make up your complete WordPress theme.

# Creating your WordPress workflow

Your work flow will pretty much look like the following:

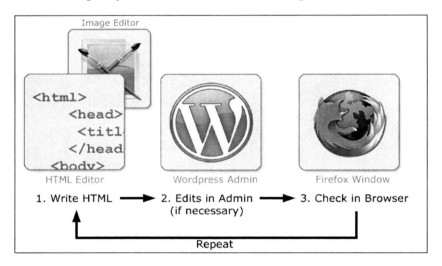

You'll be editing CSS and XHTML in your HTML editor. After each edit, you'll hit **Save**, then use *Alt + Tab* or the taskbar to switch over to your browser window. You'll then hit **Refresh** and check the results (I'll normally recommend using *Alt + Tab* to switch over to the directed window, but you can use your own way). Depending on where you are in this process, you might also have two or more browser windows or tabs open—one with your WordPress theme view and others with the key WordPress Administration panels that you'll be using.

Whether you're using Dreamweaver, or a robust text editor such as Coda, TextWrangler, or HTML-Kit, all of these let you FTP directly via a site panel and/or set up a working directory panel (if you're working locally on your own server). **Be sure to use this built-in FTP feature**. It will let you edit and save to the actual theme template files and stylesheet without having to stop and copy to your working directory or upload your file with a standalone FTP client. You'll then be able to use *Alt + Tab* to move to a browser and view your results instantly after hitting **Save**. Again, this is one of the reasons you're working on a development/sandbox installation of WordPress. You can directly save to the currently selected theme's files and not have to worry about temporarily having something "ugly" or "broken" appear on the live site.

**Be sure to save regularly and make backups!**

Backups are sometimes more important than just saving. They enable you to "roll back" to a previously stable version of your theme design, should you find yourself in a position where your XHTML and CSS has stopped playing nice. Rather than continuing to futz with your code wondering where you broke it, it's sometimes much more cost effective to roll back to your last good stopping point and try again. You can set your preferences in some editors, such as HTML-Kit, to autosave backups for you in a directory of your choice. However, you know best when you're at a good "Hey, this is great!" spot. When you get to these points, get in the habit of using the "Save a Copy" feature to make backups. Your future-futzing-self will love you for it.

# Building our WordPress theme

Have your HTML editor open and set up to display your FTP or local working directory panel, giving you access to your WordPress installation files. Also, have a couple of browser windows open with your WordPress home page loaded into one as well as the WordPress Administration panel available.

**Tabs!**

Use them. They're one of those neat built-in Firefox features we were talking about (Yes, I know. Every decent browser has them now). Keep all your WordPress development and admin views in one window. Each tab within a Firefox window is accessible via keystrokes such as *Ctrl + 1*, *Ctrl + 2*, and so on. It makes for a much cleaner work space, especially as we'll already be in constant *Alt + Tab* flip mode. Flipping to the wrong browser window gets annoying and slows you down. You'll quickly get in the habit of *Alt + Tab, Ctrl + ?* to jump right to the WordPress theme view or administration page you need.

# Starting with a blank slate: Tabula rasa

As I've mentioned, WordPress separates its themes out into many different template files. As a result, if you want to work on the main body, you'll open up the index.php file, but if you want to work on the header layout or DOCTYPE, you'll need to open up the header.php file. If you want to deal with the sidebar, you'll need to open up sidebar.php, and even then, if you want to work on a specific item within the sidebar, you might need to open up yet another file such as search.php.

When you're trying to put your theme together, initially this can be quite overwhelming. My approach to coding up your theme entails the following steps: (We'll go over each step in detail.):

1. Create a new, empty theme directory and make sure the default theme directory is easily accessible.

2. Upload your mockup's image directory as well as your index.html and style.css mockup files to the directory.

3. Rename your index.html file to index.php.

4. Add WordPress' PHP code, known as "The Loop", to your design so that WordPress content shows up.

5. Once your theme's WordPress content is loading in and your XHTML and CSS still work and look correct, then you can more easily pull it apart into your theme's corresponding template files, such as header.php, footer.php, sidebar.php, and so on.

6. Once your theme design is separated out into logical template files, you can begin finalizing any special display requirements your theme has, such as a different home page layout, internal page layouts, and extra features using template tags and API hooks so your theme works with plugins.

The other advantage to this approach is that if *any* part of your theme starts to break, you can narrow it down to WordPress PHP code that wasn't copied into its own template file correctly. You'll always have your backup files and, if nothing else, the default theme directory files to go back to with clean, basic WordPress code so you can try again.

**Why does WordPress have its theme spread across so many
template files?**

In a nutshell, WordPress does this for powerful flexibility. If your theme
design is simple and straightforward enough (that is, you're sure you
want *all* your loops, posts, and pages to look and work *exactly* the same),
you can technically just dump everything into a single index.php file
that contains all the code for the header, footer, sidebar, and plugin
elements! However, as your own theme developing skills progress
(and as you'll see with the theme we build in this book), you'll find that
breaking the theme apart into individual template files helps you take
advantage of the features that WordPress has to offer, which lets you
design more robust sites that can easily accommodate many different
types of content, layouts, and plugins.

# Create a new theme directory

To get started, we'll create a copy of the existing default theme. I'm using a
development installation of WordPress 2.8.5 on my local machine within MAMP. If
you're working remotely, you can follow my instructions using an FTP client instead
of the desktop **Copy** and **Paste** commands.

1.  Create a new directory that has a completely unique name that best suits
    your project.

2.  **Important! Don't skip this step!** Copy in your XHTML/CSS mockup files
    and the image directory. Rename your index.html file to index.php.
    WordPress template files follow what's known as the **Template Hierarchy**.
    That hierarchy looks first for an index.php page. Leaving the page as
    .html or attempting to name it anything else at this point will result in
    your template not working correctly.

3. We'll be referencing WordPress PHP code from the `default` theme. Make sure the `default` theme template files are handy (if working remotely via FTP, I like to just copy that directory down locally so I can access its template files quickly).

**Find out more about the WordPress Template Hierarchy**: Certain WordPress template pages will override other pages. Not being aware of which files override which ones within your template hierarchy can make troubleshooting your template a real pain. We'll talk about this more in Chapter 6, which deals with *WordPress Reference*, and you can read through the WordPress codex online at `http://codex.wordpress.org/Template_Hierarchy`.

4. Now, we're going to reference the default theme's `style.css` file. In your editor, open up the original stylesheet into the Code view. There are 18 lines of commented out code that contain the theme's information for WordPress. Copy those 18 lines to the top of your `style.css` sheet, **before** your style rules.

5. Leaving the text before the colons in each line alone, update the information to the right of each colon to accommodate your own theme. For instance:

```
/*Theme Name: 1 OpenSource Online Magazine
  Theme URI: http://hyper3media.com/
  Description: A WordPress Theme created originally for
  <a href="http://insideopenoffice.org">InsideOpenOffice.org</a>
  and then modified for Packt Publishing's WordPress Theme Design.
  Version: 1.4
  Author: Tessa Blakeley Silver
  Author URI: http://hyper3media.com
  The CSS, XHTML and design is released under GPL:
  http://www.opensource.org/licenses/gpl-license.php
*/
```

6. In your WordPress, go to **Administration | Appearance | Themes** (or **Administration | Design | Themes** in 2.5). There, you'll be able to select and **Activate** the new theme you just created. (Note that your theme won't have a thumbnail image, which will be displayed in the Administration panel dash board.)

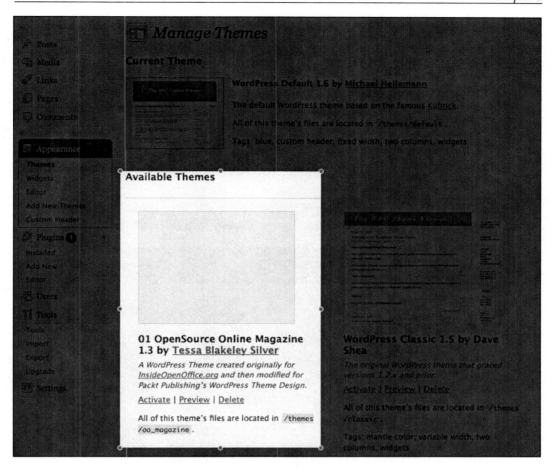

**Available Themes**

**01 OpenSource Online Magazine 1.3 by Tessa Blakeley Silver**

*A WordPress Theme created originally for InsideOpenOffice.org and then modified for Packt Publishing's WordPress Theme Design.*

Activate | Preview | Delete

All of this theme's files are located in `/themes /oo_magazine`.

**WordPress Classic 1.5 by Dave Shea**

*The original WordPress theme that graced versions 1.2.x and prior.*

Activate | Preview | Delete

All of this theme's files are located in `/themes /classic`.

Tags: mantle color, variable width, two columns, widgets

**Finding your new theme.**

I gave my theme a name that started with "01". I did this only for development purposes, so it would be easy to find in the list of many themes that come with my installation of WordPress. Before I actually deploy the theme, I'll remove the "01" from the name in the stylesheet. You may do the same when you develop, or you may choose to intentionally name your theme with a number or the letter "A" so that it shows up closer to the top within the list of themes.

# Including WordPress content

When you point your browser to your WordPress installation, you should see your mockup's unstyled XHTML.

To get your `index.php` page to read your `style.css` page, you must find the `<style..,>` tag and replace the `@import` URL code in your header with the following WordPress template tag, `bloginfo`:

```
<style type='text/cs's media='screen">
    @import url("<?php bloginfo("stylesheet_url"); ?>");
</style>
```

Congratulations! That's your first bit of WordPress code. You should now see your styled mockup when you point your browser at your WordPress installation.

In the example above, we used a bit of WordPress PHP code, called a template tag (bloginfo) to make sure that our theme can find it's own style.css file. In the upcoming sections, we'll run into several of these template tags and a few **hooks** that will help our template play well with plugins. Let's go over the basics of template tags and hooks.

# Understanding template tags

Template tags are most commonly used in templates to help you retrieve or "get" information from your WordPress CMS into your theme design. They can also be used to include or call in other template files.

The bloginfo tag was a typical example of a template tag that can be passed a parameter. In the previous section, we passed it the stylesheet_url parameter, to make sure we targeted our style.css page, but in other parts of our template we may wish to pass that template tag the name parameter or the version parameter. It's up to you where and how you might want to use a template tag. Template tags occasionally can be used to execute commands or do something.

# Getting a handle on hooks

Hooks are part of the plugin API and are mostly used by plugin developers to access and manipulate WordPress CMS data, then serve it up, for any theme to use. Your theme does need some preparation in order to work with most plugins. The most important hook we'll work with is the wp_head hook. This allows plugins to activate and write information in your WordPress theme's header files, such as CSS links to any special CSS the plugin might need or JavaScript files the plugin might use to enhance your site. We'll take a look at a few other hooks that will enhance our theme and make sure it's plugin-ready.

We're now ready to start adding WordPress theme code.

# Learning the Loop

After the bloginfo template tag, the next (and I'd say, the most important) bit of WordPress code that I like to tuck into my mockup file is called "The Loop". The Loop is an essential part of your WordPress theme. It displays your posts in chronological order and lets you define custom display properties with various WordPress template tags wrapped in your XHTML markup.

If by some chance, you have no posts to show, the default is to display WordPress' search.php file.

**Unfamiliar with the Loop?**

"The Loop" is one of those core pieces of WordPress PHP code you should brush up on. Understanding how "The Loop" works in WordPress is incredibly helpful in letting you achieve any special requirements or effects of a custom professional template. To find out more about The Loop, its uses in the main index page, other template pages, and how to customize it, check out the following links on WordPress.org's codex site:

http://codex.wordpress.org/The_Loop_in_Action

http://codex.wordpress.org/The_Loop

# Creating a basic loop

I'll start by pasting the following code (which I've copied from the default theme's index.php loop) into my widest column under my This Month: header, overwriting the sample content. This code will ensure that the sample posts I've added to my WordPress installation will show up:

```php
<?php if (have_posts()) : ?>

    <?php while (have_posts()) : the_post(); ?>

        <div <?php post_class() ?> id="post-<?php the_ID(); ?>">
            <h2><a href="<?php the_permalink() ?>" rel="bookmark"
            title="Permanent Link to <?php the_title_attribute();
                ?>"><?php the_title(); ?></a></h2>
            <small><?php the_time('F jS, Y') ?> <!-- by <?php
            the_author() ?> --></small>

            <div class="entry">
            <?php the_content('Read the rest of this entry
                            &raquo;'); ?>
            </div>

            <p class="postmetadata"><?php the_tags('Tags: ', ',
            ', '<br />'); ?> Posted in <?php the_category(', ')
             ?> | <?php edit_post_link('Edit', '', ' | '); ?>
            <?php comments_popup_link('No Comments &#187;', '1
            Comment &#187;', '% Comments &#187;'); ?></p>
        </div>

    <?php endwhile; ?>

    <div class="navigation">
        <div class="alignleft"><?php next_posts_link('&laquo;
                Older Entries') ?></div>
        <div class="alignright"><?php previous_posts_link('Newer
                Entries &raquo;') ?></div>
    </div>
```

```
<?php else : ?>

    <h2 class="center">Not Found</h2>
    <p class="center">Sorry, but you are looking for something
            that isn't here.</p>
    <?php get_search_form(); ?>

<?php endif; ?>
```

Upon reloading my page, I discover it works just fine and my five sample posts are indeed showing up. However, there's a bit of tweaking to be done:

Keeping in mind that I don't want this theme to be an "average blog", I'm going to continue to emulate my magazine-style concept—the first thing I notice about this loop is that it best suits standard blog posts. It displays the date, and although commented out, it displays the author. It also lists a **Posted in** for the **Category** and **Comments** link.

# Modifying the timestamp and author template tags

Just like any good magazine, I want to let the content loaded into this theme hang around while the month on the cover is current, and peruse its contents at my leisure. I'm concerned that leaving the full timestamp for each post will encourage some people to not read the content if it happens to be more than a few days old.

Hence, I'm going to remove the individual timestamp:

```php
<?php the_time("F jS, Y") ?>
```

I do want the author's name to show up but, again, more like a magazine article, I think it should be their full name, not just their user ID or nickname, and the author's name should appear below the post's title with a "by Author Name". So, that will have to be uncommented and tweaked to display the author's first and last name. I'll also change the XHTML a bit by adding a new CSS class reference—authorName. My author code then changes from `<!--<?php the_author() ?>-->` to the following:

```php
<p class="authorName">by <?php the_author_meta('first_name'); ?> <?php
the_author_meta('last_name'); ?> for <?php the_category(", ") ?></p>
```

**Upgrading your template to 2.7+**

In version 2.3 to 2.5, you could use the_author_firstname and the_author_lastname template tags. While those tags still work in version 2.8, they have been deprecated and the the_author_meta template tag has been introduced. This meta tag offers more flexibility than the previous template tags by allowing the theme to take advantage of all the user registration information with a single tag, as well as any additional information a custom plugin may add to the user registration database table. Be sure to check out Chapter 6 for a complete reference on essential WordPress template tags.

# Modifying the basic comments display

Because this is the Web and not a paper magazine, there are WordPress features I should take advantage of. I want to show what "Column" (a.k.a. WordPress category) the article has been posted to. I also want to take advantage of having people's comments and ideas on the article and help keep it fresh. So, I'll show how many comments have been added to the post. But again, some editing will need to happen, as I don't want those two items lumped together at the end of the article section. I've already moved my category template tag up next to my author name display, so what I'm left with is this:

```
<div class="comments"> <div class="commentIcon"><?php comments_
number("No Comment's,"<span class="bigNum">1</span> response","<span
class="bigNum">%</span> Comment's); ?></div> <?comments_popup_
link("Add Your Thought's, "Add Your Thought's, "Add Your Thought's);
?></div>
```

You'll see in the preceding code that I've changed the `comments_popup_link` template tag to always display **Add Your Thoughts** and added the `comment_number` template tag to track how many comments are made on an article. I've also again added my own custom classes called `comments`, `commentsIcon`, and `bigNum` to the markup and changed it from a `paragraph` tag to a `div` tag. (So my "left" and "right" float assignments would work within it.) It looks like this:

Even though I had most of these text elements handled in my mockup, I'm now seeing what's available to me via the WordPress template tags. You've probably noticed that the classes `authorName` and `bigNum` were not the part of my original mockup. I've decided to add them in as I'm developing the WordPress theme. This is the kind of thing I was discussing in Chapter 2's overall strategy. By making sure the XHTML/CSS mockup was handled well using more "generic" or high-level XHTML objects and container `div` tags, it's now very easy to add finishing touches and details within the template by taking advantage of CSS inheritance.

I thought that making the author's name just a little smaller would offset it nicely from the article, and as I created the comment icon, it would be cool, if there were comments, to show them in a big number floating in the middle of the icon.

You will probably come across a few details like this yourself; feel free to add them in as you see it. As long as your changes don't drastically change the layout, your client will not mind. If you think they will, it might be best to add to your original mockup and send a screenshot to the client for approval before proceeding.

**Upgrading from 2.5 to 2.7+ — making sure your sticky post "sticks":**
If you copied over the loop from the `default` theme of a 2.7+ installation, you're good to go. Mark a post as "sticky" in the Administration panel and you'll see your `.sticky` class, which we created in Chapter 2, at work.

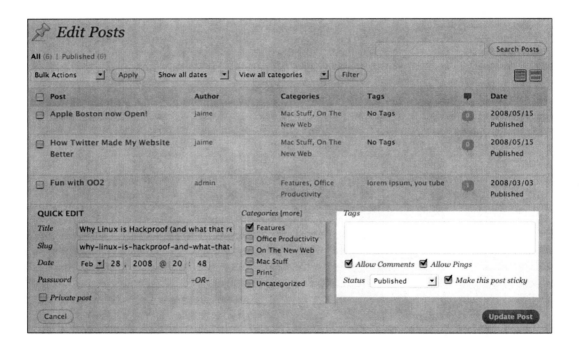

If you're updating a theme to 2.7+, you probably don't see the `.sticky` class at work. In your loop, under the `...while (have_posts())...` code, make sure you replace the class tag in the beginning `div` from this:

```
<div class="post" id="post-<?php the_ID(); ?>">
```

to this:

```
<div <?php post_class() ?> id="post-<?php the_ID(); ?>">
```

The `post_class` template tag will ensure that the `div` has all sorts of associated classes appear, such as, the original `post` class, the post's ID, and even its category name as a class! Of course, it also includes the `sticky` class, if it applies. All of these classes are nicely formatted in a `class=""` attribute.

If you don't want all of those classes to appear, you can target just the sticky class by amending your `div` code like this:

```
<div class="post<?php sticky_class(); ?>" id="post-<?php the_ID(); ?>">
```

**Within the loop (template tags):**

Once you get to rummaging around in your loop (or loops, if you create custom ones for other template pages), you'll quickly see that the default theme's template tags are a bit limiting. There are thousands of custom template tags you can call and reference within the loop (and outside of it) to display the WordPress content. Chapter 6 will have a template tag reference and you can also check out the following link to find out what template tags are available:

```
http://codex.wordpress.org/Template_Tags
```

After going through and considering everything in the previous discussion, I've come up with a main loop that looks something like the following:

```php
<!--//start content loop-->
<?php if (have_posts()) : ?>
    <?php while (have_posts()) : the_post(); ?>
        <div <?php post_class() ?> id="post-<?php the_ID(); ?>">
            <h2><a href="<?php the_permalink() ?>" rel="bookmark"
            title="Permanent Link to <?php the_title(); ?>"><?php
            the_title(); ?></a></h2>
            <p class="authorName">by <?php
                    the_author_meta('first_name'); ?> <?php
                    the_author_meta('last_name'); ?> for <?php
                    the_category(", ") ?></p>
            <div class="entry">
                <?php the_content('<br>Read the rest of this entry
                                &raquo;'); ?>
            </div>
            <div id="pagecomments">
                <?php comments_template(); ?>
            </div>
                <div class="comments"> <div class='commentIcon'><?php
                        comments_number('No Comments','<span
                        class="bigNum">1</span> response','<span
                        class="bigNum">%</span> Comments');
                        ?></div> <?comments_popup_link('Add Your
                        Thoughts', 'Add Your Thoughts', 'Add Your
                        Thoughts'); ?></div>

        </div>
    <?php endwhile; ?>
        <div class="navigation">
            <div class="alignleft"><?php next_posts_link('&laquo;
                    Previous Entries') ?></div>
            <div class="alignright"><?php previous_posts_link('Next
                    Entries &raquo;') ?></div>
        </div>
    <?php else : ?>
        <h2 class="center">Not Found</h2>
        <p class="center">Sorry, but you are looking for something
                        that isn't here.</p>
        <?php include (TEMPLATEPATH . "/searchform.php"); ?>
    <?php endif; ?>
<!--//end content loop-->
```

It displays comment posts that are normal and sticky which look like this:

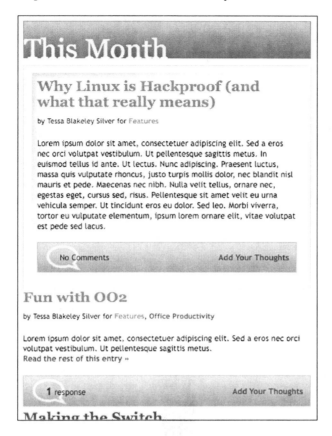

# Including threaded comments

Threaded comments were introduced in **version** 2.7. They're great in that they allow a post's commenters to interact with each other as well as commenting to the posts author. A new comment on the post will show up, as normal at the bottom (or top if that option was set in the Administration panel), but if someone wants to comment on a comment, it will show up beneath that comment "nested" in one level. You can specify how many levels deep you'd like to allow commenting to go.

This brings about a whole new level of community and contributed content. For sites that receive large amounts of comments per post or article, this can clean up and streamline the comments, while making it much more engaging and interactive for the site's users.

To implement threaded comments into your theme, you'll need to do the following:

1. First, you'll need to turn on threaded comments in your Administration panel. Go to **Administration | Settings | Discussion** and in the **Other comment settings** section, select **Enable threaded (nested) comments [#] levels deep**. Select how many levels deep you'd like to allow site users to post and reply with. The default is five, but many people find that three levels deep is ideal, as it keeps the commenting much more "focused".

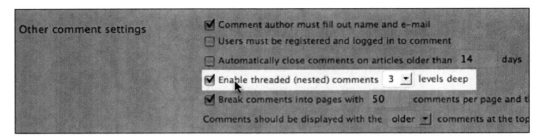

2. Once you enable threaded commenting, we'll need to do a couple of things to our theme's template files. Most importantly, you'll need to add the following bolded line of code to your `header.php` file within the `<head>` tags:

```php
<?php
...
if ( is_singular() ) wp_enqueue_script( 'comment-reply' );
wp_head();
...
?>
```

Note that the `if ( is_singular() ) wp_enqueue_script( 'comment-reply' );` code is placed **immediately** before the `wp_head();` plugin API hook function (we'll cover plugin API hooks and that function later on in this chapter). It has to come before that function in order to work properly.

3. Last, as this is a fresh, from scratch theme, we'll need some loop code that can handle comments. You'll want to go into the `default` theme that came with your 2.7+ or 2.8+ version of WordPress and copy the `comments.php` and `comments-popup.php` files over into your theme. If you happen to be tweaking an existing theme, instead of working from scratch as we are in this title, you'll want to back up your `current comments.php` file just in case. Also, again, if you've upgraded your WordPress using automatic update, you'll need the latest default theme. Just download the latest version of WordPress from `WordPress.org` and pull the `default` theme out from w̶the `wp-content/themes directory`.

If you navigate to a post that has a comment, or create a comment on a post, you should see a new little **Reply** link under the comment. If you click on that, you'll find that you can reply directly to that comment. You've probably ended up with something similar to this:

## Styling threaded comments

As you can see from the previous screenshot, some styling would help. While the output picks up a lot from our existing `style.css` and doesn't look all that bad, having the numbers and bullets seems a bit much. I'd rather just have some nice boxing and show the threading with indentation. With a solid stylesheet, like the one we created in Chapter 2, that addresses XHTML elements from the top down, you don't need a lot more to handle the basic threading. This is what I added to the theme's `style.css` file in the blog elements section underneath the other comment IDs and classes for the post page:

```
...
.commentlist {
    list-style: none;
    margin: 0;
    padding: 0;
}

.commentlist li {
```

```
    list-style: none;
}
.commentlist li ul li {
    margin-bottom:10px;
    margin-top:10px;
    background-color: #eee;
    padding:0 20px 10px 0;
}
.commentlist li ul li ul li {
    background-color: #fff;
}
...
```

The previous rules added to our `style.css` sheet give us this effect:

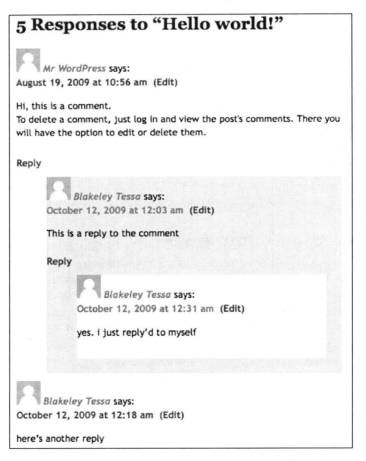

**Control all the comment details**

Chapter 6 has a full listing of all the class styles WordPress outputs for comments so that you can control your layout down to the most minute detail. Chris Harrison (cdharrison) has an excellent, comprehensive breakdown of styling WordPress 2.7 threaded comments on WordPress. org's site: `http://wordpress.org/support/topic/221693`

## Adding and styling comment pagination

Because we used the `comment.php` from the default theme, we can get going with comment pagination as well. Just go back to the **Administration | Settings | Discussion** page and turn on pagination for comments (it might already be turned on). The default is 50 comments and that seems to be a pretty good number. If a post ends up with more than 50 comments (that's 50 unique comments, not counting their threads, which will display as part of the original comment), **Newer Comments** and **Older Comments** pagination links will appear so that people can read all of the comments without having to scroll for days. I personally don't think scrolling is so bad, but again, if you're looking to keep the conversation focused and, in this case, fresh, you can use this feature to your advantage so people only see the most recent number of comments you specify.

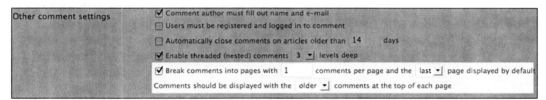

Just to get an idea of what's showing up, I set my pagination to kick off at one comment. Again, it will only display one comment and its immediate threads on a page. This is how the pagination looks initially:

Again, not terrible, thanks to our existing stylesheet, but it could certainly be a lot better. I'd like the navigation to spread the width of the content column with **Older Comments** to the left and **Newer Comments** to the right. By right-clicking and selecting **View Source**, I can see that WordPress is outputting the pagination inside a div with the class name navigation and that the **Older Comments** link has an alignleft class and the **Newer Comments** link has an alignright class like so:

```
<div class="navigation">
                <div class="alignleft"><a href="http://localhost/
?p=1&amp;cpage=1#comments">« Older Comments</a></div>
                <div class="alignright"><a href="localhost/
?p=1#comments">Newer Comments »</a></div>
        </div>
```

As a result the following CSS rules will align the links out and add a little margin, padding, and borders to separate them out from the comment content:

```
.navigation{
    clear: both;
    height: 25px;
    padding: 5px 0;
    margin: 5px 0;
    border-bottom: 1px solid #253A59;
```

```
    border-top: 1px solid #253A59;
}
.navigation .alignleft{
    border: 1px solid #ccc;
    padding: 2px;
    float: left;
}
.navigation .alignright{
    border: 1px solid #ddd;
    padding: 2px;
    float: right;
}
```

The result is a very basic style that can be easily upgraded with background images or other positioning placement:

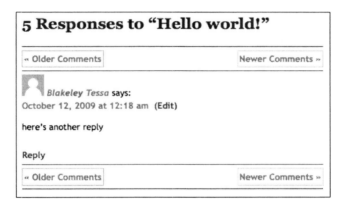

# Breaking it up: Header, footer, and sidebar template files

Now that we've got the Loop working in our theme, it's time to start breaking the theme down into template files which will help us make sure edits flow consistently across all of the various aspects of the theme.

My rule of thumb for separating markup and code into its own template file is, first and foremost, avoiding *duplicate* markup and code. Second, you'll be able to create template files to address any *unique* markup and code that should only appear in special circumstances, like on a home page, but nowhere else.

The most common template files we'll look at first are the `header.php`, `footer.php`, and `sidebar.php` template files. Each of these template fields will be used in various types of pages on the site.

The header should be the same for an article post page as for a static page. The footer should remain consistent across all types of pages on the site. If I update or change the header or footer, I'll want that change to appear everywhere it's used and not have to edit two or three different template files. The same goes for the sidebar; I may want it on several types of pages or not. This is easy to manage if it's contained in its own file and included where needed into other template files which control different page types.

These three template files are so common; they have their own include template tags in WordPress: `get_header`, `get_sidebar`, `get_footer`. The tags are used like so in your template file:

```php
<?php get_header(); ?>
```

# Creating the footer.php template file

We'll start first with the `footer.php` file, as this will remain consistent across all page types for my theme:

1. Create a new file in your theme's directory and name it `footer.php`.

2. Open up your `index.php` file and cut all the markup and WordPress PHP from the beginning of the footer in the markup:

   ```
   . . .
   <div id="footer">
   . . .
   ```

   to the end of the HTML page's last tag:

   ```
   . . .
   </html>
   . . .
   ```

3. Paste the selected code into your new `footer.php` file.

4. In your `index.php` file, where your footer code used to be, add the WordPress include template tag `get_footer`:

   ```php
   . . .
   <?php
   //get the footer information from footer.php
   get_footer();
   ?>
   ```

When you save these files and reload your WordPress site, the result should look no different than when your footer markup and code was inside the `index.php` file. Now from here on out, for each new page type we create, we can just include the footer code with the `get_footer` template tag.

## Hooking it up: Plugin API hooks

WordPress plugins take advantage of plugin API hooks placed in themes so they can execute various commands inside the plugin and/or get and write information to your website. To make sure your footer markup and code are able to play well with various plugins, include the following WordPress hook function right before the closing `</body>` tag of your XHTML markup:

```
. . .
</div><!--//container-->
    <?php wp_footer(); ?>
</body>
. . .
```

# Creating the sidebar.php template file

Currently, the main sidebar (the sidebar that's just on the right-hand side of my layout) is still just XHTML markup. Let's get it out into its own template file and included into the `index.php` file, and then see about making it more dynamic with WordPress template tags.

This will essentially be the same as creating the `footer.php` file:

1. First, create a new template file named `sidebar.php` in your theme's directory.

2. Now cut everything that makes up your sidebar markup into that file. In our case study design, that is the markup from the `Features` header:

   ```
   . . .
   <h2 class="features">Features</h2>
   . . .
   ```

   to the XHTML comment:

   ```
   . . .
   <!--//end archive list-->
   . . .
   ```

3. Once everything is copied into the `sidebar.php` file, where your markup used to be in your `index.php` file, add in the following WordPress include template tag:

   ```
   <div id="sidebarLT">
       <?php get_sidebar();?>
   </div><!--//sidebarLT  -->
   ```

If you save your `index.php` and `sidebar.php` files and refresh your WordPress site, you should see no difference in your layout.

Let's now take a look at making the sidebar dynamic.

## Making the sidebar dynamic

The default theme's `sidebar.php` file displays the following information:

- Static Page Links: This is a list of your static pages. It is the content you add via the **Administration | Page** navigation in the Administrator panel as opposed to the **Administration | Post** navigation. This list is displayed using the `wp_list_pages` template tag.
- Archive Links: Again, controlled by a template tag, `wp_get_archives`, this is set to the `type=monthly` default.
- Category Links (with how many posts per category): This displays your categories using the `wp_list_categories` template tag.
- A BlogRoll set of links: This list is controlled by the `wp_list_bookmarks` template tag which displays bookmarks found in the **Administration | Links** navigation.
- A set of "meta" links (links to information about the site): These links are hand-coded into the `sidebar.php` page in the default template.

Generally the above works out great for a more "standard" blog. But, as discussed, I would like my page links to display horizontally on top of my sidebar, and I want my theme to display a vertical sidebar that looks more like the contents page of a magazine.

Let's make our `sidebar.php` file dynamic with the following steps:

1. To start, I'll be treating my archives as **Past Issues**. I only want to display the month and the year of the "issue". Under my **Past Issues** heading, I'll add the following code which will display my archive links wrapped in unordered list elements:

```
<h2 class="pastIssues">Past Issues</h2>
<!--//start archive list-->
<ul class='tocNav'>
   <?php wp_get_archives('type=monthly"); ?>
</ul>
<!--//end archive list-->
```

**Formatting tip:**
You'll see I've wrapped each bit of PHP and its template tag in `<ul class="...">` (unordered list XHTML markup). WordPress will automatically return each item wrapped in `<li>` (list item tags). Adding the unordered list tags (or `<ol>` ordered list tags if you want) ensures I have a valid list that is easy for me to customize with my CSS.

**XHTML comments:**
You'll also note that I'm wrapping most of my WordPress code in `<!--//-->` XHTML comment tags. I do this so that scanning the markup is easier for myself and any other developer who comes across the code (a nice idea for those of you who are looking forward to creating commercial themes to make a little money; the more clear your markup, the less time you'll spend helping purchasers troubleshoot your theme). Also, indicating where WordPress code starts and ends, as well as what kind of code it is, will also come in handy when we get ready to break the code out into template pages, reducing the chance of possible cut-and-paste errors that can occur.

2. Next, my **Columns** are really just a list of my **categories**. The default sidebar lists the title as **Categories**, but as I have my own special header hand-coded into the sidebar, I've removed the following:

&title_li=<h2>Categories</h2>

I have changed it to this:

```
&title_li=
```

It gives me the code *under* my `Columns` header that looks like this:

```
<h2 class="columns">Columns</h2>
<!--//start categories list-->
<ul class='tocNav'>
    <?php wp_list_categories('show_count=1&title_li="); ?>
</ul>
<!--//end categories list-->
```

3.  Next, my Features will require a little bit of finessing. I would like WordPress to display the most recent *five* posts that are *only* in the Features category. There are a few clean template tags that will display the most recent post titles, but they don't seem to let me limit the posts to just my Features category.

    Because I understand a little PHP, I'll include a small, custom loop which will use three WordPress template tags and a formatting function to call in the post information for the last five posts in *category 3* (which is my Features category), then just display the perma link for each post and its title.

    Again, as long as you recognize what the template tags look like and how to paste them into your theme's template pages, you don't have to understand PHP or write any special scripts yourself. You can do a whole lot with just the existing template tags.

    Understanding PHP and how to craft your own bits of code and loops will enable you to have no limits on your theme's capabilities. The following script has the WordPress template tags highlighted in it, so you can see how they're used:

```
<h2 class="features">Features</h2>
<!--//start recent features list-->
<ul class='tocNav'>
    <?php
    global $post;
    $myposts = get_posts("numberposts=5&category=3");
    foreach($myposts as $post):
        setup_postdata($post);
    ?>
        <li><a href="<?php the_permalink() ?>"><?php the_title();
?></a></li>
    <?php endforeach; ?>
</ul>
<!--//end recent features list-->
```

**Custom selecting post data:**

You'll probably notice that the `setup_postdata();` function isn't listed in WordPress.org's template tag reference page; it's actually a WordPress formatting function. If you're interested in PHP and would like to learn more about being able to infinitely customize WordPress content into your themes, I'll discuss this and some other formatting functions in Chapter 6. It's also worth it to check out the topic on the WordPress codex site at `http://codex.wordpress.org/Displaying_Posts_Using_a_Custom_Select_Query`.

4. Last, I am ready for my page navigation. At the moment, the only static pages are **About** and **Contact**. I'll place the `wp_list_pages` template tag into my `top_navlist div` tags as follows:

```
<!--//start page nav list-->
<ul id="navlist">
   <?php wp_list_pages('title_li=" ); ?>
</ul>
<!--//end page nav list-->
```

Now, refreshing your WordPress site will show us our layout with current WordPress posts, categories, and archives, which we call: **Features**, **Columns**, and **Past Issues**.

## Hooking it up: Plugin API hooks

The most important WordPress hook that people like to take advantage of in their sidebar is **widgitizing** the sidebar so that it works with WordPress widgets (widgets are essentially "light" plugins, which can work independently and sometimes work *with* other more robust WordPress plugins.

There's no simple single-line function for getting your sidebar widget ready. We cover widgitizing your theme in full detail in Chapter 8.

# The header

For me, the header is more than just the beginning of the XHTML file and the specific `<head></head>` tags. It includes the opening `<body>` tag and through to the `<div id="head">` tag that make up the top half of my theme's design.

## Creating the header.php file

Create a file called `header.php` in your theme directory.

Open up your `index.php` file and cut everything from the DOCTYPE at the very top of the file down to the closing XHTML comment:

```
. . .
<!--//header-->
. . .
```

Paste that into your `header.php` file, and in your `index.php` file include the header back in with the `get_header` include template tag:

```
<?php
//includes header.php file for internal page layouts
get_header();
?>
. . .
```

## Hooking it up: Plugin API hooks

One of the important things we'll want to do to ensure that plugins can take advantage of our template is to include the `wp_head` hook into our `header.php` file. Just underneath our `style.css` include:

```
. . .
<?php wp_head(); ?>
. . .
```

# More template files: Home, internal, and static pages

As I mentioned earlier, the advantage of having your WordPress theme's parts separated into individual template pages is that your theme will be more flexible and able to accommodate a wider range of content. As nice as my theme currently looks, there are some problems with it that can only be dealt with if I break down the theme's design into further WordPress template pages.

To start, I only want that huge 300 pixel-high header graphic to load on the home page. It's neat to give the feel of a magazine cover, but once the reader has moved to a full article (a.k.a. post) or one of my static pages, I'd rather not have it there eating up screen real estate that the reader could be using to read more content without having to scroll. Likewise, the This Month header only needs to be on the home page, not on any internal page.

Also, while I do want the Features, Columns, Past Issues sidebar navigation to show up in a full article view page, I don't want that navigation sidebar on the About and Contact static pages. I'll have them click on an additional link in the top nav called The Zine to get back to the home page view.

Again, because WordPress is so flexible, it's super easy to add this extra link to the top nav by just adding the list item under the template tag like so:

```
<ul id="navlist">
    <li><a href="/">The Zine</a></li>
    <?php wp_list_pages('title_li=" ); ?>
</ul>
```

The Zine link will now let people go back to the home post page if they view one of my static pages. As my CSS style is targeting list items in the top_navigation div, the new list items automatically pick up the same styling as the WordPress-generated items.

Next, the loop needs slightly different formatting between my posts and static pages. Posts are being treated like articles, so I have template tags that announce "by Author Name for Category Name". However, on the static pages, to have "About" as the page title and then "by Author Name" is a little ridiculous.

Last, I'll need the full article pages to display comments under the article with the Add Comment's form underneath that, so if people click on the **Add Your Thoughts** link, they'll be anchor-tagged down to the form for the post.

# The home page

To ensure that the main header and This Month show up only on the home page, I'll take advantage of WordPress' template pages. Along with index.php, header.php, footer.php, and sidebar.php, you can also create a template file called home.php.

If you have a template file called home.php, WordPress will automatically use this as your theme's home page. If WordPress scans your theme's directory and finds no home.php page, WordPress will use the index.php page as the default.

Many theme developers use a home.php page to set up a static home page or "splash" page for their site. I'll be keeping the loop in mine, but it's the same idea.

Because I don't intend for my theme's blog posts (a.k.a. articles) to have a different URL location from my home page, this method for separating out some visual elements between my home page and internal pages is just fine.

However, if you do intend to have different URL locations for your blog posts versus the home page (that is http://myblogurl.com for the home page and http://myblogurl.com/blog for the blog posts page), you should heed WordPress' latest 2.1 suggestion of not naming your homepage as home.php and setting your home page up via your **Administration | Settings | Reading** panel. Not doing so may mean trouble for your "more" link. You can find out more on WordPress' site: http://codex.wordpress.org/Creating_a_Static_Front_Page.

## Creating a custom home.php template file

Because I like the way my index.php looks and works strictly as a home page, I'll start off by duplicating my index.php file and renaming it to home.php inside my theme's directory. Even though the markup is the same, WordPress is now automatically reading from the home.php page instead of the index.php page. (Making a small, temporary difference in the markup of the home.php will prove this if you'd like to test it.)

1. Now that it's done, I know that the Features, Columns, and Past Issues sidebar will be used in post pages and the home page, so I'll pull the markup and code from my #sidebarLT div and paste it into my sidebar.php page. I'll then include that page into my home.php page by using the following code:

   ```php
   <?php get_sidebar(); ?>
   ```

2. I'll do the same with my footer code, cutting and pasting everything from my footer div into the footer.php file using the following code:

   ```php
   <?php get_footer(); ?>
   ```

3. I'll test this in the browser, and, if it's working, I'll duplicate those included files from my `home.php` page into in my `index.php` page. (It will be handy to have the includes in place when we make our internal page.)

**Add the current month and year**

In my `#header` div, I have a `div` ID called `#date`. I want to display the full name for the current month and year. The best route for this is to just apply some basic PHP directly. I enter the following PHP code into my `#date` div:

```
<div id='date'><?php echo date("F Y"); ?></div>
```

## Creating a second sidebar

The very last detail I'll include is my third column. I want to be able to manually control the advertisements (be it Google AdSense or AdBrite ads) and custom feature graphic links that go in here. No one else should be able to edit this `include` through the WordPress Administration panel, so using a little of my own PHP, I'll create a page called `sidebar2.php`. I'll place this page in my own directory in the root of my WordPress installation and manually include this page with a standard PHP `include` call, like so:

```
<?php include(TEMPLATEPATH . "/sidebar2.php"); ?>
```

Including `TEMPLATEPATH` will point to your current theme directory.

## Internal pages

Now that our home page is working, it's time to modify the `index.php` file for the internal page layout.

Using the same "rapid prototyping" process we used to generate the home page layout in Chapter 2, I've created a mockup of my internal layout.

## Updating the index.php file to be an internal page

The biggest difference between my internal pages and my home page is the header. As a result, it will be easier to start off by just copying my current home.php page back over into the index.php page.

1. I'll rename the #header div ID and give it a different ID called #intHeader and create a new style that calls in my thinner, internal page header graphic and sets the height of the div accordingly.

2. Next, I'll remove the <h2> header that displays This Month. I'll also create a div ID rule for the header's #date and create a style for that which will move my magazine's PHP date code to the top-right of my internal header.

3. Next, my top_navigation ID will have to change to intTop_navlist, and I'll amend the top_navlist rules that control the unordered list.

4. Now, I just need to add the Comment's display and Add Comment's form to my index page. I'll do so by placing the following code at the end of my loop in the index.php page, under the the_content template tag like so:

```
<div class="entry">
<?php the_content("<br>Read the rest of this entry &raquo;");
?>
</div>
    <div id="pagecomment's>
    <?php comments_template(); ?>
    </div>
<p class="articleComment">
```

5. This will pull in the default theme's comments.php page, which works quite well for my purpose. It just requires that I create a few additional style elements for the input box and the submit button so that it works well with my theme.

6. I'll now just break the header div out of my index.php page and copy it into a header.php file in my theme's directory. Then in index.php, I'll call in the header block with:

```
<?php get_header(); ?>
```

This gives us an internal page that looks like this:

# Static pages

Static pages are the pages you generate in WordPress using the **Pages** menu instead of **Posts** menu. Our `index.php` page now effectively handles all the secondary requests. This is great, except my static About and Contact pages don't need the comment posted or `#sidebarLT` information to be displayed. This is where another one of those great WordPress template files comes in — the `page.php` template file.

## Creating a custom page.php template file

Create a `page.php` file and paste your `index.php` information into it.

The first quick and easy thing we can do is remove the `class="current_page_item"` from The Zine link that we've added to our page display.

1.  You can now remove WordPress' `comments_template` template tag and XHTML markup from the loop:

    ```
    <div id="pagecomment's>
       <?php comments_template(); ?>
    </div>
    ```

    You can also remove the number of comments code and the Add Your Thoughts code from the loop:

    ```
    <div class="comment's> <div class="commentIcon"><?php
    comments_number("No Comment's,"<span class="bigNum">1</span>
    response","<span class="bigNum">%</span> Comment's); ?></div>
    <?comments_popup_link("Add Your Thought's, "Add Your Thought's,
    "Add Your Thought's); ?></div>
    ```

2.  You can also completely remove the `#sidebarLT` div now:

    ```
    <div id="sidebarLT">
    <?php get_sidebar();?>
    </div><!--//sidebarLT  -->
    ```

3.  Without the side column, the content `div` doesn't have to be restricted to `430px` wide. Change the `div` ID to `pgContent` and add a new CSS rule to your `style.css` page:

    ```
    <!-- Begin #content -->
        <div id="pgContent">...
    #pgContent {
      margin:0 0 0 10px;
      width: 650px;
      float:left;
    }
    ```

# Quick review

OK, to review what we've done so far, you should have three views now:

1. One template view for your home page that shows the large home page header and link to comments.

2. One template view for your article (post) pages, which uses the internal header and displays your comments. Because this layout is for articles, The Zine link is left with the class `current_page_item`.

3. One template page view for "static" pages.

# Fun with other page layouts

Because we don't have `archive.php` and `category.php` template files in our template directory, the `index.php` template file is covering links to Categories (Columns) and archives (a.k.a. Past Issues).

This on its own is working well enough, but you can certainly improve these pages by pasting your `index.php` code into a new `archive.php` and/or `category.php` page, and then customize those page views even further.

For instance, you could place the following code into your `category.php` page, just above the loop:

```
<h3>You're reading the: <?php the_category(", ")?> column</h3>
```

It would give you the following result:

Remember, WordPress has a host of template tags to help you add content to any of your template files, be they includes or page views. We'll discuss important WordPress template tags in Chapter 6.

## Don't forget about your 404 page

Error 404 pages are where servers direct browsers when a URL seeks a missing page. While it's easy to think you won't really need a 404 page with a WordPress install, you'd be surprised. Even though all the links to the article or page you deleted are removed automatically from within your site, someone else might have created a link on their site to your post, which will no longer work. The 404.php template page is how you'll handle these requests.

You might have noticed that the PHP code we use for the `home.php` and `index.php` page loops have a "catch-all fix" in case posts are not found, which will display a nice message and the `search.php` template page. The `404.php` template page in the default WordPress theme does not do this (and it's also not set up to display our other template files and CSS).

Because the `404.php` page does not require the comments or author information to be displayed, the template page that is closest to it is our `page.php` file. However, we want to give people additional options to get back into our content, so we'll want to place the `#sidebarLT div` back into it.

## Creating a custom 404 template file

In order to create a custom 404 template file, follow these steps:

1. Copy the contents of your `page.php` template file into a new template file named `404.php` template file.

2. You can remove the entire loop from the file.

3. Place in some encouraging text and the PHP code to include the `search.php` template file:

   ```
   <h2 class="center">Not Found</h2>
   <p class="center">Sorry, but you are looking for something that
   isn't here.</p>
   <?php include (TEMPLATEPATH . "/searchform.php"); ?>
   ```

4. Add the `#sidebarLT` XHTML `div` and PHP WordPress template tag back in *under* the content `div`:

   ```
   <div id='sidebarLT'>
   <?php get_sidebar();?>
   </div><!--//sidebarLT   -->
   ```

These steps should give you a 404 error page that looks like this:

# Even more template files

We now have an `index.php` template file as well as a `footer.php`, `sidebar.php`, `header.php`, `home.php`, and `category.php` file! The fun doesn't have to stop there. Remember the whole point of these separated out template files is to reduce duplicate markup and code. While I'm an advocate of keeping things simple, if you notice that any of your markup and code is duplicated in two or more files, I would suggest you separate it out into its own template file. While WordPress only has a few include template tags, you've seen in a couple of examples how to custom include files using the `TEMPLATEPATH` WordPress PHP code inside a standard PHP include function:

```php
<?php include (TEMPLATEPATH . "/nameOfTemplateFile.php"); ?>
```

One additional piece of code that is duplicated is my main page menu. I have several page types—static, article, and category. I don't want to have to edit all three of those files just for making a change to my page menu, so I'm going to copy that out into its own template file—navlist.php and include it where needed in my page type template files:

```
. . .
<?php include(TEMPLATEPATH . '/navlist.php'); ?>
. . .
```

You can go through your theme and create as many template files as you see fit.

# Adding in the favicon

The last touch is to take the favicon.ico file we created in Chapter 2 and make sure it loads up in our theme.

## Activating the favicon

To activate the favicon, follow these steps:

1. Make sure the favicon.ico file is placed into the root of your theme's directory.

2. In your header.php file, locate your favicon link and target your theme's directory using the bloginfo template tag like so:

```
<link href="<?php bloginfo('template_directory'); ?>/favicon.ico"
rel="shortcut icon" type="image/x-icon" />
```

That should do it. When you refresh your WordPress site, you should see your new favicon load in. Again, you may have to fully clear your browser's cache to see the new favicon load in.

# Summary

We've now completed the OpenSource Online Magazine WordPress theme. Great Job!

It's probably clear that you can take advantage of all sorts of custom WordPress template hierarchy pages and template tags to endlessly continue to tweak your theme, in order to display custom information and layouts for all types of different scenarios.

How much customization your theme requires depends entirely on what you want to use it for. If you know exactly how it's going to be used and you'll be the administrator controlling it, then you can save time by covering the most obvious page displays the site will need to get it rolling and occasionally create new page view files should the need arise. If you intend to release the theme to the public, then the more customized page views you cover, the better. You never know how someone will want to apply your theme to their site.

You've now learned how to set up your development environment and an HTML editor for a smooth workflow. You now have a theme design that uses semantic, SEO-friendly XHTML and CSS, and has been broken down into WordPress template pages for flexibility in your layouts. Believe it or not, we're not quite done!

In the next chapter, we'll continue working with our XHTML and CSS layout, showing you some tips and tricks for getting it to display properly in all the browsers, debugging IE quirks, as well as running it through a thorough validation process.

# Debugging and Validation

As you work further and develop your own WordPress themes, you will no doubt discover that life will be much smoother if you debug and validate at each step of your theme development process, as follows:

1. Adding some code.
2. Checking if the page looks good in Firefox.
3. Validating.
4. Checking it in IE and any other browsers that you or the site's audience might use.
5. Validating again, if necessary.
6. Adding the next bit of code.
7. Repeating, as necessary, until your theme is complete.

In this chapter, I'm going to cover the basics:

- Debugging and validation; you will be employing these throughout your theme's development
- The W3C's, XHTML, and CSS validation services
- Using Firefox's JavaScript/Error Console for robust debugging
- Using the Firebug extension and the Web Developer Toolbar
- Troubleshooting some of the most common reasons why a "good code goes bad", especially in IE, and the various ways to remedy the problems

# Testing other browsers and platforms

I'll mostly be talking about working in Firefox and then "fixing" for IE. Perhaps this is quite unfair, assuming you're working on Windows or a Mac OS, and that the source of all your design woes will (of course) be Microsoft IE's fault. But as I mentioned in Chapter 1, this book is not about only using Firefox! You must check your theme in all browsers and, if possible, other platforms, especially the ones you know your audience uses the most.

I surf with Opera a lot and find that sometimes JavaScripts can "hang" or slow that browser down, so I debug and double-check the scripts for that browser. (We'll discuss more on JavaScripts in Chapter 8.) I'm a freelance designer and find a lot of people who are also in the design field use a Mac OS (like me), and visit my sites using Safari. So, I occasionally take advantage of this and write CSS that cater to the Safari browser. (Safari will interpret some neat CSS 3 properties, which other browsers don't as yet.)

Generally, if you write valid markup and code that looks good in Firefox, it will look good in all the other browsers (including IE). Markup and code that go awry in IE are usually easy to fix with a workaround.

**Firefox is a tool, nothing more!**

That's the only reason why this book tends to focus on Firefox. It contains features and plugins that we'll be taking advantage of to help us streamline the theme development process and aid in the validation and debugging of our theme. Use it just like you use your HTML/code editor or your image editor. When you're not developing, you can use whatever browser you prefer.

# Introduction to debugging

Do you remember our initial workflow chart from Chapter 3?

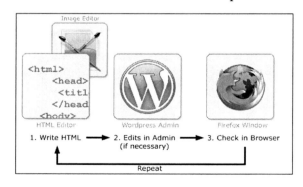

I was insistent that your workflow pretty much be "edit, check it, then go back and edit some more". The main purpose of visually checking your theme in Firefox, after adding each piece of code, is to ensure it looks fine; if it doesn't, debug that piece of code. Running a validation check as you work doubly ensures you're on the right track.

So, your workflow ends up looking something more like this:

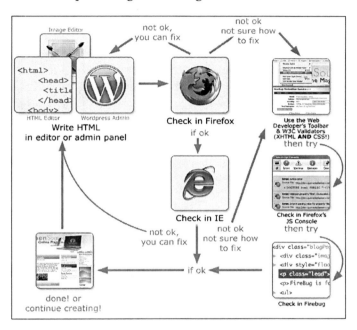

You want to work with nice, small pieces or "chunks" of code. I tend to define a chunk in XHTML markup as no more than one `div` section, the internal markup, and any WordPress template tags it contains. When working with CSS, I try to work only with one id or class rule at a time. Sometimes, while working with CSS, I'll break this down even further and test after every property I add to a rule, until the rule looks as I intend and validates.

As soon as you see something that doesn't look right in your browser, you can check for validation and then fix it. The advantage of this workflow is that you know exactly what needs to be fixed and what XHTML markup or PHP code is to blame. You can ignore all the code that was looking fine and was validating before. The recently added markup and code is also the freshest in your mind, so you're more likely to realize the solution needed to fix the problem.

If you add too many chunks of XHTML markup or several CSS rules before checking it in your browser, and then discover something has gone awry, you'll have twice as much sleuthing to do in order to discover which bit (or bits) of markup and code are to blame. Again, your fail-safe is your backup.

You should be regularly saving backups of your theme at good stopping points. If you discover that you just can't figure out where the issue is, rolling back to your last stable stopping point and starting over might be your best bet to getting back on track.

As mentioned in Chapter 2, you'll primarily design for Firefox and then apply any required fixes, hacks, and workarounds to IE. You can do that for each piece of code you add to your theme. As you can see in the preceding figure, first check your theme in Firefox and if there's a problem, fix it for Firefox first. Then, check it in IE and make any adjustments for that browser.

At this point, you guessed it, more than half of the debugging process will depend directly on your own eyeballs and aesthetics. If it looks the way you intended it to look and works the way you intended it to work, check that the code validates and move on. When one of those three things doesn't happen (it doesn't look right, work right, or validate), you have to stop and figure out why.

# Troubleshooting basics

Suffice to say, it will usually be obvious when something is wrong with your WordPress theme. The most common reasons for things being "off" are:

- CSS rules that use incorrect syntax or conflict with other CSS rules
- Misnamed, mistargeted, or inappropriately-sized images
- Markup text or PHP code that affects or breaks the **Document Object Model (DOM)** due to being inappropriately placed or having syntax errors in it
- WordPress PHP code or template tags and hooks that are copied over incorrectly, producing PHP error displays in your template rather than content

The second point is pretty obvious when it happens. You see no images, or worse, you might get those little ugly "x'd" boxes in IE if they're called directly from the WordPress posts or pages. Fortunately, the solution is also obvious: you have to go in and make sure your images are named correctly if you're overwriting standard icons or images from another theme. You also might need to go through your CSS file and make sure the relative paths to the images are correct.

For images that are not appearing correctly because they were mis-sized, you can go back to your image editor, fix them, and then re-export them, or you might be able to make adjustments in your CSS file to display a height and/or width that is more appropriate to the image you designed.

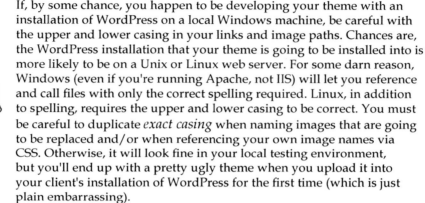

**Don't forget about casing!**

If, by some chance, you happen to be developing your theme with an installation of WordPress on a local Windows machine, be careful with the upper and lower casing in your links and image paths. Chances are, the WordPress installation that your theme is going to be installed into is more likely to be on a Unix or Linux web server. For some darn reason, Windows (even if you're running Apache, not IIS) will let you reference and call files with only the correct spelling required. Linux, in addition to spelling, requires the upper and lower casing to be correct. You must be careful to duplicate *exact casing* when naming images that are going to be replaced and/or when referencing your own image names via CSS. Otherwise, it will look fine in your local testing environment, but you'll end up with a pretty ugly theme when you upload it into your client's installation of WordPress for the first time (which is just plain embarrassing).

For the latter two points, one of the best ways to debug syntax errors that cause visual "wonks" is not to have syntax errors in the first place (don't roll your eyes just yet).

This is why, in the last figure of our expanded workflow chart, we advocate you not only visually check your design as it progresses in Firefox and IE, but also test for validation.

# Why validate?

Hey, I understand it's easy to add some code, run a visual check in Firefox and IE, see everything looks fine, and then flip right back to your HTML editor to add more code. After all, time is money and you'll just save that validation part until the very end. Besides, validation is just icing on the cake—right?

The problem with debugging purely based on visual output is that all browsers (some more grievously than others) will try their best to help you out and properly interpret less than ideal markup. One piece of invalid markup might very well look fine initially, until you add more markups and then the browser can't interpret your intentions between the two types of markup anymore. The browser will pick its own best option and display something guaranteed to be ugly.

You'll then go back and futz around with the last bit of code you added (because everything was fine until you added that last bit, so that must be the offending code), which may or may not fix the problem. The next bits of code might create other problems and what's worse is that you'll recognize a code chunk that you know should be valid! You're then frustrated, scratching your head as to why the last bit of code you added is making your theme "wonky" when you know, without a doubt, it's perfectly fine code!

The worst case scenario I tend to see of this type of visual-only debugging is that the theme developers get desperate and start randomly making all sorts of odd hacks and tweaks to their markup and CSS to get it to look right.

Miraculously, they often do get it to look right, but in only one browser. Most likely, they've inadvertently discovered what the first invalid syntax was and unwittingly applied it across all the rest of their markup and CSS. Thus, that one browser started consistently interpreting the bad syntax! The theme designer then becomes convinced that the other browser is awful and designing these non-WYSIWYG, dynamic themes is a pain.

Avoid all that frustration! Even if it looks great in both browsers, run the code through the W3C's, XHTML, and CSS validators. If something turns up invalid, no matter how small or pedantic the validator's suggestion might be (and they do seem pedantic at times), incorporate the suggested fix into your markup, before you continue working. This will keep any small syntax errors from compounding future bits of markup and code into big visual "uglies" that are hard to track down and troubleshoot.

# PHP template tags

The next issue you'll most commonly run into is mistakes and typos that are created by copying and pasting your WordPress template tags and other PHP code incorrectly. The most common result you'll get from invalid PHP syntax is a "Fatal Error". Fortunately, PHP does a decent job of trying to let you know what file name and line of code in the file the offending syntax lives in (yet another reason why in Chapter 3 I highly recommended an HTML editor that lets you view the line number in the code view).

If you get a "Fatal Error" in your template, your best bet is to open the filename that is listed and go to the line in your editor. Once there, search for missing `<?php ?>` tags. Your template tags should also be followed with parenthesis followed by a semicolon such as `();`. If the template tag has parameters passed in it, make sure each parameter is surrounded by single quote marks, for example, `template_tag_name('parameter name', 'next_parameter');`.

**Be aware of proper PHP notation**

The proper way to notate PHP is as I mentioned earlier, with a `<?php //code ?>`. PHP on a server will look for the `<?php` tag and start processing the PHP. However, many servers are set up to have shorthand support and will recognize PHP with just a `<?` (no php added). As a result, many PHP programmers will just start their scripts with a `<?`, which works fine on their server or local sandbox, but not on other servers. If you have a problem with a template tag or a plugin, check to make sure you're notating PHP properly with the `<?php //code ?>` tags and, for maximum support, it's recommended that you always start your PHP tags with `<?php`.

# CSS quick fixes

Finally, your CSS file might get fairly big, fairly quickly. It's easy to forget you already made a rule and/or just accidentally created another rule of the same name. It's all about cascading; so whatever comes last overwrites what came first.

**Double rules:** It's an easy mistake to make, but validating using W3C's CSS validator will point this out right away. However, this is not the case for *double properties* within rules! W3C's CSS validator will not point out double properties if both properties use correct syntax. This is one of the reasons why the !important hack returns valid. (We'll discuss this hack just a little further down in this chapter under *To hack or not to hack*.)

Perhaps you found a site that has a nice CSS style or effect you like, and so you copied those CSS rules into your theme's style.css sheet. Just like with XHTML markup or PHP code, it's easy to introduce errors by miscopying the bits of CSS syntax in. A small syntax error in a property towards the bottom of a rule may seem fine at first, but may cause problems with properties added to the rule later. This can also affect the entire rule or even the rule after it.

Also, if you're copying CSS, be aware that older sites might be using deprecated CSS properties, which might be technically correct if they're using an older HTML DOCTYPE, but won't do for the XHTML DOCTYPE you're using.

Again, validating your markup and CSS as you're developing will alert you to syntax errors, depreciated properties, and duplicate rules that could compound and cause issues in your stylesheet down the line.

# Advanced troubleshooting

Take some time to understand the XHTML hierarchy. You'll start running into validation errors and CSS styling issues if you wrap a "normal" (also known as a "block") element inside an "inline" only element such as putting a header tag (<h1>, <h2>, and so on) inside an anchor tag (<a href, <a name, and so on) or wrapping a div tag inside a span tag.

# Quirks mode

Quirks mode is one of the "modes" modern browsers run in (the other being strict mode) and use to interpret your CSS. Running more strictly was great for designers who learned the standards and were generating new pages; strict mode is great! But what about older sites and pages? Regardless of the fact that they should be updated, it's not nice to force people to update their sites, so quirks mode came into existence.

On the whole, quirks mode does make things go smoother, yet for ultimate smoothness, you really want to avoid triggering quirks mode in IE. This, if nothing else, is one of the most important reasons for using the W3C HTML validator.

Unfortunately, the IE browser itself doesn't seem to want to tell you if it's running in quirks mode. It doesn't seem to output that information anywhere (that I've found). However, if any part of your page or CSS isn't validating, it's a good way to trigger quirks mode in IE. Also, as I've mentioned before, IE has some well-documented wonks, and there are individuals and third parties who have created tools that exploit those wonks to determine if IE is running in quirks mode.

Find out more about quirks mode at
`http://www.quirksmode.org/css/quirksmode.html`.

I've found this little JavaScript bookmarklet from David Dorward quite valuable in determining which mode IE is in (and all other browsers, which can run in quirks mode too, but don't usually display your CSS so radically different as IE does), just drag the QorSMode link to your bookmarklet bar in all your testing browsers:
`http://dorward.me.uk/www/bookmarklets/qors/`.

The first way to avoid quirks mode is to make sure your DOCTYPE is valid and correct. If IE doesn't recognize the DOCTYPE (or if you have huge conflicts such as you have an XHTML DOCTYPE but use all-cap HTML 4.0 tags in your markup), IE will default into quirks mode and, from there onwards, who knows what you'll get in IE?

**My template stopped centering in IE!**

The most obvious thing that happens when IE goes into quirks mode, is that IE will stop centering your layout in the window properly if your CSS is using the: `margin: 0 auto;` technique. If this happens, immediately fix all the validation errors in your page. Another big obvious item to note is if your `div` layers with borders and padding are sized differently between browsers. If IE is running in quirks mode, it will incorrectly render the box model (we'll learn more about this in the next section), which is quite noticeable between Firefox and IE if you're using borders and padding in your `div` tags. This can also cause problems with font size rendering in your template. Your fonts may appear larger than expected.

Another item to keep track of is to make sure you don't have anything that will generate any text or code above your `DOCTYPE`.

Firefox will read your page until it hits a valid DOCTYPE and then proceed from there, but IE will just break and go into quirks mode.

# Fixing CSS across browsers

If you've been following our "debug and validate" method described in the chapter, then for all intents and purposes, your layout should look pretty spot-on between both the browsers.

## Box model issues

In the event that there is a visual discrepancy between Firefox and IE, in most cases it's a box model issue arising because you're running in quirks mode in IE. Generally, box model hacks apply to pre-IE6 browsers (IE5.x) and apply to IE6 if it's running in quirks mode. Again, running in quirks mode is to be preferably avoided, thus eliminating most of these issues. If your markup and CSS are validating (which means you shouldn't be triggering quirks mode in IE, but I've had people swear to me their page validated yet quirks mode was being activated), you might rather "live with it" than try to sleuth what's causing quirks mode to activate.

Basically, IE 5.x and IE 6 quirks mode don't properly interpret the box model standard. So, it will squish your borders and padding inside your box's width, instead of adding to the width as the W3C standard recommends.

However, IE does properly add margins! This means if you've a div set to 50 pixels wide, with a 5 pixel border, 5 pixels of padding, and 10 pixels of margin in Firefox, your div is actually going to be 60 pixels wide with 10 pixels of margin around it, taking up a total space of 70 pixels.

In IE quirks mode, your box is kept at 50 pixels wide (meaning it's probably taller than your Firefox div because the text inside is having to wrap at 40 pixels), yet it does have 10 pixels of margin around it. You can quickly see how even a one pixel border, some padding, and a margin can start to make a big difference in layout between IE and Firefox!

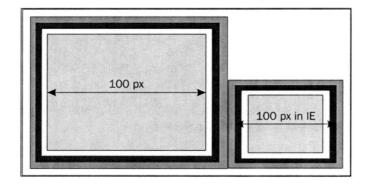

# Everything is relative

Most Windows users are still predominately using IE, though Firefox and other browsers are now gaining. When it comes to validating and debugging for IE, I find that as long as I stay in strict mode and not fall into quirks mode, I don't have too many issues with box model rendering. Occasionally, I still notice that relative CSS values such as % or .ems render a little differently, but that's not a box model issue so much as an issue with how the two browser engines interpret, say 20% to be in pixels. Even so, as long as your layout doesn't look weird, it's generally fine if your template's container div tags are a hair wider in one browser over the other. If you're using relative values to measure everything out, your layout placement will stay intact.

**What are the major browsers?**

According to W3schools, at the time of this writing, IE6, 7, and 8 combined together make up *just under* half of the total users! Firefox comes in first! Use this link to keep up on browsing trends: http://www.w3schools.com/browsers/browsers_stats.asp.

As I mentioned at the beginning of this chapter, you still need to look and make sure your site is rendering properly in as many browsers as you have access to. As a bonus, if you have access to multiple platforms (such as Linux or Mac, if you're on a PC), it's good to check and see how popular browsers who have distributions for those OSs look on them too.

If you're using a valid markup, you'll be pleasantly surprised to find out that your site looks great in all sorts of browsers and platforms. Occasionally, if you run into a situation where something doesn't look right, you can decide if that browser is critical to your users and if you'd like to fix it.

# To hack or not to hack

If, for some reason, you feel you know what you're getting into and have intentionally used markup syntax that's triggering quirks mode in IE (or you just can't figure out why, or maybe your client insists on designing for IE5.x for Windows), then it's time for some hacks.

The cleanest hack is the !important hack. I like it because it lets CSS still render as valid. However, you should note that the !important value is the valid syntax and meant to be used as an accessibility feature of CSS. It's not a value that was ever meant to affect the design.

The fact that IE does not recognize it is a bug and, though it's very simple and easy to implement, it's not recommended to be used liberally as a design fix. The understanding is, eventually (or already), IE will fix this bug so that it adheres to accessibility standards and then your hack will no longer work (especially if IE doesn't change anything about how it runs in quirks mode). In fact, this bug is supposed to be fixed in IE7 and IE8, but I've used it to fix a background property recently in IE7. It does appear to be fixed in IE8.

 **Remember:** All CSS hacks rely on exploiting various bugs in IE to some extent and may or may not continue to work with future service patches and upgrades to IE.

To implement the !important hack, take the width, height, margin, or padding property that has the discrepancy in it and duplicate it. Place the value that looks best in Firefox first and add the !important value after it. Then, place the value in the duplicate property that looks best in IE below the first property. You should have something that looks like this:

```
.classRule{
    height: 100px !important;
    height: 98px;
}
```

Firefox and all other browsers will read the value with the !important value after it, as if it were the last value in the rule. IE ignores the !important value and thus regular-old cascading kicks in, so it reads the actual last property value in the rule.

Other IE hacks include using the star selector bug hack (*) and the underscore hack (_). Both hacks work on the same general principle as the !important hack—IE does or doesn't recognize something that all the other browsers do or don't recognize themselves. You can find out more about the underscore hack from WellStyled.com (http://wellstyled.com/css-underscore-hack.html). A good overview of the star selector bug can be found at Info.com (http://www.info.com. ph/~etan/w3pantheon/style/starhtmlbug.html).

Be aware, those last two hacks will show up as validation errors in your CSS. Plus, the star and underscore hacks are rumored to no longer be viable in IE7 (ah! fixing those bugs!). You must choose to use these three hacks at your discretion.

# Out of the box model thinking

Your best bet is again to *not use hacks*. This is achieved in a couple of ways. First, you can break your XHTML markup down a little more. That means, for example, instead of one `div` layer:

```
<div id="leftSide">...</div>
```

with the assigned rule:

```
#leftSide{
width: 200px;
border: 2px;
padding: 10px;
}
```

This is clearly going to give you problems in quirks mode IE, because the `div` will stay at 200 pixels wide and squish your border and padding inside it. It would be better to tuck an extra `div` or other XHTML element inside the `leftSide` id such as:

```
<div id="leftSide"><div>...</div></div>
```

Then, you can control the width and borders much more accurately using CSS that looks as follows:

```
#leftSide{
width: 200px;
}
#leftSide div{
border: 2px;
padding: 10px;
}
```

Using a fix like that, your `div` will always be 200 pixels wide (despite the border and padding) in all the browsers, regardless of quirks mode. Plus, your XHTML markup and CSS stays valid.

**Container divs:**

I find working with CSS and XHTML markup like this also keeps you from getting into other trouble; let's say we do the math to figure our column widths and margins out, but then, either forget to account for borders and padding in the design or maybe just decide to add them later. In browsers such as Firefox, a miscalculation or late addition like that will throw columns off, especially if their containing `div` is set to an exact width. This results in ugly, stacked columns. As you noted in Chapter 2, when we built the theme mockup, I used lean containing `div` tags to control only placement, width, and margins. Then, I let inner `div` tags (which will by default, expand to the width of the containing `div`) take on borders, padding, and other visual stylings. This is a good way to get your math right and keep it right, no matter what design additions may come later.

Your final alternative is to just create two stylesheets for your theme—one for general browser use and one for IE browsers—and let each browser call them in.

This isn't as bad as it seems. The bulk of your CSS can stay in your main CSS file; you'll then call in the following specific IE stylesheet code, which will load additionally only if the browser is IE.

In the IE stylesheet, you'll duplicate the rules and correct the properties that were not looking correct in Firefox. Because this stylesheet will load in underneath your main stylesheet, any duplicated rules will overwrite the original rules in your first stylesheet. The result is CSS styling that's perfect in Firefox and IE. However, if you run the CSS validator in IE, it will alert you to the double rules.

In your `header.php`, `home.php`, or `index.php` template file (whichever file has your `<head>` tags in it), add the following code after your full stylesheet call:

```
<!--[if IE]>
    <link rel='stylesheet' type='text/css' href="ie-fix.css"
                            media='screen, projection' />
<![endif]-->
```

**Is that a conditional comment?!**

Yes it is. In the past, your best bet to loading in the proper stylesheet would have been using a server-side script to detect the browser with something like PHP. You could use a JavaScript as well, but if someone had JavaScript disabled in their browser, it wouldn't work. Not everyone can be a PHP whiz, hence I advocate the just discussed method for loading in your two stylesheets with minimal hassle. This method is also best for keeping your two stylesheets as simple as possible (having a main one, then one with IE fixes), but you can apply all sorts of control to the conditional comment above, giving you quite a bit of power in how you dole out your CSS. For instance, you can specify what version of IE to check for (IE5, IE6, or IE7). You can also invert the condition and only load in the CSS if the browser is not IE, by placing another exclamation point (!) in front of the IE (for example, `<!--[if !IE]>` `...<![endif]-->`). Learn more about this conditional CSS tag at `http://www.quirksmode.org/css/condcom.html`.

You have to add that code in the theme's template file or files that contain the `<head>` tags. I usually put it in under my main stylesheet call. Yes, it would be nice if something like this could be implemented into the actual CSS file and then only parts of our CSS would need to be specific, and we'd only need to keep track of one file, but alas, you have to add it to your theme's `header.php` or files that contain the header tags.

Also, please note that while I advocate using the `@import` method for bringing in stylesheets, that method will not work within the `<![if IE]>` CSS check. Use the standard link import tags that are used in this `include` method.

**CSS troubleshooting technique:**

The best way to quickly get a handle on a rule that's gone awry is to set a border and general background color to it. You'll notice I did this in Chapter 3 to the initial layout. Make the color something obvious and not part of your color scheme. Often, using this technique will reveal quite unexpected results, like showing that a `div` was inadvertently set somehow to just "500" wide instead of "500 px" wide, or perhaps that another `div` is pushing against it in a way you didn't realize. It will quickly bring to your attention all the actual issues affecting your object's box model that need to be fixed to get your layout back in line.

# The road to validation

You'll always want to validate your XHTML first. This is just as well because W3C's CSS validator won't even look at your CSS, if your XHTML isn't valid.

Go to `http://validator.w3.org/` and if your file is on a server, you can just enter in the URL address to it. If you're working locally, from your browser you'll need to choose **Save Page As** and save an HTML file of your theme's WordPress output and upload that full HTML file output to the validator using the upload field provided.

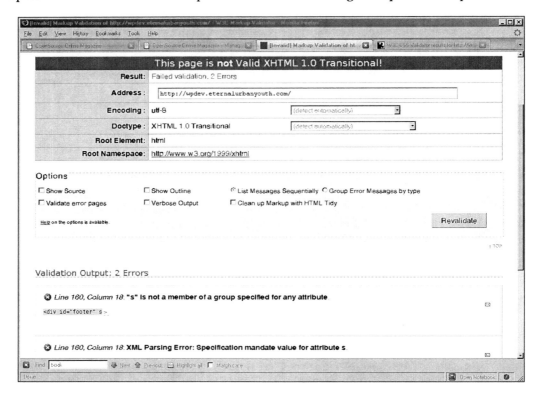

In this example, you can see that we have a typo in one of our `div` tags (looks like an odd "s" got in there somehow), and we have an image tag that doesn't have the proper closing (/) in it. Wherever possible, you'll note that the validator tries to tell us how to fix the error. Whenever a recommendation is made, go ahead and implement it.

We'll need to fix those two errors and run the validation again to make sure we're now validating. Don't just think you can fix the errors listed and move on without validating again. Occasionally, an error will be so grievous that it will block other errors from being picked up until it's fixed. Always "validate, fix, validate", until you get that happy green bar telling you that you're good to move on.

**Where's my error?**

The validator tells us which line the offensive code appears in; that is why we love HTML editors that display the line number to the left in our code view. However, once your theme is pulling in the content from WordPress, the line in which the offense appears in is not necessarily the same code line in your specific theme template anymore. So where's the error? Well, you have to know your template files enough to recognize where the error might be, for instance, I know that `<div id="footer">` is in my `footer.php` template file. Once I know the general file, I work around this by copying some unique text from the error, (in my case, `s>`). You can also use text from an `alt` or `id` tag within the reported object. Then, use the **Find** option in your editor to directly locate the error.

Ideally, when you run your XHTML through the validator, you'll get a screen with a green bar that says **This Page Is Valid XHTML 1.0 Transitional!**.

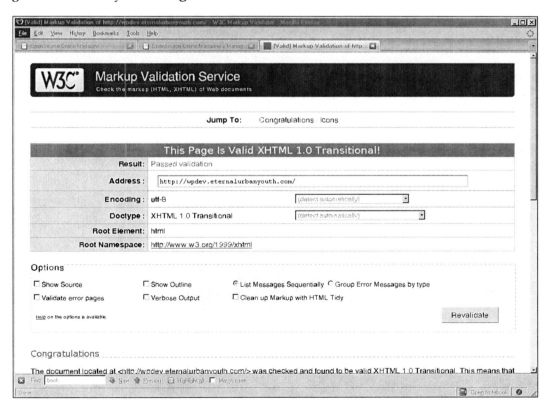

You can then move on to checking your CSS.

Open up another tab in your browser and go to `http://jigsaw.w3.org/css-validator/`. Again, same deal! If you're working off a server, then just enter the address of your CSS file on the development site and check the results. Otherwise, you'll have to use the **Validate by File Upload** tab and upload a copy of your CSS file.

Here you'll want to see another screen with a green bar that says **Congratulations! No Error Found.**

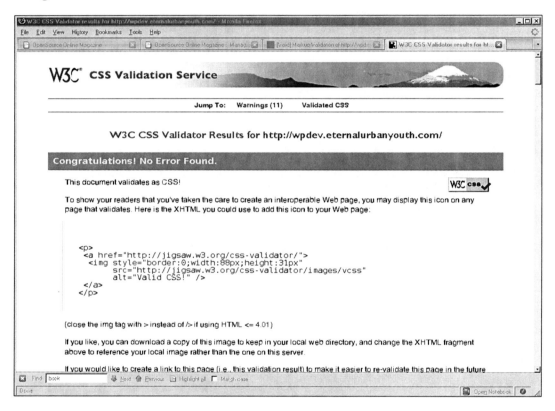

If you don't get the green bar, the validator will display the offending error and again offer suggestions on how to fix it. The CSS validator will also show you the line of code the offense takes place on. This is handy, as your stylesheet is not affected by WordPress output, so you can go right to the line mentioned and make the suggested fix.

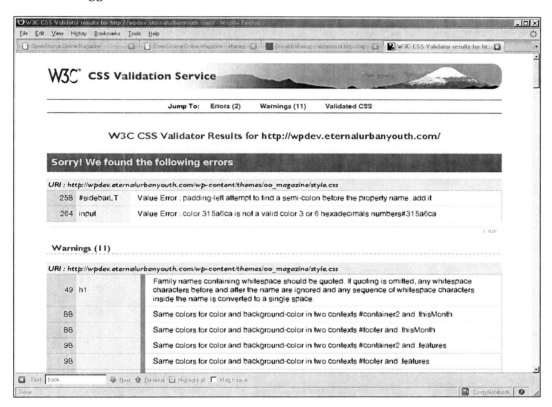

# Advanced validation

Perhaps you've discovered (because you are talented indeed and would find something like this) that your XHTML and CSS validates, yet somehow something is still wrong with your layout. Or maybe, you're using some special JavaScripts to handle certain aspects or features of your theme. W3C's XHTML and CSS tools won't validate JavaScript. If you find yourself in this situation, you're going to have to dig a little deeper to get to the root of the problem and/or make sure all aspects (such as JavaScripts) of your theme's files are valid.

# Firefox's JavaScript/Error Console

You can use Firefox's JavaScript/Error Console (called the JavaScript Console in 1.x and Error Console in 2.x) to debug and validate any JavaScripts your theme is using. Go to **Tools | Error Console** in your browser to activate it; you can also activate it by typing **JavaScript:** into your address bar and hitting *Enter* on your keyboard.

You will be pleasantly surprised to find out that the console will also spit out several warnings and errors for CSS rules that the W3C's validators probably didn't tell you about. The Error Console does hold a log of all errors it encounters for all pages you've looked at. Therefore, the best way to proceed with the **Error Console** is to first hit **Clear** and then reload your page to be sure that you're looking only at current bugs and issues for that specific page.

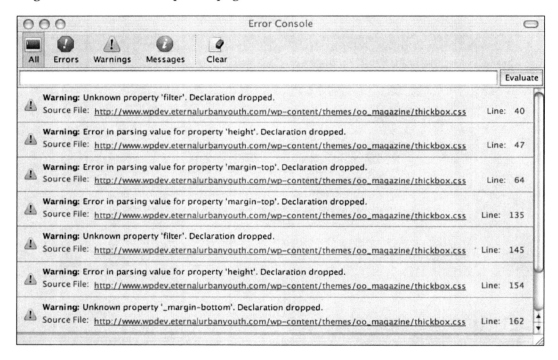

Again, the **Error Console** will let you know what file and line the offending code is in, so you can go right to it and make the suggested fix. In my previous screenshot, it looks like the console is taking issue with the `thickbox.css` file. (Thickbox is a web user interface feature we'll look at in Chapter 9.)

# The Web Developer Toolbar

This is a great extension that adds a toolbar to your Firefox browser. The extension is also available for the Seamonkey suite and the new Flock browser, both of which are like Firefox, powered by the open source code of Mozilla.

Get it from `http://chrispederick.com/work/web-developer/`.

The toolbar lets you link directly to the DOM browsers and Error Consoles, and W3C's XHTML, and CSS validation tools. It also lets you toggle and view your CSS output in various ways, and lets you view and manipulate a myriad of information your site page is outputting on-the-fly. The uses of this toolbar are endless. Every time I'm developing a design I find some feature that I have never used previously, and which is quite useful.

# Firebug

A more robust tool is Joe Hewitt's Firebug extension for Firefox (there's a "Firebug Lite" version for Internet Explorer, Safari, and Opera available at `http://www.getfirebug.com/`).

This extension is a powerhouse when combined with the features of the Web Developer Toolbar and even on its own, will find them all—XHTML, CSS, JavaScript, and even little "weirdo" tidbit things happening to your DOM (Document Object Model), on-the-fly. There's a variety of fun inspectors and just about all of them are invaluable.

Here is an extract from the Firebug FAQ site about Linux and Firebug (`http://www.getfirebug.com/faq.html`):

> *Firebug does work on Linux, but some distributions don't compile Mozilla correctly, and it is missing the components that Firebug depends on. Even more common is the case of individual Linux users compiling their own Firefox binaries incorrectly.*

Once you have Firebug installed into your browser, you can turn it off and on by hitting *F12* or going to **View | Firebug**.

My favorite Firebug features are the options for reviewing HTML, CSS, and the DOM. Firebug will show you your box models and let you see the measurements of each ledge. Plus, the latest version of Firebug lets you make edits on-the-fly to easily experiment with different fixes before committing them to your actual document. (There are features that let you do this using the Web Developer Toolbar as well, but I find the Firebug interface more in-depth; see the following screenshot.)

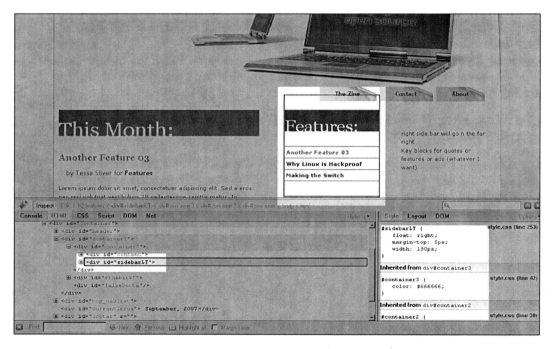

**DOM?**

We've mentioned DOM a few times in this book. Learning about the Document Object Model can really enhance your understanding of your XHTML for WordPress themes (or any web page you design), as well as help you better understand how to effectively structure your CSS rules and write cleaner and accurate JavaScripts. For more information, you can refer the W3C website (http://w3schools.com/htmldom/default.asp).

# Checking your work in Internet Explorer

Remembering that you'll need to check your work in all browsers, at some point you're going to switch over and check everything out in various versions of Internet Explorer. Here are a few tools I've found useful:

## Run multiple versions of IE

As much as I would love to stop supporting IE6, I have quite a few clients who just won't move up to IE7. I also have clients who've been in IE8 as a beta for quite some time already. Worse, each version of IE6, IE7, and IE8 does something completely unique and special with different CSS parameters, depending on if it's running in standard or quirks mode. Worse still, Microsoft seems to insist you have only one IE browser on your computer system.

To get all three versions on my machine, I use TredoSoft's Multiple IE tool to install IE6. I then have IE8 as my "official IE install" and use its "compatibility view" to test for IE7.

I'm on a Mac with Windows XP installed on Parallels. I don't know if this install runs on Vista yet. Get Multiple IE from http://tredosoft.com/Multiple_IE.

## IE Developer Toolbar

Although going through the methods in this chapter with the W3C validation tools and Firefox extensions will suffice, IE has a Developer Toolbar that gives you very similar access to your DOM, CSS, JavaScript, and a few other options as FireFox's Web Developer Toolbar. Sometimes it's useful (if not interesting) to be able to poke through the details on both the browsers. You can get the toolbar from Microsoft's site. You can just search in Google for "IE Developer Toolbar"; however, here is the URL: `http://www.microsoft.com/downloads/details.aspx?familyid=e59c3964-672d-4511-bb3e-2d5e1db91038&displaylang=en`.

## Don't forget about the QorSMode bookmarklet

I mentioned this great little JavaScript bookmarklet earlier in this chapter. You can use it (refer to the `http://dorward.me.uk/www/bookmarklets/qors/` site) in all your testing browsers to see if you're in quirks or standards mode.

# Optimizing for text and mobile browsers

If you want a better understanding of how text-only browsers or some users on mobile devices are viewing your site (not including the new iPhone or iPod Touch and similar graphical interface mobile browsers), you can use Google's mobile viewing tool to give you an idea. This may help you visualize how to better arrange your site semantically for users in these categories.

To use this Google tool, type the following into your browser:

`http://www.google.com/gwt/n?u=http://yoursitegoeshere.com.`

You'll now be able to see how your complete site looks without CSS styling. You can even turn off images. Use this to think about if your WordPress content is loading in logically and in the order of importance you prefer for your viewers. Also keep in mind, this is very similar to how a search engine bot will crawl your page from top to bottom and thus the order in which the content will be indexed.

# The new mobile Safari browser

The good news about your site and iPhone/iPod Touch users is that Mobile Safari (the mobile web browser Apple products use) is graphical. This means the browser seems to be able to take snapshots of your site fully rendered and shrink it down into the mobile browser, allowing a user to zoom in and out on the content.

Mobile Safari attempts to be standards compliant and, apparently, does a pretty good job of it. If you've followed this book's guidance on creating W3C standards-compliant XHTML markup and CSS in the creation of your template, your WordPress site will most likely show up stunningly on an iPhone or iPod Touch. The only major drawback I've seen in the Mobile Safari browser is the lack of Flash support; that is tough if your site has (or relies on) Flash content (this includes embedded YouTube, Google Video, or Jumpcut clips) on your site.

**Want more information on designing for mobile devices?**

A List Apart (as always) has some great information on designing for devices including the iPhone: http://www.alistapart.com/articles/putyourcontentinmypocket.

**Interested in Mobile Safari?**

Check out this great O'Reilly Digital ShortCut by August Trometer: Optimizing your website for Mobile Safari, ensuring your website works on the iPhone and iPod touch (Digital ShortCut). It's a digital PDF you can purchase and download from inFormIt.com: http://www.informit.com/store/product.aspx?isbn=0321544013.

# Summary

In this chapter, we reviewed the basic process of debugging and validating your theme's XHTML markup, PHP code, and CSS. We learned how to use W3C's, XHTML, and CSS validation tools, and we further explored using Firefox as a valuable development tool by using its Error Console and available extensions such as the Web Developer Toolbar and Firebug.

Next, it's time to package up the design and send it to our client!

# 5

# Putting Your Theme into Action

Now that we've got our theme designed, styled, and looking great, we just have one last thing to do. It's time to share your theme with your client, friends, and/or the rest of the WordPress community. This is the whole point of creating a theme in WordPress; your designs are separate from the WordPress CMS content and therefore easily shareable. This means that, anyone can create a WordPress theme and anybody else can install that theme into their WordPress installation. You are not restricted to only certain themes working with certain WordPress installations.

In this chapter, we'll discuss how to:

- Properly set up your theme's `style.css` so that it loads into WordPress installations correctly
- Compress your theme files into the ZIP file format
- Run some test installations of your theme package in WordPress' Administration Panel

## A picture's worth

Before we begin wrapping up our theme package, we'll need one more asset—the theme's preview thumbnail. Take a screenshot of your final layout, resize it, and save it out to be about 200 pixels wide. Place your image in your theme's root directory structure and ensure that it's named `screenshot.png`.

WordPress offers previews of themes using `screenshot.png`. It's in your best interest to take advantage of it. If you don't add a screenshot, WordPress will simply display a grey box. As mentioned, many shared hosting solutions pre-install many themes with their installations of WordPress. It can be difficult to scroll through all the textual names trying to find the theme you just installed by remembering its name. As most people will know what the theme they want to activate looks like, having the `screenshot.png` preview set up will help them out.

In a nutshell, there's not a whole lot involved in getting your new theme together and ready for the world. By using the default theme as our base for file reference and following good testing and validation standards, we already pretty much have a WordPress-approved theme according to their *Designing Themes for Public Release* document.

For other tips, including how to promote your new WordPress theme, check out the document I just mentioned:

`http://codex.wordpress.org/Designing_Themes_for_Public_Release`

# Theme packaging basics

To make sure your template is ready to go public, run through the following steps before packaging it up:

1. Remove all the unnecessary files hanging out in your theme's root directory! As I work on a theme, I often copy in files from the default theme in order to quickly reference them. I make sure to name them something like `orig_header.php`, and so on, for quick and easy reference of template tags that I will use in my theme, but those *must be cleared out* before you package up. Be sure that only the files required to run the theme are left in your directory. Don't forget to test your theme one more times *after* deleting files to ensure you didn't accidentally delete a file your theme uses!

2. Open up the `style.css` sheet and make sure that all the information contained in it is accurate. I had you fill this out in the beginning of Chapter 3 when we were setting up our development theme directory, but I'll review it in detail in the following section.

3. Create a `ReadMe.txt` file. Let your users know what version your theme is compatible with, how to install it, and if it has any special features or requirements.

4. Zip it up and put it out there! Get some feedback and install it in your client's installation of WordPress, upload it to your own website, or to your favorite user group, or post it directly on `http://themes.wordpress.net/`. The choice is yours!

# Describing your theme

We very briefly discussed this in Chapter 3, just to get our development going, but let's review exactly what kind of information you can place into your stylesheet which will show up in the WordPress **Theme Administration** Panel. Essentially, the first 18 lines of the `style.css` sheet are commented out and without changing anything that comes before a colon (:), you can fill out the following information about your template:

1. **Theme Name**: This is where you'll put the full name of your theme.

2. **Theme URI**: Here you'll place the location from where the theme can be downloaded.

3. **Description**: It's a quick description of what the theme looks like, any specific purpose it's best suited for, and/or any other theme it's based on or inspired by.

4. **Version:** If this is your theme's debut, you may want to put 1.0. If the theme has been changed, had bug fixes, or been reincarnated in any way, you may feel a higher version is appropriate. As this is essentially the same theme I've created for another project, I've just changed its color scheme, graphics, and reduced its functionality. I've numbered it version 1.3 (for the three major visual revision processes it's gone through).

5. **Author:** Your name as the theme's author goes here.

6. **Author URI:** It's a URL to a page where people can find out more about you.

7. **The CSS, XHTML, and design are released under __:** This is optional. You can use this area to describe any licensing conditions you want for your theme. The WordPress Administration Panel will not display it though; only people who've downloaded your theme and viewed the `style.css` file will see it.

**Links in the Themes tab:**

WordPress works some impressive "PHP magic" to run through that comment and parse the URI links into the appropriate places. You can also add your own URL's by hand-coding `<a href>` links into comments. Just test the output in the **Administrator | Themes** area (or **Administrator | Design | Themes** in 2.5+x, **Administrator | Presentation | Themes** in version 2.3.x) to ensure your link syntax is correct and not broken!

# Licensing

You'll find that most WordPress themes you found on the web either do not mention licensing or use the GNU General Public License (GPL) license. If you're not familiar with the GNU GPL, you can learn more about it at `http://www.gnu.org/copyleft/gpl.html`.

You may wish to do the same with your theme, if you want it to be freely distributed, available to all, and changeable by all, with no permissions necessary as long as they acknowledge you.

If you've created a completely original design that you intend to sell commercially, or just want to be able to grant permission for any other possible use, you'll want to place specific copyright information and the name of the person or organization that holds the copyright. Something like © 2008 My Name, All Rights Reserved, is generally recognized as legal with or without any formal copyright filing procedures (but you should look up how to best formally copyright your design material!).

This book's theme has been leveraged from another project of mine for Packt Publishing for educational purposes. While the GNU GPL is more than adequate, its text is a bit more "software-ish" and "tech-heavy" than I'd like, so I'm going to redistribute the Open Source Magazine theme under a more general-public-friendly Creative Commons license (`http://creativecommons.org`).

I'll use the CC Labs DHTML License Chooser to assist me in selecting an appropriate license (`http://labs.creativecommons.org/dhtmllicense/`):

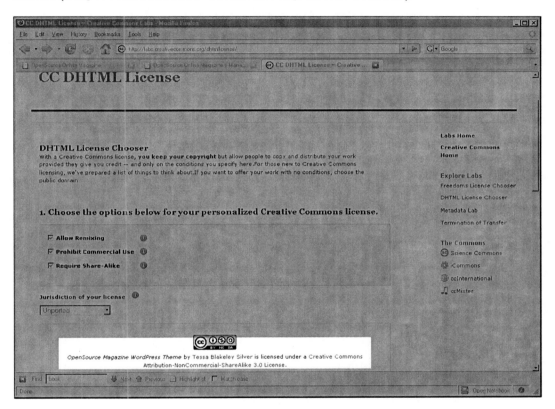

I'll of course allow sharing of the theme, and let others "Remix", which means, derive new themes from this theme with proper credit. I will, however, prevent it from being sold commercially by another entity (commercial sites are welcome to download it and use it), and require the "Share-Alike" option. This means that no one can legally take the theme package and offer it for sale or use it in such a way that it generates income for them without my permission. If they reuse or redesign the package in any other non-commercial way, they're free to do so; they're simply required to give me and Packt Publishing credit where credit is due.

My licensing agreement looks like the following:

**OpenSource Magazine WordPress Theme by Tessa Blakeley Silver is licensed under a Creative Commons Attribution-NonCommercial-ShareAlike 3.0 License.**

The end result is a license that keeps to the spirit of the GNU GPL, but is much less technical-vocabulary heavy. It tells the user upfront that it allows sharing, which is important to us for educational purposes and prevents commercial distribution without permission, and by requiring "Share-Alike," encourages a continued friendly WordPress-esque atmosphere of open source collaboration. It also expressly states the version number of the license, making it very easy for anyone to look up and read in detail.

# Creating a ReadMe.txt file

You're now ready to create a `ReadMe.txt` file. ReadMe files have a long history with computers, often accompanying software installation. This has carried over to the Web where anything that gets added or installed into a web service usually has a ReadMe file included. Many theme authors choose to make the ReadMe file a `.rtf` or `.html` file so that they can include formatting. You may deliver it in any format you wish. I prefer `.txt` files because it ensures that everyone can simply click to open the file, and the lack of formatting options ensures I keep my text as clear and concise as possible.

ReadMe files are not required for your theme to work, but if you want to have happy theme users, they're highly recommended. Your ReadMe file is generally your first defense against theme users with installation and usage questions.

These are the basics of what you should cover in your WordPress theme ReadMe file:

- Inform theme users what your theme and template files will do (what kind of site it works best with, if any plugins work with it, if it's "Widit-ized", and so on—WordPress will let you know that a theme is widget-ready once you've activated it, not before, so it's nice to let people know in advance).

- Inform theme users of any deficiencies in your theme (any plugins it does not play well with or types of content it doesn't handle well, that is; I've seen good themes that don't do well with YouTube content due to column width, among others).

- Discuss any specific modifications you've made to the theme (especially if it's a newer version of a theme you've previously released) and what files contain the modifications (it's always good to have comments in those files that explain the modification as well).

- Reiterate the basic steps for installing a WordPress theme (not everyone is keen on reading through WordPress' codex site and will know how to unzip the theme or where to upload the file). Also, mention any special requirements your theme has. For instance, if you included some custom PHP code that requires special CHMOD (a.k.a. RewriteRules) or anything like that, specifically list the steps of action a user should take to get your theme running.

- As mentioned in Chapter 4, try and test your theme across platforms and browsers and mention any rendering issues that certain browsers may have on specific platforms.

- Reiterate the copyright information that you placed into your `style.css` sheet and provide your contact information (web page or e-mail) so that people can reach you for support and questions.

**ReadThisToo.txt:**

As long as your ReadMe file includes the points just discussed, you're generally good to go! However, if you're gearing up to release themes for commercial sale, Tonya Engst's article on writing a ReadMe file is great. It's geared toward software developers, but can provide invaluable insight to your theme's ReadMe file (if the following URL is too long, you can also just go to `mactech.com` and use the Google search bar to search for **ReadMe file**):

`http://www.mactech.com/articles/mactech/Vol.14/14.10/`
`WritingAReadMeFile/index.html`

# Zipping it up

We're now ready to zip up our theme files and test an installation of our theme package. Zipping is just the file compression type WordPress prefers, though it's suggested you offer at least two kinds of compression, such as `.zip` and `.rar` or `.tar`. If you're a Windows PC user, chances are you're very familiar with zipping files. If you're a Mac user, it's just as easy. As a new Mac user, I was thrilled to discover its built-in support for creating ZIP archives similar to Windows XP (and I assume Vista). Select your theme's directory and right-click or *Ctrl*-click to select **Create Archive**.

Even if you're working off a server, rather than locally, it's probably best if you download your theme's directory and zip them up on your local machine. Plus, you'll want to test your install and almost everyone will be uploading your file off their local machine.

# No way to zip?

If you're on an older computer and don't have compression software, you'll have to take a little tour of the Internet to find the very best zip solution for you. There are tons of free archiving and compression tools that offer the ZIP format.

So let's start with the obvious. If you don't have any compression tools, head over to `http://www.stuffit.com/`. You'll find that StuffIt software is available for Mac or PC and lets you compress and expand several different types of formats including `.zip`. The standard edition is most likely all you'll ever need, and while there's nothing wrong with purchasing good commercial software, you'll have plenty of time to play with the trial version. The trial for the standard software is 15 days, but you might find that it lasts longer than that (especially if you're patient while the continue trial button loads). If you're on a PC, you also have WinZip as an option (`http://www.winzip.com/`) where again, you're given a trial period that does seem to last longer than the suggested 45 days.

WinZip and StuffIt are considered "industry standard" software. They've been around for a good while and are stable products with which, for under $50, you can't go too wrong.

**Come on, where's the free open source stuff?**

If you must have truly free compression software and are on a PC, there is 7-Zip (`http://www.7-zip.org/`). I've only minimally played around with 7-Zip, but it does create and expand ZIP files and can even compress in a new format (called 7z) that gives better compression than standard ZIP files. Unfortunately, not too many people are readily using the 7z format yet, so make sure you're also creating a standard zip version of your theme when you use it.

Each compression utility has its own interface and procedures for creating a standard .zip file. I'll assume that you have one, or have chosen one from above, and have made yourself familiar with how to use it.

# Performing one last test

You're now ready to test the package. Start from scratch. If at all possible, don't install the theme back into your sandbox installation (especially if it's on your local machine). If your sandbox is all you have for some reason, I recommend you rename your existing development theme directory or back it up (so you're sure to be testing your package).

Ideally, you'll want to install your theme on a web server installation, preferably the one where the theme is going to be used (if it's a custom design for a single client) or under the circumstances you feel your theme's users are most likely to use it (for example, if you're going to post your theme for download on WordPress' theme directory, then test your theme on an installation of WordPress on a shared hosting environment that most people use).

Don't assume the ZIP or compression file you made is going to unzip or unpack properly (files have been known to get corrupted). Follow the procedure you know your client will be using or the procedure that someone finding your theme on the Web will perform:

1.  Unzip the directory (if applicable, download it from wherever it will be accessed from, and then try to unzip the directory).

2.  FTP the directory to the `wp_content/themes` directory.

3.  Go to **Administration | Themes** (or **Administration | Design | Themes** in 2.5+.x, **Administration | Presentation | Themes** in 2.3.x) and see if your theme is there.

4.  Select the theme and make sure it displays properly.

With the successful installation and testing of your theme, you now have an understanding of the entire WordPress theme development process — from conception to packaging.

# Getting some feedback and tracking it

You're not quite done! Great design doesn't happen in a vacuum. If you've developed your theme for private use by a client, then you've probably already gone through a rigorous process of feedback and changes during the theme's development. But if you're developing a theme for commercial sale, free distribution, or even just for yourself, you'll want to get some feedback. How much feedback is up to you. You might just want to e-mail a handful of friends and ask them what they think. If you plan to widely distribute your theme freely or commercially, you really should offer a way for people to review a demo of your theme and post comments about it.

At first glance, if you're happy with something, you might not want anyone else's input. Having to hear criticism is hard. However, there's a scientific term called "emergence", and it basically dictates that "we" is smarter than "me". It's the basis behind a lot of things, from how ants form food routes for their colonies, to how people in urban areas create neighborhood niches, and why the Web is transforming itself into a huge social network. As far as feedback goes, if you have a group of people guess how many jelly beans are in a jar, the average of everyone's answer will be closer to the exact amount than anyone's single guess. Now, design aesthetics are a lot more ambiguous than the correct number of jelly beans in a jar, but using this principle in receiving feedback is still something your theme can really take advantage of.

See how people use your theme. You'll be surprised at the situations and circumstances they attempt to use it in, as you may never have thought of these on your own. After several feedback comments, you'll probably be able to detect patterns: what kind of hosting they're using, what kind of sites (discussed in Chapter 2) they are applying it to, and most importantly, what about the theme is working for them and what drawbacks they are encountering.

You'll be able to offer version upgrades to your theme by being able to see if it needs any tweaks or additions made to it. More importantly, you'll also see if there's anything in your theme that can be pared down, removed, or simplified. Remember that more isn't always better!

# Summary

In this chapter, we reviewed describing our theme in the `style.css` commented header and how to package up your finished theme into a working ZIP file that anyone should be able to upload into their own WordPress installation.

Congratulations! You now know about getting a WordPress theme design off that coffee shop napkin and into the real world! In the next few chapters, we'll get down into the "real-world" nitty-gritty of getting things done quickly with our theme Markup Reference and "how to" chapters. We'll cover the key design tips and cool "how to's," such as how to set up dynamic drop-down menus, best practices for integrating Flash, AJAX techniques, useful plugins, and more.

# 6

# WordPress Template Tag, Function, and CSS Reference

If you like quick reference guides and cheatsheet charts, this chapter is for you. It's one thing to be walked through a general development and another when you're developing on your own. Often, you'll just need the syntax of a function or template tag or know what all the CSS classes a function outputs.

This chapter will cover information to help you with your WordPress theme development. It includes:

- A comprehensive listing of essential template tags
- The various CSS class styles generated by Template Tags, include tags, and functions
- WordPress' template hierarchy
- A breakdown of The Loop
- A few other functions and features you can take advantage of such as Shortcodes

I'll review the essentials with you and how to expand on them and then give you key links to bookmark, should you be interested in more detail.

# Class styles generated by WordPress

As we learned in Chapter 3, WordPress content is generated mostly by those bits of PHP code known as template tags, which look like `have_posts` or `the_category`, and so on.

Until recently, WordPress template tags did not output many CSS styles. In Chapter 3, we used the `wp_list_pages` tag and learned it output a few classes that could be used to style menu items. With the release of 2.7 and now 2.8, we have a few new template tag functions that output quite a few class styles.

What I find particularly nice about WordPress' class styles is they're *descriptive* and *useful* and if you choose, *optional*. I would recommend that you do leverage them and be sure you account for them in your theme's style sheet.

**Styling tip**

Remember, you can set CSS styling rules not only for CSS classes such as `.classname`, but also for XHTML markup objects such as h2, li, p, div, form, and so on, and for IDs such as `#idname`. In targeting objects, classes, and IDs you have quite a bit of power in controlling your theme's layout!

# The search bar ID

WordPress outputs a few ID names on XHTML markup objects, but almost all of these also have a class name added as well for styling. The only WordPress generated ID names that I consistently find the need to create styles for is the `#searchform`, s, and searchsubmit ID which is assigned to the search bar like so:

```
<form method="get" id="searchform" action="http://yourdevurl.com/">
<div><input value="" name="s" id="s" type="text">
<input id="searchsubmit" value="Search" type="submit">
</div>
</form>
```

In order to control the search bar effectively, you'll find that creating CSS rules for the above IDs will help you have more control over the search form. I find, at the very minimum, I need to create a rule for `#searchformsubmit`.

```
. . .
#searchsubmit{
 width: 150px;
 border: 1px solid #253A59;
 background-color: #8BA8BA;
 color: #ffffff;
}
. . .
```

The previous code produces markup that looks like this:

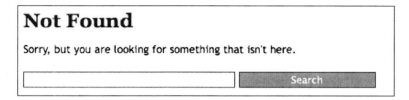

## Classes output by the media manager

The following are the options available when uploading an image using WordPress' media manager:

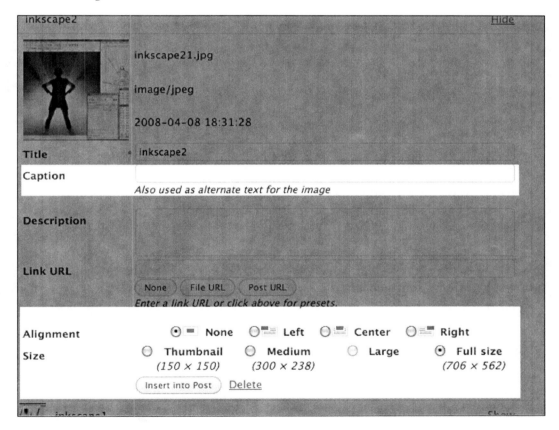

Any images uploaded through WordPress' media manager will have the following classes elegantly applied, depending on the options you selected when uploading the image:

- `.aligncenter`: This style is generated if you select **Center**. A good way to ensure this style is centered is:

```
...
div.aligncenter {
    display: block;
    margin-left: auto;
    margin-right: auto;
}
...
```

- `.alignleft`: This class is generated if you select **Left**.
- `.alignright`: This class is generated if you select **Right**.

Your best bet for the `.alignleft` and `.alignright` classes is to simply assign floats like so:

```
...
.alignleft {
    float: left;
}

.alignright {
    float: right;
}
...
```

In addition to the alignment, if you choose to write a caption for your image, the following classes will be generated:

- `.wp-caption`: Wraps the image and the caption text in a `div` which also includes the alignment class from above if you selected one.
- `.wp-caption-text`: Wraps the specific text in a `p` tag with this class assigned. This class appears inside the outer `div` with the `.wp-caption` class assigned to that `div`, like so:

```
...
<div id="attachment_12" class="wp-caption alignleft" style="width:
160px;">

<img class="size-thumbnail wp-image-12" title="plant2"
```

```
src="http://yourdevurl.com/wp-content/uploads/2008/03/plant21-
150x150.jpg" alt="this is my caption" height="150" width="150"/>

<p class="wp-caption-text">this is my caption</p>
</div>
...
```

As you can see, WordPress takes your caption and adds it to the `alt` attribute of the image tag. The `wp-caption` class is added to the outer containing and alignment `div` and the actual caption text is added again, to a paragraph tag with the `wp-caption-text` class, which is tucked under the image tag, all neatly wrapped inside the containing alignment `div`.

This arrangement gives you a lot of flexibility with CSS rules while designing. For example, you may wish to just style `.wp-caption-text` or, you may want to have images that have captions, styled differently than images that don't have captions. By creating a style for `.wp-caption`, you could achieve that.

# Classes output by the sidebar widgets

The following classes are output by the various default widgets available in WordPress:

- `.widget`: If you use the standard function to register a sidebar and "widigtize" your theme, this class will be appended to every `<li>` tag produced by a widget. You can customize the register sidebar function so that this class will not appear.

- `.textwidget`: This class is added to text generated by the Text widget.

- `.blogroll`: This class is generated by the Links widget (your blogroll). It is added to the main `ul` wrapper.

- `.linkcat`: This class is added to the `<li>` of every link that has a `href` link for a category.

# Classes output by the wp_list_pages template tag

We first discussed the `wp_list_pages` template tag in Chapter 2. In Chapter 3, we discovered that if you pass this template tag a parameter of `title_li=`, WordPress assumes you're going to use the list as a set of navigation links, so it helps you out by adding the following class styles to the `<li>` tags generated by the template:

- `.page_item`: This is applied to each list item tag in a page list (even page lists generated by the **Page** widget).

- `.page-item-(number)`; for example, `.page-item-23`: This is the specific page number applied to the list item. If you know what the page number is, you can write a style specifically for just a single page item if you want.

- `.current_page_item`: This class is assigned to the currently selected page. You can use this class to highlight the current page in the navigation (this is great for "tabbed" navigation effects, like in this book's case study).

- `.current_page_parent`: If the currently selected page has a parent page, that parent will have this class appended to it. This is useful for nested list displays of page navigation; you can highlight the main page parent as well as the current page in a display list.

- `.current_page_ancestor`: For multilevel, nested page display lists, if the current page selected is say, three levels or more deep, the immediate parent will get the `.current_page_parent` class applied and any "ancestors" of that parent page will have this class applied. Again, this is most useful for drop-down lists or nested list displays, as you'll be able to highlight the entire page hierarchy "trail" to a currently selected page.

A sample of some nested page links may look like this:

```
. . .
<li class="page_item page-item-2 current_page_ancestor current_
page_parent"><a href="http://yourdevurl.com/?page_id=2"
title="About">About</a>
<ul>
        <li class="page_item page-item-19"><a href="http://yourdevurl.
com/?page_id=19" title="Open Resources">Open Resources</a></li>
        <li class="page_item page-item-16 current_page_item"><a
href="http://yourdevurl .com/?page_id=16" title="What is Open
Source">What is Open Source</a></li>
. . .
```

As you can see, WordPress takes advantage of a CSS feature which lets you apply as many CSS class styles as you'd like to a single XHTML object. You simply leave a space in between each class name.

By applying those two classes to the `wp_page_list()` template tag, WordPress enables you to create a very flexible navigation layout using pure CSS.

If you wanted to use WordPress as a full CMS, you could have many pages and their subpages displayed in a clean navigation menu. In fact, in Chapter 8, I'll cover how to use this template tag's output to create a great dynamic drop-down menu.

# Classes output by the wp_list_categories template tag

This template tag works very similarly to the `list_pages` template tag (it also includes category lists output by your sidebar widget):

- `.cat-item`: This is applied to each `li` item in a category listing
- `.cat-item-`(number); for example, cat-item-23: This is also applied to each listing for the specific category number
- `.current-cat`: If a category is currently selected, this will display in the `li` item
- `.current-cat-parent`: If a category is nested and selected, this will display in the `li` item of that parent

# post_class class styles

This function, released with WordPress 2.7 generates CSS styles on the post and allows us to style the new sticky post feature that was released with version 2.7 along with several other distinctions.

Most importantly, the `post_class` tag will spit out the `.sticky` class if the post has been marked as sticky in the Administration panel.

You call the `post_class` in the loop by placing it in the main `div` (as we did in Chapter 3):

```
...
<?php while (have_posts()) : the_post(); ?>
        <div <?php post_class() ?> id="post-<?php the_ID(); ?>">
...
```

The `post` spits out these specific CSS classes that you can style for:

- `.post`: Lets you style the class as a post
- `.hentry`: This is actually a microformat, but of course you could style to it instead of using `post`
- `.sticky`: Defines and allows additional styling if the post has been marked sticky
- `.category-(name of category)`; for example, `.category-features`: Lets you create custom styling for whatever category the post is assigned to (this is great—you can create CSS rules for different categories; just be careful of multiple category assignments)
- `.tag-(name of tag)`; for example, `.tag-images`: Defines what tags the `post` has assigned to it (you can further add CSS customization based on this similar to the category style lists)

# body_class class styles

As of WordPress 2.8, we now have the `body_class()` function. This function works similar to the `post_class` function and can be placed directly, out of the loop, in the beginning `<body>` tag.

Simply add the body class function to the template file that your opening `<body>` tag is placed in, like so:

```
<body <?php body_class(); ?>>
```

When you check the **View Source** on your theme in the browser, depending on what type of content has loaded, you'll notice and be able to target (on a larger scale than just posts) any of the following class styles:

- `archive`
- `attachment`
- `attachment-(mime-type of file)`; for example, `.attachement-zip`
- `attachmentid-(id number)`; for example, `attachementid-23`
- `author`
- `author-(user_nicename)`; for example, `author-admin`
- `author-paged-(page number)`; for example, `author-paged-23`
- `blog`
- `category`
- `category-(category name)`; for example, `.category-images`
- `category-paged-(page number)`; for example, `category-paged-23`

- date
- date-paged-(page number); *for example,* dated-paged-23
- error404
- home
- logged-in
- page-child
- parent-pageid-(id); *for example,* parent-pageid-4
- page-paged-(page number); *for example,* page-paged-23
- page-parent
- page-template
- page-template-(template file name); *for example,* .page-template-dynamic
- paged
- paged-(page number); *for example,* paged-23
- rtl
- search
- search-no-results
- search-paged-(page number)
- search-results
- single
- postid-(id); *for example,* postid-4
- single-paged-(page number); *for example,* single-paged-23
- tag
- tag-(tag name); *for example,* tag-images
- tag-paged-(page number); *for example,* tag-paged-23

**For more information**

The WordPress Codex actually has some pretty sparse information on these two very powerful template tags. For a detailed look at the body class tag, check out WPEngineer at http://wpengineer.com/wordpress-28-body_class-automatic_feed_links/ and Nathan Rice at http://www.nathanrice.net/blog/wordpress-2-8-and-the-body_class-function/. For more information on the post class, check out Lisa's http://justagirlintheworld.com/take-advantage-of-the-new-sticky-post-feature-in-wordpress-27/ and the WordPress Codex at http://codex.wordpress.org/Migrating_Plugins_and_Themes_to_2.7.

## Why add custom class styles to template tags?

At first glance, it seems like a bit of work to add CSS styles, especially as it's so easy to just add the class directly to the theme's template page XHTML markup! Adding custom classes will help keep your template page markup clean (especially if you're just going to add the full list tag that generates the entire class) Also, it helps ensure that your template users can't mess up the page too much. If you're planning on distributing a theme for the masses, this keeps your template files a little cleaner looking and your end user may try to tweak the XHTML or CSS, but will stay away from template tags. If you've tucked your CSS into these tags, it's just another way to keep end users from inadvertently breaking your design too badly and pushes them to do more of their tweaking in the CSS sheet instead of in the template pages.

# Using the template selector feature

In Chapter 3, I intended my pages (About and Contact) to be static. So I removed the `comments_template` and `comments_number` template tag from the `page.php` template. But what if I want (or want my theme users to be able) to create a static page that lets users leave comments? This is easily achieved by creating a custom page template:

# Creating a custom page template

Let's use the following steps for creating a custom page template in our theme:

1. Create a new file that contains the markup, CSS styles, and template tags you'd like your optional template page to have. I made a copy of my `page.php` and called it `page_dynmc.php`. I then copied the following comment loop back into it:

```
. . .
<div id="pagecomments">
      <?php comments_template(); ?>
</div>
<div class="comments"> <div class="commentIcon"><?php
    comments_number("No Comments","<span class="bigNum">1</span>
    response","<span class="bigNum">%</span> Comments"); ?></div>
<?comments_popup_link("Add Your Thoughts", "Add Your Thoughts",
"Add Your Thoughts"); ?></div>
. . .
```

2. At the very top of the page, before any other coding, you'll want to include this comment inside PHP brackets:

```php
<?php
/*
Template Name: Dynamic Page
*/
?>
...
```

3. You can then log in to your Administration panel, and by going to **Administration | Write** (or **Manage**) **Page**, select the page you want to have a unique template, and underneath the editor window, select your new template from the page **Template** selector drop-down:

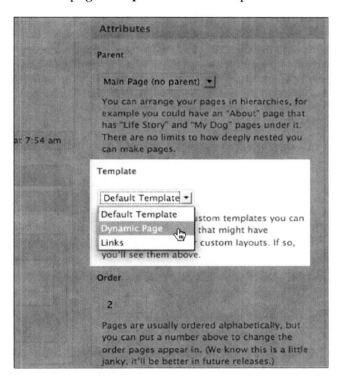

# Template hierarchy

After the work we've done on our theme, you've probably noticed that certain WordPress template pages will override other template pages. Not being aware of which standard file names can override other file names within your template hierarchy can cause problems in troubleshooting your template.

Essentially, you can have 14 different default page templates in your WordPress theme, not including your `style.css` sheet or includes such as `header.php`, `sidebar.php`, and `searchform.php`. You can have more template pages than that if you take advantage of WordPress' capability for individual custom page, category, and tag templates.

For instance, if you've created a category whose ID is "4", and then created a template page in your theme called `category-4.php`, WordPress will *automatically* pull that template page in before accessing the `category.php` or `index.php` page when that category *is selected*. Same goes for tags; if I have a tag named "office", and create a template called `tag-office.php`, WordPress will pull that template page in before pulling the `tag.php` or `index.php`.

**Can't find your category ID?**

If you want to create a specific category template page, but don't want to take time to use the `the_ID()` template tag to display the ID in your theme, and you don't have your WordPress **Administration | Settings | Permalinks** set to default, you can still easily figure out a category's ID number by using the Administration panel's URI to discover the ID (this works for discovering the post and page IDs as well):

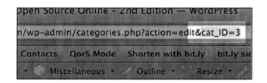

The following are the general template hierarchy's rules. The absolute simplest theme you can have must contain an `index.php` page. If no other specific template pages exist, then `index.php` is the default. You can then begin expanding your theme by adding the following pages:

- `archive.php` trumps `index.php` when a category, tag, date, or author page is viewed.
- `home.php` trumps `index.php` when the home page is viewed.
- `single.php` trumps `index.php` when an individual post is viewed.
- `search.php` trumps `index.php` when the results from a search are viewed.
- `404.php` trumps `index.php`, when the URI address finds no existing content.
- `page.php` trumps `index.php` when looking at a static page.
    - ◦ A custom template page, selected via the Administration panel, trumps `page.php`, which trumps `index.php` when that particular page is viewed.

- category.php trumps archive.php. This then trumps index.php when a category is viewed.
  - ° A custom category-ID.php page trumps category.php. This then trumps archive.php, which trumps index.php.
- tag.php trumps archive.php. This in turn trumps index.php when a tag page is viewed.
  - ° A custom tag-tagnam.php page trumps tag.php. This trumps archive.php, which trumps index.php.
- author.php trumps archive.php. This in turn trumps index.php, when an author page is viewed.
- date.php trumps archive.php, This trumps index.php when a date page is viewed.

You can find a detailed flowchart of the template hierarchy here:

http://codex.wordpress.org/Template_Hierarchy

WordPress' template tags go through revisions with each release. New and useful tags are introduced and some tags become deprecated (which means that one of the template tags has been superseded by a more efficient template tag). Tags that are deprecated usually still work in the current version of WordPress, but at some point their functionality will be removed.

Do not use a deprecated template tag in a new theme. If you have an older theme that now has deprecated tags, you'll want to update it to the new template tag equivalent and offer a new release of your template. Keeping up with the template tags page on WP's codex will help you keep your theme up-to-date.

Let's take a look at what I consider some of the more useful template tags to be. I won't list them all here; you can easily review them all in detail and clearly see what's been deprecated at http://codex.wordpress.org/Template_Tags.

# Template tags

As we saw in Chapter 3, within your template files you can use tags. Some need to be in the loop, while others can be called outside the loop. I'll start with some of my more recent, favorite tags; we'll then move on to the essentials you need to know.

The WordPress template tag library is extensive and the creative ways you can use the tags in your themes can just stretch to infinity. I've included the tags that make a template useful and great, but by all means, do check out the codex: http://codex.wordpress.org/Template_Tags.

# Author template tag updates in 2.8

Depending on your site type, you might want to reference author information in your theme. In this book's case study, the author's information really helps give it a magazine feel, with a subtle focus on the authors. WordPress 2.8 saw the release of the_author_meta and the newly modified author tags. We used the_author_meta tag in our loop in Chapter 3. While the_author(param) still works, its parameters are being deprecated, as are a host of author template tags that directly pull information that can now be accessed via the_author_meta.

Again, those template tags still work, but you can access all of that information via the_author_meta using the following field parameters:

```
the_author_meta(field, ID);
```

The following bullets describe the parameters that can be placed into the field parameter area of the_author_meta() tag:

- user_login: You most likely wouldn't display this on the site, unless it's the same as the author's nickname. It's their WordPress login username.
- user_pass: You obviously wouldn't use this in your theme at all, but that's how powerful this tag is. If you get into plugin development, I'm sure there are lots of interesting applications of this parameter in the_author_meta tag. It displays the user's password (MD5 encrypted).
- user_nicename: This also appears to display the author's username (that is, admin, or other assigned username) similar to user_login.
- user_email: Displays the author's e-mail address.
- user_url: Displays the author's URL.
- user_registered: Displays the author's registration timestamp.
- user_activation_key: Shows the user's activation key if it has not been reset with a password.
- user_status: Displays the numeric value of the user's status.
- display_name: Display varies, depending on what you've set this to in the drop-down field, either your nickname or a combination of first and last names.
- nickname: Displays the author's nickname.
- first_name: Displays the author's first name.
- last_name: Displays the author's last name.
- description: Displays the bio information if filled out.
- jabber: Displays the jabber account information if filled out.
- aim: Displays the AOL instant messenger account information if filled out.
- yim: Displays the Yahoo instant messenger account information if filled out.

- `user_level`: Displays the user's level (10 or lower).
- `user_firstname`: Same as `first_name`.
- `user_lastname`: Same as `last_name`.
- `user_description`: Same as `description`.
- `rich_editing`: Displays true or false depending on user settings.
- `comment_shortcuts`: Displays true or false depending on user settings.
- `admin_color`: Displays the name of the admin color scheme the user is using, that is "fresh" or "classic", or any other installed admin theme.
- `plugins_per_page`: Displays how many plugins are used in the user's post or page.
- `plugins_last_view`: Displays the timestamp of the last time the user looked at the plugins panel.
- `ID`: Displays the users ID number (if you use this tag outside the loop, you can manually add the ID number as a second parameter).

# Template tags for tags

If you're interested in using the "tags" feature of WordPress, then all five will be of interest to you.

> Tags are not intended to replace categories. Categories provide a more hierarchical structure for your content. Tags are not hierarchical at all and function more like meta-information about your posts, letting you "crosslink" them.

While you can assign multiple categories to your content (such as placing a post in "Features" and also in "On The Web"), tagging additional keywords in that article, especially words that you might not want to set up a full category for, makes it easier for your site's users to find relevant information.

For instance, if I write two articles and one goes into "On The Web" and another goes into "Office Productivity", but both articles happen to talk about text-to-speech technology, I don't really want to create a whole category called "text-to-speech" (especially as my site sparingly uses categories as "monthly columns"), but I'll certainly add the tag to those items. This way, when someone who is interested in text-to-speech stumbles upon one of my articles, they can simply click on the tag "text-to-speech" and be able to see all my relevant articles, regardless of what individual categories the content belongs to.

# Adding tag display to your theme

In the interest of keeping things straightforward and concise, we didn't include tag-display capability to our theme in Chapter 3. That's OK, we'll do it now. This feature is very easy to add using the `the_tags()` template tag.

Within any pages that display The Loop in your theme, decide where you'd like your tags to be displayed. I prefer them to be on top, under the author's name and category display.

I'll add the following template tag just under the author and category tags in my loop:

```
. . .
<p class="authorName">by <?php the_author_firstname(); ?> <?php the_
author_lastname(); ?> for <?php the_category(", ") ?>
<br/><em><?php the_tags(); ?></em></p>
            <div class="entry">
. . .
```

The result is this:

The coolest template tag is `wp_tag_cloud()`. It lets you easily generate one of those neat text clouds that show all your tags and have the most used tags sized from larger to smaller accordingly. This tag is used in the TagCloud widget as well.

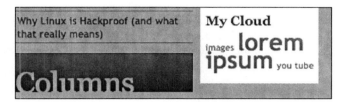

Here's a breakdown of all the Template Tags that handle the tag features:

| Template tag | Description | Parameters |
|---|---|---|
| `the_tags()`<br><br>Sample:<br><br>`the_tags("before",`<br>`"separator",`<br>`"after");` | Displays links to the tags that a post belongs to. If an entry has no tags, the associated category is displayed instead.<br><br>**Note**: Use this tag in The Loop. (see Chapter 3 for how to set up The Loop)<br><br>For more information, refer to:<br><br>`http://codex.wordpress.org/Template_Tags/the_tags` | Any text characters you want to appear before and after the tags, as well as, to separate them:<br><br>`("Tags:","|","<br/>")`<br><br>Default: No parameters will be displayed.<br><br>Tags: tagName, tagName. |
| `get_the_tags()`<br>Sample:<br>`<?php`<br>`$posttags =`<br>`get_the_tags();`<br>`if ($posttags) {`<br>`foreach($posttags`<br>`as $tag) {`<br>`echo $tag->name . "`<br>`";`<br>`}`<br>`}`<br>`?>;` | This tag does not display anything by itself. You have to sort through it using a basic PHP statement—`foreach`—to display the information you want (see sample to the left).<br><br>**Note**: Use this tag in The Loop. (see Chapter 3 for how to set up The Loop)<br><br>For more information, refer to: `http://codex.wordpress.org/Template_Tags/get_the_tags` | You can use the following parameters within the `foreach` statement to display the tag information:<br><br>`$tag->term_id, $tag->name, $tag->slug, $tag->term_group, $tag->description, $tag->count.` |

| Template tag | Description | Parameters |
|---|---|---|
| `get_the_tag_list()`<br><br>Sample:<br><br>`echo`<br><br>`get_the_tag_`<br>`list("<p>Tags: ",",`<br><br>`",","</p>");` | This tag does not display anything by itself. If you use the PHP echo statement (see sample to the left), it can display XHTML markup of the tags assigned to the post.<br><br>**Note**: Use this tag in The Loop. (See Chapter 3 for how to set up The Loop.)<br><br>For more information, refer to:<br><br>`http://codex.wordpress.`<br>`org/Template_Tags/get_`<br>`the_tag_list` | Similar to `the_tags()`, you can place any text characters you want to appear before and after the tags as well as separate them:<br><br>`("<p>Tags: ",",`<br><br>`",","</p>")` |
| `single_tag_title()`<br><br>Sample:<br><br>`single_tag_`<br>`title("This Tag: ");` | Displays the title of the tag the user is viewing or sorting by.<br><br>For more information, refer to:<br><br>`http://codex.wordpress.`<br>`org/Template_Tags/`<br>`single_tag_title` | Any text characters you want to appear before the tag name can be added — `("This Tag:")`.<br><br>You can also add a Boolean of true or false afterwards if you don't want the text to display — `("","false")`.<br><br>Default: The Boolean default is "true" and no parameters will display — `()` tagName. |

# General template tags—the least you need to know

The following are the top WordPress template tags I find most useful for basic theme development:

| Template tag | Description | Parameters |
|---|---|---|
| `bloginfo()`<br><br>Sample:<br><br>`bloginfo("name");` | Displays your blog's information supplied by your user profile and general options in the Administration panel.<br><br>For more information, refer to:<br><br>`http://codex.wordpress.org/Template_Tags/bloginfo` | Any text characters you want to appear before and after the tags, as well as to separate them—`name`, `description`, `url`, `rdf_url`, `rss_url`, `rss2_url`, `atom_url`, `comments_rss2_url`, `pingback_url`, `admin_email`, `charset`, `version`.<br><br>Default: No parameters will display "anything". You must use a parameter. |
| `wp_title()`<br><br>Sample:<br><br>`wp_title("--",true,"");` | Displays the title of a page or single post.<br><br>**Note:** Use this tag anywhere outside The Loop.<br><br>For more information, refer to:<br><br>`http://codex.wordpress.org/Template_Tags/wp_title` | Any text characters you want to use to separate the title—`("--")`.<br><br>You can set up a Boolean to display the title—`("--", "false")`.<br><br>As of 2.5+: You can decide if the separator goes before or after the title—`("--",t'rue", "right")`.<br><br>Default: No parameters will display the page title with a separator if a separator is assigned its default to the left. |

| Template tag | Description | Parameters |
|---|---|---|
| `the_title()`<br><br>Sample:<br><br>`the_title("<h2>", "</h2>");` | Displays the title of the current post.<br><br>**Note**: Use this tag in The Loop. (See Chapter 3 for how to set up The Loop.)<br><br>For more information, refer to:<br><br>`http://codex.wordpress.org/Template_Tags/the_title` | Any text characters you want to appear before and after the title— (`"<h2>"`, `"</h2>"`).<br><br>You can also set a Boolean to turn the display to false— (`"<h2>"`, `"</h2>"`, `"false"`).<br><br>Default: No parameters will display the title without a markup. |
| `the_content()`<br><br>Sample:<br><br>`the_content("more_link_text", strip_teaser, "more_file");` | Displays the content and markup you've edited into the current post.<br><br>**Note**: Use this tag in The Loop. (See Chapter 3 for how to set up The Loop.)<br><br>For more information, refer to:<br><br>`http://codex.wordpress.org/Template_Tags/the_content` | As you can add text to display the "more link", a Boolean to show or hide the "teaser text", there is a third parameter for `more_file` that currently doesn't work— (`"Continue reading"`.`the_title())`).<br><br>You can also set a Boolean to turn the display to false— (`"<h2>"`, `"</h2>"`, `"false"`).<br><br>Default: No parameters will display the content for the post with a generic "read more" link. |
| `the_category()`<br><br>Sample:<br><br>`the_category(", ");` | Displays a link to the category or categories that a post is assigned to.<br><br>**Note**: Use this tag in The Loop. (See Chapter 3 for how to set up The Loop)<br><br>For more information, refer to:<br><br>`http://codex.wordpress.org/Template_Tags/the_category` | You can include text separators in case there's more than one category— (`"&gt;"`).<br><br>Default: No parameters will display a comma separation if there is more than one category assigned. |

| Template tag | Description | Parameters |
|---|---|---|
| `the_author_meta()`<br><br>Sample:<br><br>`the_author_meta();` | Displays the author of a post or a page.<br><br>**Note**: Use this tag in The Loop. (See Chapter 3 for how to set up The Loop.)<br><br>For more information, refer to:<br><br>`http://codex.wordpress.org/Template_Tags/the_author_meta` | This tag accepts a large amount of parameters. They are covered in the previous sections. You can also check out the codex. |
| `wp_list_pages()`<br>Sample:<br><br>`wp_list_pages(t'itle_li=");` | Displays a list of WordPress pages as links.<br><br>For more information, refer to:<br><br>`http://codex.wordpress.org/Template_Tags/wp_list_pages` | `title_li` is the most useful as it wraps the page name and link in list tags `<li>`. The other parameters can be set by separating with an "`&`": `depth`, `show_date`, `date_format`, `child_of`, `exclude`, `echo`, `authors`, `sort_column`.<br><br>Default: No parameters will display each title link in a `<li>` list and include a `<ul>` tag around the list (not recommended if you want to add your own custom items to the page navigation). |
| `next_post_link()`<br>Sample:<br><br>`next_post_link("<strong>%title</strong>");` | Displays a link to the next post which exists in chronological order from the current post.<br><br>**Note**: Use this tag in The Loop. (See Chapter 3 for how to set up The Loop.)<br><br>For more information, refer to:<br><br>`http://codex.wordpress.org/Template_Tags/next_post_link` | Any markup and text characters you want to appear—(`<strong>%title</strong>`).<br><br>`%link` will display the permalink; `%title` will display the title of the next post.<br><br>Default: No parameters will display the next post title as a link followed by angular quotes (>>). |

| Template tag | Description | Parameters |
|---|---|---|
| `previous_post_link()`<br><br>Sample:<br><br>`previous_post_`<br>`link("<strong>%title</`<br>`strong>");` | Displays a link to the previous post which exists in chronological order from the current post.<br><br>**Note**: Use this tag in The Loop. (See Chapter 3 for how to set up The Loop.)<br><br>For more information, refer to:<br><br>`http://codex.wordpress.`<br>`org/Template_Tags/`<br>`previous_post_link` | Any markup and text characters you want to appear—<br>`(<strong>%title</`<br>`strong>)`.<br><br>`%link` will display the permalink; `%title` will display the title of the next post.<br><br>Default: No parameters will display the previous post title as a link preceded by angular quotes (`<<`). |
| `comments_number()`<br><br>Sample:<br><br>`comments_number("no`<br>`responses","one`<br>`response","%`<br>`responses");` | Displays the total number of comments, Trackbacks, and Pingbacks for a post.<br><br>**Note**: Use this tag in The Loop. (See Chapter 3 for how to set up The Loop.)<br><br>For more information, refer to:<br><br>`http://codex.wordpress.`<br>`org/Template_Tags/`<br>`comments_number` | Lets you specify how to display if there are 0 comments, only 1 comment, or many comments— `("no`<br>`responses","one`<br>`response","%`<br>`responses")`.<br><br>You can also wrap items in additional markup— `("No`<br>`Comments","<span`<br>`class="bigNum">1</`<br>`span>`<br>`response","<span`<br>`class="bigNum">%</`<br>`span> Comments")`.<br><br>Default: No parameters will display:<br><br>No comments, or 1 comment, or ? comments. |

| Template tag | Description | Parameters |
|---|---|---|
| `comments_popup_link()`<br><br>Sample:<br><br>`comments_popup_link("Add Your Thoughts");` | If the `comments_popup_script` is not used, this displays a normal link to comments.<br><br>**Note**: Use this tag in The Loop. (See Chapter 3 for how to set up The Loop.)<br><br>For more information, refer to:<br><br>`http://codex.wordpress.org/Template_Tags/comments_popup_link` | Lets you specify how to display if there are 0 comments, only 1 comment, or many comments— (`"No comments yet"`, `"1 comment so far"`, `"% comments so far (is that a lot?)"`, `"comments-link"`, `"Comments are off for this post"`).<br><br>Default: No parameters will display the same default information as the `comments_number()` tag. |
| `edit_post_link()`<br><br>Sample:<br><br>`edit_post_link("edit", "<p>", "</p>");` | If the user is logged in and has permission to edit the post, this displays a link to edit the current post.<br><br>**Note**: Use this tag in The Loop. (See Chapter 3 for how to set up The Loop.)<br><br>For more information, refer to:<br><br>`http://codex.wordpress.org/Template_Tags/edit_post_link` | Any text you want to be present in the name of the link, plus markup that you'd like to come before and after it— (`"edit me!"`, `"<strong>"`, `"</strong>"`).<br><br>Default: No parameters will display a link that says "edit" with no additional markup. |
| `the_permalink()`<br><br>Sample:<br><br>`the_permalink();` | Displays the URL for the permalink to the current post.<br><br>**Note**: Use this tag in The Loop. (See Chapter 3 for how to set up The Loop.)<br><br>For more information, refer to:<br><br>`http://codex.wordpress.org/Template_Tags/the_permalink` | This tag has no parameters. |

| Template tag | Description | Parameters |
|---|---|---|
| `the_ID()`<br>Sample:<br>`the_ID();` | Displays the numeric ID of the current post.<br>**Note**: Use this tag in The Loop. (See Chapter 3 for how to set up The Loop.)<br>For more information, refer to:<br>`http://codex.wordpress.org/Template_Tags/the_ID` | This tag has no parameters. |
| `wp_get_archives()`<br>Sample:<br>`wp_get_archives(t'ype=monthly");` | Displays a date-based archives list.<br>For more information, refer to:<br>`http://codex.wordpress.org/Template_Tags/wp_get_archives` | You can set parameters by separating them with an `"&"` – (`"type=monthly&limit=12"`).<br>The other parameters are: `type`, `limit`, `format`, `before`, `after`, `show_post_count`.<br>Default: No parameters will display a list of all your monthly archives in HTML format without before or after markup and `show_post_count` set to false. |
| `get_calendar()`<br>Sample:<br>`get_calendar(false);` | Displays the current month/year calendar.<br>For more information, refer to:<br>`http://codex.wordpress.org/Template_Tags/get_calendar` | A Boolean value can be set which will display a single-letter initial (`S` = Sunday) if set to true. Otherwise, it will display the abbreviation based on your localization (`Sun` = Sunday) – (`true`).<br>Default: No parameters will display the single-letter abbreviation. |

# Conditional tags

The conditional tags can be used in your template files to change what content is displayed and how that content is displayed on a particular page depending on what conditions that page matches. For example, you might want to display a snippet of text above the series of posts, but only on the main page of your blog. With the `is_home()` conditional tag, that task is made easy.

There are conditional tags for just about everything; out of all of them, these are the three I find I need most in my theme development:

- `is_page()`
- `is_single()`
- `is_sticky()`

All of those functions can take the following parameters: the `post ID` or `page ID` number, the post or page `title`, or the post or page `slug`.

As great as themes are, I'm sure you've run into the conundrum that you or your client doesn't want the exact same sidebar on every single page or post.

I use these so that specific pages can have particular styles or `divs` of content turned on and off and display or not display specific content. These three tags really help give my client's custom themed sites a true, custom website feel and not that standard "nice design, but every page has the exact same sidebar; this is probably another WordPress site" feel.

The conditional tag fun doesn't end there. There are many more that you may find invaluable in aiding your theme's customization:

`http://codex.wordpress.org/Conditional_Tags`

# Including tags into your themes

The following is a list of all the tags and file names you can include into your theme:

| Include tag | Description |
| --- | --- |
| `get_header();` | Finds and includes the file `header.php` from your current theme's directory. If that file is not found, it will include `wp-content/themes/default/header.php` in its place. |
| `get_footer();` | Finds and includes the file `footer.php` from your current theme's directory. If that file is not found, it will include `wp-content/themes/default/footer.php` in its place. |
| `get_sidebar();` | Finds and includes the file `sidebar.php` from your current theme's directory. If that file is not found, it will include `wp-content/themes/default/sidebar.php` in its place. |
| `comments_template();` | Finds and includes the file `comments.php` from your current theme's directory. If that file is not found, it will include `wp-content/themes/default/comments.php` in its place. |
| `include(TEMPLATEPATH . "/filename.php");` | TEMPLATEPATH is a reference to the **absolute path** (not the URL path) to the current theme directory. It does not include a / at the end of the path. You can use it to include any file into your theme using the standard PHP include statement (see the sample to the left). This is how theme developers include the `searchform.php` file into their themes. |

# Creating custom header, footer, sidebar includes

WordPress 2.7 introduced the ability to create custom header, footer, and sidebar templates for a theme. You simply create your custom header, footer, or sidebar and call it using the standard include template tag (which we'll get to later in this chapter). Be sure to add a file prefix of `header-`, `footer-`, or `sidebar-` and your own name. You can then call your custom template file like so. In Chapter 3, I updated my second sidebar include, from using the TEMPLATEPATH call, to the following much more elegant solution:

- `get_header('customHeader')` will include `header-customHeader.php`

- `get_footer('customFooter')` will include `footer-customFooter.php`

- `get_sidebar('customSidebar')` will include `sidebar-customSidebar.php`

**Warning**

As mentioned in some of the previous tables, if you use `get_header()`, `get_footer()`, or `get_sidebar()` calls (with or without the new parameters) and your theme contains no `header.php`, `footer.php`, or `sidebar.php` files, then WordPress will include those files from the default theme.

# Completely custom—streamlining your theme

In Chapter 3, we included our own custom sidebar using the previous technique. You can also use the WordPress TEMPLATE path inside a basic PHP `include` function. This technique can come very handy in helping you streamline your theme's code and help keep it easily updatable.

For instance, my `index.php`, `page.php`, and `category.php` pages have different headers and slightly different uses of The Loop, but they all have the exact same page navigation code. This bit of code is small yet, if I ever want to tweak my internal navigation layout, I'll need to touch all three of those pages.

# Creating a custom include in your theme

Creating a custom include will not require me to edit all three pages. I only need to edit one page as follows:

1. Open up your `index.php` page and select everything from the `<div id="intTop_navlist">` down to the end `div` tag and `<!--//top_navlist-->` comment.

2. Cut that code out and paste it into a new template page—`navlist.php`.

3. Go back to the `index.php` page and add this include file where all that code used to be:

   ```php
   <?php include(TEMPLATEPATH . "/navlist.php"); ?>
   ```

4. Test your internal page views out. You should see your layout working just fine.

You can now replace that same code in your `page.php` and `category.php` template pages with the include line you just created. Test out those internal page views again to be sure the include is working. Now any time you want to update your internal navigation, you only have to edit the `navlist.php` file.

You can get really granular with this technique. Feel free to really look through your theme and find ways to separate out parts into includes so that you don't have to worry about duplicating your markup.

# The Loop functions

Chapter 3 will really help you understand how to put each of these functions together into The Loop. The following is a description of each part of The Loop:

| Loop functions | Description |
| --- | --- |
| `<?php if(have_posts()) : ?>` | This function checks to make sure there are posts to display. If so, the code continues to the next function. |
| `<?php while(have_posts()) : the_post(); ?>` | This function shows the posts that are available and continues to the next function. |
| `<?php endwhile; ?>` | This function closes the `while(have_posts...` loop that was previously opened, once the available posts have been displayed. |
| `<?php endif; ?>` | This function ends the `if(have_posts...` statement that was previously opened, once the `while(have_posts...` loop has completed. |

# Plugin hooks

Whether you're developing for the public or for a specific client, or just yourself, you'll still want to create a theme that's robust and can "play well with others". the "others" being plugins. Plugins can be created to add additional functionally to WordPress for just about anything you can imagine, so long as the plugin API offers a "Hook" for it. In general, unless you're a plugin developer, you probably don't have much need to pour over the plugin API. There are, however, a few hooks that should be placed into your theme in order for plugins to work effectively with your theme and be able to reference and display information in your theme, as well as know when to run specific WordPress functions.

We placed three of these four "Action Hooks" into our theme in Chapter 3; here's a little more detail on them:

- `wp_head`: Place within the `<head>` tags of a `header.php` template:

  `<?php wp_head(); ?>`

- `wp_footer`: Place within the `footer.php` template:

  `<?php wp_footer(); ?>`

- wp_meta: You'll most likely place this hook within the sidebar.php template. However, it's best to add this hook wherever you intend plugins and widgets to appear:

```php
<?php wp_meta(); ?>
```

- comment_form: Goes in comments.php and comments-popup.php, before the </form> closing tag:

```php
<?php do_action('comment_form'); ?>
```

# WordPress core functions

In Chapter 3, I wrote a custom display loop that showed the top five most recent post titles in my Features category. I used a WordPress function called setup_postdata().

I mentioned you might notice that the setup_postdata() function isn't listed in WordPress.org's template tag reference page. Template tags are WordPress functions that are defined for use specifically within themes; the setup_postdata function is part of WordPress' core functions.

Core functions are primarily useful to plugin developers and the developers customizing WordPress' overall functionality for themselves. Occasionally, as we discovered in Chapter 3, some of the functions can be useful to theme developers who want highly specialized functionality within their themes.

I won't take time to break down any core functions into a table, as most people won't really need these for their theme development. I just want to make you aware of the existence of core functions so that if you ever do find WordPress' template tags to be limiting, you can see if getting creative with a core function might solve your problem.

The most useful core functions I've found as a theme developer are part of a class called WP_query. The setup_postdata() function is part of this class. Functions within this class let you call specific posts and manipulate post data and how it's displayed. You can find out more about this class at:

http://codex.wordpress.org/Function_Reference/WP_Query

**A class that doesn't have anything to do with CSS?**

This might seem to take us off topic from theme development, but it never hurts to understand WordPress a little better. You might only be familiar with the term "class" as used in CSS. This is different. A class is also a term used in Object Oriented Programming (which is how WordPress is written using the PHP language). It can best be described as a "package" or "collection" of functions and rules that define what an object could have done to it and how that object will behave. Objects are instances of their class which hold actual data inside them (such as blog post or page data, for example, in the case of WordPress). The data inside the object can be retrieved and manipulated via the functions available in that object's class (such as the setup_postdata() function).

Again, you can find out more about using the setup_postdata() function, as mentioned in Chapter 3, here:

```
http://codex.wordpress.org/Displaying_Posts_Using_a_Custom_Select_
Query
```

If you use PHP or are interested in it and would like to learn more about WordPress' core functions, you can find out more here:

```
http://codex.wordpress.org/Function_Reference
```

# WordPress shortcodes

While we're on the topic of WordPress' core functions, we should take a quick look at shortcodes. They were first introduced in version 2.5. If you're comfortable with writing functions in WordPress, shortcodes can help you take longer bits of code (such as custom loops and complex template tag strings) or even just markup and text that you feel you'd use a lot in your theme (or plugin) and allow you to compress them into cleaner, simpler bits of reusable code.

You can add shortcodes to your theme's functions.php file. This can enable your theme's template pages to be a little cleaner and streamlined, thus, less confusing to anyone who uses your theme.

You're probably familiar with shortcodes and may not realize it. If you've ever taken a look at how WordPress' media manager inserts captions into images, you've probably noticed something like:

```
. . .
[caption id="attachment_12" align="alignleft" width="150"
caption="this is my caption"]<img src.../>[/caption]
. . .
```

That's a built in shortcode for captions and alignment in WordPress.

To create a shortcode, you need to create a PHP function in your theme's `functions.php` file. If your theme does not have a `functions.php` file, simply create a new file, name it `functions.php`, and place it in the root of your theme's directory.

# Creating a basic shortcode

We'll start off by opening up our `functions.php` file and at the end of it, create a simple function that returns a string of text and markup for our shortcode like so:

```php
<?php
...

function quickadd() {

    //code goes here
    $dontateText = 'Open Source Online Magazine is free, but please
<a href="#">donate</a>';

    return $donateText;
}

?>
```

Now, to really take advantage of shortcodes, you do need to know some PHP which, to fully cover, is a bit beyond the scope of this title. But even without much PHP experience, if you follow this example, you'll start to see how flexible this WordPress feature is in saving you time not just in your theme, but in your day-to-day use of WordPress.

In the previous sample, *inside* our function brackets { }, I set up a very basic variable `$donateText` and assigned it a string of text and markup.

The `return` statement is a very basic PHP function that will make sure our `quickadd` function passes back whatever has been assigned to that variable.

We're now ready to use WordPress' `add_shortcode()` function by adding it just *underneath* our `quickadd` function that we set up in the previous sample. The `add_shortcode` function has two parameters. For the first parameter, you'll enter in a reference name for your shortcode and in the second, you'll enter in the name of the function you'd like your shortcode to call, like so:

```php
...
add_shortcode('donate', 'quickadd');
?>
```

Now the fun part: Pick any template page in your theme and use the donate shortcode by simply adding in:

```
. . .
[donate]
. . .
```

Wherever you paste that [donate] shortcode in your theme's template files, the "Open Source Online Magazine is free, but please donate" text, with a link to the donate page, will appear! Bonus: You are not restricted to using this shortcode in just your template files! Paste it directly into a post or page via the Administration panel and you'll get the same result.

Shortcodes are a wonderful way to shortcut your time if you're a busy WordPress content author. Even if you're not creating your own theme from scratch, you can easily add your own shortcodes to any theme's functions.php file and ramp up your productivity.

Those of you more comfortable with PHP can take a look at WordPress' Shortcode API and see how to extend and make your shortcodes even more powerful by adding parameters to them: http://codex.wordpress.org/Shortcode_API.

# Summary

Aside from a handful of CSS style classes output by a few template tags, WordPress lets you completely control your own XHTML markup and CSS styles, even through the template tags! We've reviewed WordPress' template hierarchy, top template tags, as well as *include* and *loop* functions that will help you with your theme. I've also introduced you to the "under-belly" of WordPress' core functions and shortcodes, should you choose to venture far out into the world of WordPress theme and plugin development. Dog-ear this chapter and let's get ready to start cooking. First up: AJAX, Dynamic Content, and Interactive Forms.

# 7
# AJAX / Dynamic Content and Interactive Forms

AJAX—it's the buzzword that hit the Web with a bullet in 2005, thanks to Jesse James Garrett, a user-experience expert who founded `www.AdaptivePath.com`. If you're totally new to AJAX, I'll just point out that at its core, AJAX is nothing that scary or horrendous. AJAX isn't even a new technology or language!

Essentially, **AJAX** is an acronym for **Asynchronous JavaScript and XML**, and it is the technique of using JavaScript and XML to send and receive data between a web browser and a web server. A big advantage with this technique is the fact that you can dynamically update a piece of content on your web page or web form with data from the server (preferably formatted in XML), without forcing the entire page to reload. The implementation of this technique has made it obvious to many web developers that they can start making advanced web applications (sometimes called **RIAs—Rich Interface Applications**) that work and feel more like software applications, instead of like web pages.

Keep in mind that the word AJAX is starting to have its own meaning (as you'll also note its occasional use here as well as all over the Web as a proper noun, "Ajax", rather than an all-cap acronym). For example, a web developer using a Microsoft web server may develop his/her page using a browser scripting language called VBScript instead of JavaScript, to sort and display content transformed into a lightweight data format called JSON instead of XML. Today, that developer's site would still be considered an AJAX site, rather than an AVAJ site (yes, AJAX just sounds cooler).

In fact, it's getting to the point where just about *anything* on a website (that isn't in Flash) that slides, moves, fades, or pops up without rendering a new browser window is considered an *Ajaxy* site. In truth, a large portion of these sites don't truly qualify as using AJAX, they're just using straight-up JavaScripting. Generally, if you use cool JavaScripts in your WordPress site, it will probably be considered *Ajaxy*, despite not being asynchronous or using any XML.

In this chapter, we're going to take a look at:

- The most popular methods to get you going with AJAX in WordPress, using plugins and widgets to help you include dynamic self-updating content.
- We'll also look at some cool JavaScript toolkits, libraries, and scripts you can use to appear *Ajaxy*.

**Want more info on this AJAX business**?

The W3Schools website (`http://w3schools.com/ajax/`) has an excellent introduction to AJAX, explaining it in straightforward, simple terms. They even have a couple of great tutorials that are fun and easy to accomplish, even if you only have a little HTML, JavaScript, and server-side script (PHP or ASP) experience (no XML experience required) .

# Preparing for dynamic content and interactive forms

Gone are the days of clicking, submitting, and waiting for the next page to load, or manually compiling your own content from all your various online identities to post into your site.

A web page using AJAX techniques (if applied properly) will give the user a smoother and leaner experience. Click on a drop-down option and the checkbox menus underneath are updated immediately with the relevant choices—no submitting, no waiting. Complicated forms which, in the past, took two or three screens to process can be reduced into one convenient screen by implementing the form with AJAX.

As wonderful as this all sounds, I must again offer a quick disclaimer. I understand, as with drop-down menus and Flash, you may want or your clients are demanding that AJAX be in their sites. Just keep in mind that AJAX techniques are best used in situations where they truly benefit the user's experience of the page—for example, being able to add relevant content via a widget painlessly or cutting a lengthy web process from three pages down to one. In a nutshell, using an AJAX technique simply to say your site is an AJAX site is probably not a good idea.

You should be aware that, if not implemented properly, some uses of AJAX can compromise the security of your site. You may inadvertently end up disabling key web browser features such as back buttons or the history manager). Then there are all the basic usability and accessibility issues that JavaScript, in general, can bring to your site.

Some screen readers may not be able to read a "new" screen area that's been generated by JavaScript. If you cater to users who rely on tabbing through content, navigation may be compromised once new content is updated. There are also interface design problems that AJAX brings to the table (and Flash developers can commiserate). Many times, while trying to limit screen real estate and simplify a process, developers actually end up creating a form or interface that is complex and confusing, especially when your user is expecting the web page to act like a normal web page! So, how exactly do you go about getting something *Ajaxy* into your WordPress site? Let's take a look at how we can do that.

# Assessing if AJAX is appropriate for your site

Fine! You're here and reading this chapter because you want AJAX in your WordPress site. I would ask you to consider what we just discussed and do one or more of the following to prepare:

- Help your client assess their site's target users first. If everyone is "Web 2.0" aware, using newer browsers, and are fully "mouse-able" (meaning, navigation by tabbing is not disabled), then you'll have no problems; AJAX away.

- But if any of your users are inexperienced with RIA (Rich Interface Application) sites or have accessibility requirements, take some extra care. Again, it's not that you can't or shouldn't use AJAX techniques; just be sure to make allowances for these users.

- You can easily adjust your site's user expectations upfront, by explaining how to expect the interface to act. Again, you can also offer alternative solutions and themes for people with disabilities or browsers that can't accommodate the AJAX techniques.

*Don't Make Me Think! A Common Sense Approach to Website Usability* is an excellent book on website design for usability and testing that anyone who has anything to do with website development or design can greatly benefit from. You'll learn why people really leave websites, how to make your site more usable and accessible, and even how to survive those executive design whims. You can find out more at Steve's site (http://www.sensible.com/).

Also, if you're really interested in taking on some AJAX programming yourself, I highly recommend *AJAX and PHP: Building Responsive Web Applications* by Cristian Darie, Bogdan Brinzarea, Filip Chereches-Tosa, and Mihai Bucica. In it, you'll learn the ins and outs of AJAX development, including handling security issues. You'll also do some very cool stuff such as making your own Google style autosuggest form and a drag-and-drop sortable list (and that's just two of the many fun things to learn in the book).

So, that said, you're now all equally warned and armed with all the knowledgeable resources that I can think of throwing at you. Let's get to it.

# Do it yourself or use plugins

In this chapter and the next one, I'll discuss how to use some of these techniques yourself and will also direct you to comparable plugins. In the case of more complex techniques, I will show you plugins that do the job and point you in the direction for learning more about doing it yourself. As to the question, "should I use plugins or do it myself?", it depends on a few things such as the following:

- Available time
- Your technical comfort level
- The level of control you want over the theme
- Whether your theme is unique, for use on a single site, or if you plan on its wide distribution

# Plugin pros and cons

If you're new to web development, especially using PHP, and/or you just don't have the time to create a completely custom solution, WordPress plugins are a great way for you to go. If you've been developing with various web technologies for a while and you want to have exact detailed control over your theme, then you might want to create a theme having various JavaScript and/or AJAX features embedded directly in it.

The other consideration is the usage of your theme. If you're developing a theme that is for a specific client, to be used only on their site, then you might want to implement a solution directly into your theme. This will enable you to have detailed control over its display via your theme pages and `style.css` sheet. On the other hand, if you plan to sell your theme commercially or otherwise want it to be widely distributed, your best bet is to make it *widgetized* and as **plugin friendly** as possible. (By "plugin friendly", I simply mean, make sure the standard **Plugin API hooks** we discussed in Chapter 3 are in place and test your theme with popular plugins to make sure they work well with your theme).This way, your theme users have greater flexibility in how they end up using your theme and aren't locked-in to using any features you've enabled in the theme.

# The AJAX factor

First up, we'll just cut to the chase. Aside from the many-interface enhancing, time-saving benefits of AJAX, most of the time, you just simply want to "fascinate" your site visitors. It's easy to give your site an *Ajaxy* feel, regardless of asynchronously updating it with server-side XML, just by sprucing up your interface with some snappy JavaScripts. The easiest way to get many of these effects is to reference a JavaScript library (sometimes called a toolkit or framework, depending on how robust the provider feels the code is). A few of the leading favorites in the AJAX community are:

- jQuery: `http://jquery.com/`
- Prototype: `http://www.prototypejs.org/`
- MooTools: `http://mootools.net/`

There's also the following:

- Script.acilo.us: `http://script.aculo.us/`
- Moo.fx: `http://moofx.mad4milk.net/`

And then there's:

- Dojo: `http://dojotoolkit.org`
- YUI (Yahoo User Interface Library): `http://developer.yahoo.com/yui/`

Prototype and MooTools are both pretty solid little frameworks (here "little" is used to indicate "compact"). Script.acilo.us and Moo.fx are add-on toolkits/libraries mostly used for neat effects and easily traversing, selecting, and handling objects in the DOM. In fact, Script.acilo.us references and requires the Prototype framework. Moo.fx requires either Prototype or Mootools (your choice). So, if you use Script.acilo.us or Moo.fx, be sure to check out Prototype's site or Mootools' site and try to understand how each of those frameworks work. I know learning curves are a bear, but reading through the quick start or introduction documentation will save you quite a few headaches.

Dojo and YUI are extremely robust and are considered RIA frameworks. Unless you're planning on branching out beyond WordPress themes and attempting to create a complex WordPress plugin, these two JavaScript frameworks are probably overkill for a WordPress theme project (but it's good to know they're out there; you never know).

jQuery is my personal favorite and it's enjoying a lot of popularity on the web right now. I originally used Prototype and Script.acilo.us, then moved on to Moo.fx. Both Script.acilo.us and Moo.fx are good and did their job as expected. However, from my very first experience with jQuery, I was hooked. I'm a convert at this point, I actually can't remember the last time I wrote a JavaScript that wasn't jQuery scripting or at least referenced or was aided by jQuery in some way. For me, the power I got out of jQuery with a very minimal learning curve pretty much did it for me.

jQuery bills itself as a JavaScript library, yet it pretty much stands on its own without needing to be backed up by an additional framework (such as Prototype or MooTools). You can still do some very robust and very clever things with it by manipulating data and objects in the DOM. It's also packed with tons of neat visual effects, similar to Script.acilo.us and Moo.fx. jQuery also has an impressive library of UI tools and third-party plugins. The options for using it are endless.

# jQuery now comes bundled with WordPress

As of WordPress 2.7, jQuery is now bundled and available with a handy function called `wp_enqueue_script`. Actually, WordPress has had jQuery and quite a few other JavaScript includes (such as Script.acilo.us with Prototype) bundled into the `wp-includes` directory. But from version 2.5 to 2.7, these includes were not so easily accessible.

# Including jQuery in WordPress

You can activate WordPress' bundled jQuery in two different ways:

- Place the following code in your `header.php` file *before* closing the `</head>` tag:

```php
<?php wp_enqueue_script("jquery"); ?>
    <?php wp_head(); ?>
    <script type="text/javascript">
     //add jQuery code here
    jQuery(document).ready(function() {
     jQuery("p").click(function() {
      alert("Hello world!");
     });
    });
    </script>
```

- Alternatively, you can register the `wp_enqueue_script` (and any custom jQuery code you write) in your theme's `functions.php` file. If your theme doesn't have a `functions.php` file, simply create a new file named that and place it in your theme's root directory with your other template files. (`functions.php` is a standard template file that's covered in Chapter 6's reference; we'll go over using it further later in this chapter.) Place the following in your `functions.php` file:

```php
<?php wp_enqueue_script('jquery');
    function jq_test(){
?>
<script type="text/javascript">
 jQuery(document).ready(function() {
    jQuery("p").click(function() {
     alert("Hello world!");
    });
 });
</script>
<?php
}
add_filter('wp_head', 'jq_test');?>
```

# Avoiding problems registering jQuery

The first time I attempted to load up jQuery using the `wp_enqueue_script` (both in the `functions.php` file and in the `header.php` file), I just could not get it to work. After some hair pulling and a few hours on WordPress Codex, I finally realized the following:

- If you're loading directly into your `header.php` template file, make sure the `wp_enqueue_script` function is above your `wp_head` function. Your custom jQuery code must go below the `wp_head` function.

- If you're registering the `wp_enqueue_script` in the `functions.php` file, make sure it comes before any custom functions that load via the `add_filter` function into the `wp_head`.

- Finally, because WordPress and jQuery are anticipating other libraries to be loaded which may use the short variable, `$`. The `wp_enqueue_script` ensures jQuery is loaded up in *noConflict* mode . Therefore, make sure to write your custom jQuery code in *noConflict* mode syntax. The easiest way to do this is to replace the `$` variable (common in many jQuery scripts) with the full `jQuery` variable, as I've done in my two previous samples.

  You can also set any variable you want to replace the standard `$` variable as follows:

  ```
  <script type="text/javascript">
  var $jq = jQuery.noConflict();
    $jq(document).ready(function() {
      $jq("p").click(function() {
        alert("Hello world!");
      });
    });
  </script>
  ```

# Linking to jQuery from Google Code's CDN

Personally, I am a little torn about registering and referencing the copy that comes with WordPress. I've discovered loading the library from **Google Code's CDN (content distribution network)** is sometimes a better way to go. The CDN saves on bandwidth, allowing you some parallel processing in downloading other scripts on your site. Plus, if I want, I can ensure that I'll always get the most current version of jQuery. Also, the library loads very quickly from Google's CDN. And, as a bonus, the library will already be cached if the site's user has previously visited another site that delivers jQuery from Google Code's CDN.

It's very simple to include jQuery from Google Code's CDN. The most straightforward way is to include the `js` using a standard `script` include:

```
<script src="http://ajax.googleapis.com/ajax/libs/jquery/1.3.2/
jquery.min.js" type="text/javascript"></script>
```

Google offers a great versioning system that allows you to be as precise as you want, or just pull the latest stable version. Consider the following example (note the bold number `1` in the following example):

```
<script src="http://ajax.googleapis.com/ajax/libs/
        jquery/1/jquery.min.js" type="text/javascript">
</script>
```

That script include will reference version 1.3.2 of jQuery (the most recent version as of writing this). When jQuery's developers release a new version, say, 1.3.6, that version will *automatically* be called by that same URL because I did not pinpoint the version's specifics. In the same vein, I could choose to call ...jquery/1.2/jquery... that would give me 1.2.6, the highest version in the 1.2 release. Generally it's good practice to always have the most recent library load, but you never know, you may use a jQuery plugin or write some of your own code that doesn't work well with a newer version. You'd then want to target the last specific version of the library that works with your plugins or custom scripts until you can fix and update them.

You can also reference Google's JavaScript API and load in JavaScripts using the `google.load()` function as follows:

```
<script src="http://www.google.com/jsapi"></script>
 <script type="text/javascript">
    google.load("jquery", "1.3.2");
    google.setOnLoadCallback(function() {
        // Your code goes here.
    });
</script>
```

# Using WordPress' bundled includes versus including your own or using a CDN

As I mentioned earlier, the `wp_enqueue_script` function allows for a safe load of jQuery (and other includes) into *noConflict* mode. Loading your own version from Google Code or from your own site has the potential for problems down the line. For one thing, some plugins may also use the jQuery library (from WordPress' bundle or included directly in their own plugin), and they are going to load it up as well. They may load in older versions of jQuery or even a newer one. Having multiple versions of the same library loaded, not to mention other libraries and frameworks loaded (depending on the plugins you've installed), can cause problems even if you're using *noConflict* mode with your code. There's still the potential for libraries loaded up from other plugins to conflict with WordPress' bundled includes, but you'll cut down on what to troubleshoot if you use WordPress' bundled includes.

Lastly, for development, I find it nice to have jQuery already running locally on my MAMP server, if I'm developing a theme yet have disconnected from the Web due to traveling (or the need for enhanced productivity. Distracted? Who me?).

Ultimately, whether or not to use plugins or include features directly in your theme, you have to judge how you think your theme is going to be used. When I create themes that I'm sure of how they're going to be used and exactly what plugins will be installed (if any), I'll opt to directly reference Google's CDN in my `header.php` template file and take advantage of their server and library updates.

Yet occasionally, I create themes that I just have no idea how they'll end up being used or with what plugins. Either the site is huge with several administrators and editors and could go in any direction, or the theme is for public release and anyone can download it and do anything they want with it. For the later two scenarios, I play it safe and load up jQuery using the `wp_enqueue_script` function.

**Read up on the `wp_enqueue_script` function!**

It actually does a lot more than just load up jQuery! There are well over fifty JavaScript toolkits, frameworks, user interface libraries, plugins, and helpers that you can load up safely using the `wp_enqueue_script` function. Check it out here: `http://codex.wordpress.org/Function_Reference/wp_enqueue_script`.

If you opt to include a specific version of jQuery via Google Code's CDN or via a downloaded copy in your theme's `js` directory, make sure to update your `ReadMe.txt` file. Tell people why you've locked in this version of jQuery with your theme and warn them about potential conflicts with plugins and how your theme references jQuery's *noConflict* mode.

# jQuery plugins

The fun doesn't stop here! If you don't have time to go read up on how to use a JavaScript library such as jQuery—don't be afraid! There are many other JavaScript effect plugins which are built using the above libraries.

One of the most popular scripts that makes a big hit on any website is Lightbox JS: `http://www.huddletogether.com/projects/lightbox2/`.

**Lightbox JS** is a simple, unobtrusive script used to overlay images on the current page. It's great, but it uses both the Prototype and Script.aculo.us libraries to achieve its effects. Also, unfortunately, I've found Lightbox JS was a bit limited in terms of using it with a CMS that has a WYSIWYG editor like TinyMCE (that didn't stop clients from wanting it on their site).

# Problem with setting up a Lightbox effect in WordPress

While Lightbox JS is simple to add to your template (remember, Script.aculo.us and Prototype are available in WordPress via that `wp_enqueue_script` function). However, in order for Lightbox JS to work, you need to add a custom `rel="lightbox"` attribute to each `<a href...` tag that will call an image into the Lightbox. I find this very easily done by flipping over to the HTML view in your WordPress **Post** or **Page** editor and just adding it in to the XHTML markup. Well, easy for me and maybe you, but not so easy for many of my clients (and probably a hassle for you to have to flip over to the HTML view).

Even for my clients who did learn how to add that `rel` attribute, upon reloading the content in from the WordPress database into the **View** screen, WordPress' default WYSIWYG editor (TinyMCE) sometimes likes to help out and do some "cleaning up" for you. That `rel="lightbox"` attribute in any link in the page can sometimes drop out (and sometimes it stays; if you have several links to images, some may break and others may work). The result is a site editor who has to call you to fix the problem (upset, as they thought they'd be maintaining their own site).

While it's easy to get annoyed with non-XHTML savvy clients, the truth is, this is exactly the reason they've invested in using WordPress. They need an easy way to manage their site's content, sometimes with multiple editors, many of whom don't have the foggiest idea what an HTML tag or attribute is.

## jQuery lightBox

jQuery lightBox by Leandro Vieira Pinho is very similar to Lightbox JS, in that it has a very nice, smooth animation as the image loads up. On the positive side, it uses only the jQuery library. Also it doesn't require any custom markup to your `<a href>` tags. You can download it from here:

`http://leandrovieira.com/projects/jquery/lightbox/.`

# Adding jQuery lightBox to your template

This is an extremely easy-to-implement plugin. (Don't get confused, this is not a WordPress plugin. jQuery refers to packaged scripts that use its library as plugins.)

After downloading it, place the lightBox files somewhere they make sense in your theme's root directory (I like to place the plugins `.js` and `.css` files inside my `js` directory and any images the plugin uses inside my `images` directory).

First, make sure you are already referencing the core jQuery library, either from the lightBox script in your theme, via Google Code's CDN, or via the `wp_enqueue_script` function as we discussed above. Add the plugins' `.js` and `.css` files inside your `header.php` file, below the `wp_head` function.

```
. . .
<?php wp_head() ?>
. . .
<script type="text/javascript" src="<?php
  bloginfo('template_directory'); ?>/js/jquery.lightbox
0.5.js"></script>
. . .
```

You'll also add in a call to the jQuery lightBox CSS file:

```
. . .
<link rel="stylesheet" type="text/css" href="<?php
  bloginfo('template_directory'); ?>/js/jquery.lightbox-0.5.css"
  media="screen" />
. . .
```

Don't forget to upload the images in the ZIP package to your template's image directory and update the `jquery.lightbox-0.5.js` file's image paths in lines 30 to 34 with your theme's path (this is a tad inelegant, but it works and the plugin is great):

```
. . .
        imageLoading:          '/wp-content/themes/oo_magazine/images/
lightbox-ico-loading.gif',        // (string) Path and the name of the
loading icon

        imageBtnPrev:          '/wp-content/themes/oo_magazine/images/
lightbox-btn-prev.gif',           // (string) Path and the name of the
prev button image

        imageBtnNext:          '/wp-content/themes/oo_magazine/images/
lightbox-btn-next.gif',           // (string) Path and the name of the
next button image

        imageBtnClose:         '/wp-content/themes/oo_magazine/images/
lightbox-btn-close.gif',          // (string) Path and the name of the
close btn
```

```
        imageBlank:              '/wp-content/themes/oo_magazine/images/
lightbox-blank.gif',            // (string) Path and the name of a blank
image (one pixel)
```

Now, we're ready to activate the jQuery lightBox plugin. This is the beauty of jQuery. It has a robust DOM and CSS selector feature, and that means we don't have to put any special `class` or `rel` tags in our markup. We can generally target `<a href>` links by placing a small jQuery JavaScript in our `header.php` file (below our `.js` and `.css` file calls) as follows:

```
...
<script type="text/javascript">
jQuery(function() {
    jQuery('a').lightBox(); // Select all links in an XHTML area with
page ID
});
</script>
...
```

Now, you can create a post or page in your Administration panel using the easy method of **Add New** and then adding content to it.

I uploaded the images via WordPress' built-in image uploader, which you can find at the top-right of the edit area. I then inserted my thumbnail version into the page and created a link to the full image using the image uploader's options. That's it!

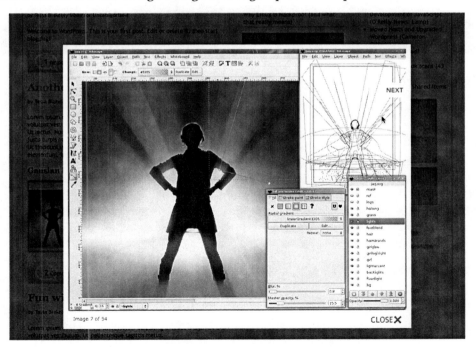

# Implementing lightBox

Unfortunately, there's a small drawback in implementing lightBox. Because I'm targeting all the `<a href>` links inside WordPress, my page navigation links, any outbound link, or link to download something that's not a link to an image, gets an unexpected result. As you can see in the following screenshot, after clicking on a link to another page, the results are "interesting".

This is easily remedied if you know a bit about jQuery's selectors.

First off, we'll simply target the area we want to focus on a bit more:

```
jQuery('.post a').lightBox();
```

This will only activate `<a href` inside the `post` class, inside `<p>` (paragraph) tags. This will keep my main navigation and any links in my sidebar from activating lightBox, but it doesn't totally fix our problem—my post's headers are usually linkable and they're inside my post class! Rather than going into my otherwise well-working template and reorganizing how the loop works, we'll zero in a little more with jQuery selectors as follows:

```
jQuery('.post:not(h2) a').lightBox();
```

This is great; using the `not` selector option, my main navigation, sidebar, and linked post h2 headings don't activate lightBox. Oh, but I know my clients. They're going to create lots of articles, using nothing but the WYSIWYG editor, with no clue as to what markup they're actually creating. They will not only upload images with links for the lightBox, but they'll probably also throw in a bunch of other links to other stuff that shouldn't kick off the lightBox. They can be so "link-happy" sometimes. Well, that's fine too. We'll simply amend the a selector a bit more:

```
jQuery('.post:not(h2) a:has(img)').lightBox();
```

Now we've got it. By adding `a:has(img)`, only the `<a href...` tags, in the `.post` class, that are **not** h2 headers that also wrap around images will activate the jQuery lightBox plugin.

You now have a foolproof lightBoxing method that the most sloppy HTML mess-making WYSIWYG editors will be hard pressed to break!

**Learn more about jQuery selectors**

In order to make jQuery lightBox work well with your template, you should get to understand selectors. Karl Swedberg has two excellent articles on targeting anything you want with jQuery selectors at the following URL: `http://www.learningjquery.com/2006/12/how-to-get-anything-you-want-part-2`.

You can also use jQuery's reference guide at: `http://docs.jquery.com/Selectors`.

# jQuery's ThickBox and ColorBox plugins

**ThickBox** installs and works very similar to jQuery's lightBox. However, in addition to handling images similar to Lightbox JS, it can also handle inline content, iFrame content, and AJAX content (be sure to check out the examples on the Thickbox page): `http://jquery.com/demo/thickbox/`.

The downside is ThickBox requires that you add a special `class="thickbox"` to your `<a href` tag markup. The good news is, because it's a class attribute, TinyMCE doesn't strip this out, but you'll need to have content editors that know how to add that class to their content in the HTML view. ThickBox also doesn't do that neat, smooth animation that jQuery lightBox does when images are different sizes. This is a trade-off I've made when I've occasionally decided it's more important to be able to display additional content such as PHP forms or Flash video players in a lightBox within my WordPress themes.

**ColorBox** seems to be the best of both worlds. I've only used it experimentally, but I've been very pleased with the results and it may very well replace ThickBox for my more robust needs. It can load images, inline HTML, external HTML, and iFrames like ThickBox, but you can target with selectors just like jQuery lightBox. The built-in skins are great too. You can download ColorBox here: `http://colorpowered.com/colorbox/`.

# Plugins and widgets

In these next few sections, we're going to cover plugins and widgets. Plugins and widgets are not a part of your theme; they are additional files that use WordPress-compatible, PHP code, and are installed separately into their own directories in your WordPress installation (again, not in your theme's directory). Once installed, they are available to be used with any theme that is also installed in your WordPress installation.

Even though plugins and widgets are not a part of your theme, you might have to prepare your theme to be compatible with them. We'll get to that in the following section.

# Plugins

WordPress has been built to be a lean, no-frills publishing platform. It simply means that with a little coding and PHP know-how, you can easily expand WordPress' capabilities to accommodate your site's specific needs. Plugins were developed so that even without a little coding and PHP know-how, users could add extra features and functionality to their WordPress site painlessly, via the Administration panel. These extra features can be just about anything — from enhancing the experience of your content and forms with AJAX, to adding self-updating "listening/watching now" lists, Flickr feeds, Google Map Info, along with events and calendars. You name it, and someone has probably written a great WordPress plugin for it.

Take a look at the WordPress plugin page to see what's available: `http://wordpress.org/extend/plugins/`.

# Widgets

**Widgets** are basically just another plugin! The widget plugin was developed by AUTOMATTIC (`http://automattic.com/code/widgets/`), and it allows you to add many more kinds of self-updating content bits and other useful bits to your WordPress site. Widgets are intended to be smaller and a little more contained than a full, standalone plugin, and they usually display within the sidebar of your theme (or wherever you want; don't panic if you're designing a theme without a sidebar).

As of WordPress 2.2 later, the widget plugin is part of WordPress itself, so you no longer need to install it before installing widgets. Just look through the widget library on WordPress' widget blog at `http://widgets.wordpress.com/` and see what you'd like!

**Trying to download widgets, but the links keep taking you to plugin download pages?**

You'll find that many WordPress widgets "piggyback" on WordPress plugins, which means you'll need the full plugin installed in order for the widget to work or the widget is an additional feature of the plugin. So, don't be confused when searching for widgets and all of a sudden you're directed to a plugin page.

WordPress widgets are often intended to perform much the same way Mac OS's Dashboard Widgets and Windows Vista Gadgets work. They're there to offer you a quick overview of content or data and maybe let you access a small piece of often-used functionality from within a full application or website, without having to take the time to launch the application or navigate to the website directly. In a nutshell, widgets can be very powerful; while at the same time, just don't expect too much.

# Getting your theme ready for plugins and widgets

Let's move forward and take a look at what needs to be done to prepare your theme for plugins and widgets.

# Preparing your theme for plugins

In Chapter 3, we included the following plugin API hooks--`wp_head`, `wp_footer`.

If you have those two hooks in your template, you're pretty much compatible with a host of plugins out there. Plugins will leverage the `wp_head` and `wp_footer` files to include JavaScripts (as we just saw earlier) and any special CSS files that help define the plugin. Plugins can also use these hooks to help them know when to "kick off" or activate functions and additional scripts. If a plugin needs to activate a function as soon as the entire site and theme has been loaded, waiting for the `wp_footer` hook to load is a good indicator that the site has completely loaded (of course, also provided you put the `wp_footer` hook in the footer of your theme!)

If a plugin requires that a theme have any additional hook in place, that plugin's documentation will need to disclose clearly what hook and what template file it should optimally go in, in order to work with the plugin.

# Installing a plugin

As long as you followed the preparations above (which we did in Chapter 3), most WordPress plugins can be installed and will work just fine with your theme, with no extra effort on your part. You'll generally upload the plugin into your `wp_content/plugins` directory and activate it in your Administration panel. Here are a few quick tips for getting a properly displayed plugin in your theme:

- When getting ready to work with a plugin, read all the documentation provided with the plugin before installing it and follow the developer's instructions for installing it (don't assume just because you've installed one plugin, they all get installed the same way).

- Occasionally, a developer may mention the plugin was made to work best with a specific theme, and/or the plugin may generate content with XHTML markup containing a specific CSS `id` or `class` rule. In order to have maximum control over the plugin's display, you might want to make sure your theme's stylesheet accommodates any `id` or `class` rules the plugin outputs.

- If the developer mentions the plugin works with, say, the *kubrick* theme, then, when you install the plugin, view it using the *kubrick* theme (or any other theme they say it works with), so you can see how the plugin author intended the plugin to display and work within the theme. You'll then be able to duplicate the appropriate appearance in your theme.

# Installing the AJAX comment preview plugin

There are tons of plugins that aid with AJAX. Just go to the plugins directory at (`http://wordpress.org/extend/plugins/`) and search for "AJAX".

Here's a nice one that caught my attention, a nice clean comment preview. Moderating comments on a site is pretty much given nowadays. But for the rare and cherished, "real person" who would like to leave a comment and see what it looks like before they submit and get the **Thank you. Your comment is pending approval** message, this is a great little plugin.

It uses AJAX to display the preview and let the user hit **Submit All** without having to reload the page.

Let's download and install the Ajax comment preview plugin in our installation of WordPress:

1. Get the plugin from here: `http://wordpress.org/extend/plugins/ajax-comment-preview/`.

2. Place the unzipped directory inside your `wp-content/wp-plugins` directory, then go to **Administration | Plugins** to activate it.

3. You'll then need to go to **Administration | Settings | AJAX Comment Preview** (or **Administration | Options | AJAX Comment Preview** if you're using version 2.6 or older) and set your display preferences.

4. Once activated, you can pretty much just start using it! If you go to your **Comment** form on your site, you'll note that you now have a **Preview** button underneath your **Submit Comment** button. Your site users can select **Preview!!** to see their comment styled.

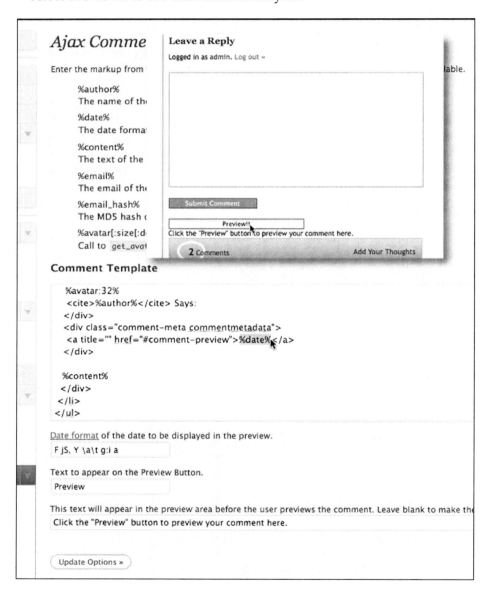

# Preparing your theme for widgets

Some plugins, like the widget plugin (again you don't have to install this if you're using WordPress version 2.2 and up), do require your theme to go through some more formal preparation. You'll need to do the following to make your theme compatible with widgets (also known as "widgetized").

## Making your theme compatible with widgets

In order to make your theme compatible with widgets, go through the following points:

1.  Your sidebar should ideally be set up using an unordered list format. If it is, you can add the following code within your sidebar. (If your sidebar is not set up using an unordered list format, ignore this step, and go to Step 3.)

```
<ul id="sidebar">
    <?php if ( !function_exists('dynamic_sidebar')
    || !dynamic_sidebar() ) : ?>
      <li id="about">
        <h2>About</h2>
        <p>This is my blog.</p>
      </li>
</ul>
```

2.  Earlier in this chapter, you created a `functions.php` file to include in WordPress' bundled jQuery library. If you don't have a `functions.php` file yet, you simply need to create one in your themes directory and add this code to it:

```
<?php
    if ( function_exists('register_sidebar') )
        register_sidebar(array(
            'before_widget' => '<li id="%1$s"
                                    class="widget %2$s">',
            'after_widget' => '</li>',
            'before_title' => '<h2 class="widgettitle">',
            'after_title' => '</h2>',
        ));
?>
```

3. My problem is that my sidebar format is much more customized and it's not in a simple unordered list. Plus, I have two sidebars. I'd want the second sidebar that holds my Google AdSense to contain a widget or two, but not my "Table of Contents" sidebar. Not a problem! The code we entered above in the functions.php file helps us with our more traditional div-header-list structure. Add the following code to your non-unordered list sidebar:

```
<div id="sidebar">
  <?php if ( !function_exists('dynamic_sidebar')
          || !dynamic_sidebar() ) : ?>
    <div class="title">About</div>
    <p>This is my blog.</p>
    <div class="title">Links</div>
      <ul>
        <li><a href="http://example.com">Example</a></li>
      </ul>
  <?php endif; ?>
</div>
```

4. If you have two sidebars and you want both of them to be dynamic, then instead of register_sidebar(), use register_sidebars(n), where n is the number of sidebars. Place them before the array bit of code if you're using a non-unordered list sidebar, as follows:

```
<?php
if ( function_exists('register_sidebar') )
    register_sidebar(2, array(
            'before_widget' => '<p>',
            'after_widget' => '</p>',
            'before_title' => '<h2>',
            'after_title' => '</h2>',
    ));
?>
```

5. Then place the appropriate number in the dynamic_sidebar() function, starting with 1. For example:

```
...
<div id="sidebar1">
  <?php if ( !function_exists('dynamic_sidebar')
              || !dynamic_sidebar(1) ) : ?>
<div class="title">About</div>
...
```

This will give you your sidebar options that look like as follows in your widget panel:

Alternatively, you can use the `name` attribute and register two separate sidebars. It takes a bit more code, but it makes it a lot easier for a less technical end user to use in the Administration panel. Set up two side bars in your `function.php` file as follows:

```php
if ( function_exists('register_sidebar') )
    register_sidebars(1, array(
            'name' => 'top sidebar',
        'before_widget' => '<p>',
        'after_widget' => '</p>',
        'before_title' => '<h2>',
        'after_title' => '</h2>',
 ));
        register_sidebars(1, array(
        'name' => 'bot sidebar',
        'before_widget' => '<p>',
        'after_widget' => '</p>',
        'before_title' => '<h2>',
        'after_title' => '</h2>',
    ));
?>
```

You'd then call the sidebar you require in your theme's template files as follows:

```php
...
<?php if ( !function_exists('dynamic_sidebar')
        || !dynamic_sidebar('bot sidebar') ) : ?>
<?php endif; ?>
....
```

This will give you sidebar options that look like the following screenshot in your Administration widget panel:

Your theme is now officially "widgetized". For those of you who are looking forward to creating commercial themes, be sure to tell everyone your theme is "widgetized" or widget friendly.

**So, you like widgets?**

Learn all about how to control their display in your theme and even develop your own. Check out AUTOMATTIC's Widget API Documentation at http://automattic.com/code/widgets/api/.

**Additional Considerations**: There are no concrete standards for widgets as of now. However, the W3C is working on it (http://www.w3.org/TR/widgets/). Many WordPress widgets such as Google Reader are flexible and can handle just about any size column. Some widgets may require a minimum column size! You may need to adjust your theme if the widget has an inflexible size. Some widgets (especially the ones that display pay-per-check for your site) have display requirements and restrictions. Be sure to thoroughly investigate and research any widget you're interested in, before installing it on your site.

# Google Reader widget

I do a lot of online reading, thank goodness for RSS feeds. I used to load in all sorts of RSS feeds to my site to show people what I was reading, but that's not very accurate. It only shows what sites I usually go to, and what I might have read on that site. With all the new sites and blogs coming and going, I'd have old feeds left on my site, it got to be ugly, and I eventually stripped them all out.

Google Reader has a shared feed that lets people know exactly what I really have been reading and what I'm interested in. Thanks to this handy widget by James Wilson—I can share what I'm reading, quickly and easily. Once your theme is widget-compatible, it's pretty much just as simple to get a widget up and running as a plugin.

Get the Google Reader widget from: `http://wordpress.org/extend/plugins/google-reader-widget/`.

**Check what version of WordPress, plugins and widgets are compatible with.**

I originally installed this widget in a 2.5 site (in the first edition of this book). I then upgraded it to my 2.7.1 site. I've since upgraded to 2.8.4 and, while this widget's page says it's compatible up to 2.7.1, it seems to be working just fine in 2.8.4. When installing widgets and plugins, you'll want to take care to note what version of WordPress they've been tested and are compatible with. If a widget or plugin is compatible up to only an old version of WordPress, you might have problems with it and the plugin may no longer be actively supported or developed.

## Installing the Google Reader widget

The following are the steps to install a Google Reader widget:

1. Unzip and drop `googlereader.php` file into the `wp-content/plugins` directory. (Depending on the widget, be sure to read the author's instructions. Some will want you to install to the `wp-content/plugins` directory and some will want you to install to the `wp-content/plugins/widgets` directory. You might have to create the widget directory.)

2. Go to **Administration | plugins** and **Activate** the plugin.

3. Go to **Administration | Appearance | Widgets** (or **Administration | Presentation | Widgets** in 2.6 and older versions) and drag the widget to your sidebar area.

4. View it on your site.

Locally, using MAMP, this worked fine! But on my web server I ran into a snag with the Google Reader widget. See the following screenshot:

## A small problem you may run into while installing the Google Reader widget

I had to read the FAQ for the Google Reader widget to learn that my hosting provider doesn't approve of the `file_get_contents()` method (`http://wordpress.org/extend/plugins/google-reader-widget/faq/`). So, I had to modify my `googlereader.php` file at line 57 with the following workaround that the widget author recommended:

```
$ch = curl_init();
$timeout = 5; // set to zero for no timeout
   curl_setopt ($ch, CURLOPT_URL, $uri);
   curl_setopt ($ch, CURLOPT_RETURNTRANSFER, 1);
   curl_setopt ($ch, CURLOPT_CONNECTTIMEOUT, $timeout);
   $stories = curl_exec($ch);
curl_close($ch);
```

After making this tweak, the widget worked fine, as in the following screenshot:

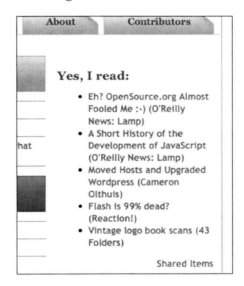

# AJAX—it's not just for your site's users

I've already mentioned how, when applied properly, AJAX can aid in interface usability. WordPress attempts to take advantage of this within its own Administration panel by enhancing it with relevant information and compressing multiple page forms into one single screen area. The following is a quick look at how WordPress uses AJAX to enhance its Administration panel forms:

# New work space features

As of 2.7, WordPress lets you configure your workspaces infinitely, adjusting the panels in the order and configuration you use most.

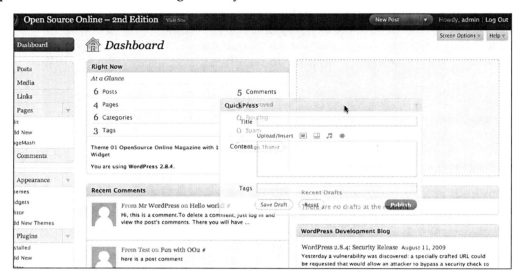

Even in the main **Posts** and **Pages** editor, great, subtle uses of AJAX can be seen, giving you a helping hand in ensuring your site management tasks are handled as fluidly as possible.

# pageMash

Plugins aren't just for your site's users. Despite all the nice AJAX interface elements in the 2.7+ Administration panel, I still find this plugin, pageMash, immensely useful in managing sites with several pages. For example, if your WordPress site has a lot of pages and/or you display your page links as drop-down menus (as discussed in Chapter 8), then Joel Starnes' pageMash plugin is for you.

**pageMash** is a great little plugin that uses the MooTools framework and Moo.fx library. Instead of having to go into each individual page's editor view and then use the **Page Parent** view to manipulate your pages around into your hierarchical structure, this plugin lets you reorder and assign pages as parents and subpages on-the-fly, by dragging-and-dropping them in the order and hierarchy you choose.

## Installing the pageMash plugin

Following are the steps to install the pageMash plugin and use it to organize our pages:

1. Download the pageMash plugin from: `http://wordpress.org/extend/plugins/pagemash/`.

2. Unzip the files and upload the pageMash directory to your `/wp-content/plugins/` directory.

3. Go to **Administration | plugins** and **Activate** it. pageMash will then show up under the **Administration | Manage** tag.

I hope you can get an idea from the following screenshot about how much easier and quicker it is to arrange your WordPress pages with pageMash.

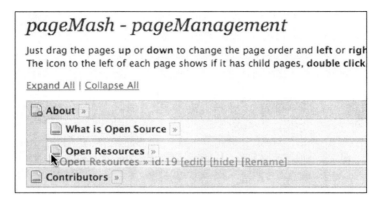

## Summary

In this chapter, we reviewed a few ways to take advantage of AJAX on your WordPress site. We optimized our theme for plugins and got it "wigitized". We also downloaded and installed a couple of useful plugins and widgets, and looked at various ways to include the jQuery library into our theme and used the jQuery lightBox plugin to enhance post and page content. Let's now enhance our theme a bit more by creating custom drop-down menus for it, and looking at different ways to include, without much hassle, Flash content into the theme itself and into the WordPress site.

# 8
# Dynamic Menus and Interactive Elements

As was the case in the previous chapter, most of the techniques that I'm about to discuss in this chapter are often used inappropriately and needlessly. They can create issues with usability and accessibility standards, but if you haven't already been asked for one or more of these features, you will be!

Chances are that clients have already asked you for drop-down menus, slick Flash headers, You Tube embeds, and other interactive content that they insist will give their site "pizazz!"

In this chapter, we'll take a look at:

- Developing custom, dynamic drop-down menus
- Various ways to embed Flash as part of your theme, and into your content

**Be sure to check out that Steve Krug book I mentioned in Chapter 7**
*Don't Make Me Think, by Steve Krug*; again, it's a great resource for help with any interface usability questions you may run into.

## Dynamic menus

This is the nice thing about WordPress—it's all "dynamic". Once you install WordPress and design a great theme for it, anyone with the right level of administrative capability can log into the Administration Panel and add, edit, or delete content and menu items. But generally, when people ask for "dynamic menus", what they really want are those appearing and disappearing drop-down menus which, I believe, they like because it quickly gives a site a very "busy" feel.

I must add my own disclaimer—I don't like dropdowns. Before you get on to my case, I will say it's not that they're "wrong" or "bad"; they just don't meet my own aesthetic standards and I personally find them *non-user friendly*. I'd prefer to see a menu system that, if subsections are required, displays them somewhere consistently on the page, either by having a vertical navigation expand to display subsections underneath, or showing additional subjections in a set location on the page if a horizontal menu is used.

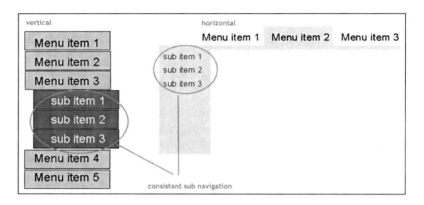

I like to be able to look around and say, "OK, I'm in the **New Items | Cool Drink** section and I can also check out **Red Dinks** and **Retro Dinks** within this section". Having to constantly go back up to the menu and drop-down the options to remind myself of what's available and what my next move might be, is annoying. Still haven't convinced you not to use drop-downs? OK, read on.

# Drop-down menus

So you're going to use dropdowns. Again it's not "wrong"; however, I would strongly caution you to help your client take a look at their target users before implementing them. If there's a good chance that most users are going to use the latest browsers that support the current JavaScript, CSS, and Flash standards, and everyone has great mobility and is "mouse-ready", then there's really no problem in going for it.

If it becomes apparent that *any* percentage of the site's target users will be using older browsers or have disabilities that prevent them from using a mouse and will limit them to tabbing through content, you must consider not using drop-down menus.

I was especially negative about drop-down menus as, until recently, they required bulky JavaScripting or the use of Flash, which does not make clean, semantic, and SEO-friendly (or accessible) XHTML. Enter the Suckerfish method developed by Patrick Griffiths and Dan Webb.

This method is wonderful because it takes valid, semantically accurate, unordered lists (WordPress' favorite!), and using almost pure CSS, creates dropdowns. The drop-down menus are not tab accessible, but they will simply display as a single, clear unordered list to older browsers that don't support the required CSS.

 IE6, as per usual, poses a problem or two for us, so there is some minimal DOM JavaScripting needed to compensate and achieve the correct effect in that browser.

If you haven't heard of or worked with the Suckerfish method, I'm going to recommend you to go online (right now!) and read Dan and Patrick's article in detail (`http://alistapart.com/articles/dropdowns`).

More recently, Patrick and Dan have revisited this method with "Son-of-a-Suckerfish", which offers multiple levels and an even further pared down DOM JavaScript. Check it out at `http://www.htmldog.com/articles/suckerfish/dropdowns/`.

I also suggest you play around with the sample code provided in these articles so that you understand exactly how it works. Go on, and read it. When you get back, I'll review how to apply this method to your WordPress theme.

# DIY SuckerFish menus in WordPress

All done? Great! As you can see, the essential part of this effect is getting your menu items to show up as unordered lists with sub unordered lists. Once you do that, the rest of the magic can be easily handled by finessing the CSS that Patrick and Dan suggest into your theme's CSS and placing the DOM script in your theme's header tag(s), in your `header.php` and/or `index.php` template files. Seriously, that's it!

The really good news is that WordPress already outputs your content's pages and their subpages using unordered lists. Right-click on the page links in Firefox to **View Selected Source** and check that the DOM inspector shows us that the menu is, in fact, being displayed using an unordered list.

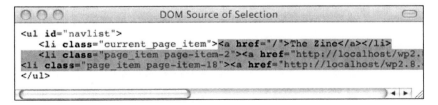

Now you can go into your WordPress Administration panel and add as many pages and subpages as you'd like (**Administration | Page | Add New**). You'll use the **Page Parent** tab on the right to assign your subpages to their parent.

If you installed pageMash with me in the previous chapter, it's even easier! You can drag-and-drop your created pages into any configuration you'd like. Just be sure to hit the **Update** button when you're done.

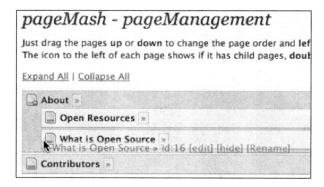

Once you've added subpages to a page, you'll be able to use the **DOM Source of Selection** viewer to see that your menu is displayed with unordered lists and sublists.

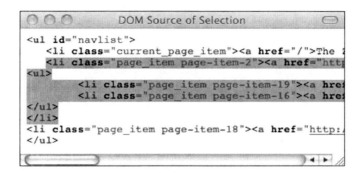

# Applying CSS to WordPress

We're going to use the new and improved "Son-of-a-Suckerfish" method so that our menu can handle multilevel dropdowns. To start, let's just take Dan and Patrick's suggested code and see what happens. Their unordered list CSS looks like the following:

```
#nav, #nav ul { /* all lists */
    padding: 0;
    margin: 0;
    list-style: none;
    line-height: 1;
}

#nav a {
    display: block;
    width: 10em;
}

#nav li { /* all list items */
    float: left;
    width: 10em; /* width needed or else Opera goes nuts */
}

#nav li ul { /* second-level lists */

position: absolute;
    background: orange;
    width: 10em;
    left: -999em; /* using left instead of display to hide menus
                    because display: none isn't read by screen
                    readers */
}
```

```
#nav li ul ul { /* third-and-above-level lists */
    margin: -1em 0 0 10em;
}

#nav li:hover ul ul, #nav li:hover ul ul ul, #nav li.sfhover ul ul,
#nav li.sfhover ul ul ul {
    left: -999em;
}

#nav li:hover ul, #nav li li:hover ul, #nav li li li:hover ul,
#nav li.sfhover ul, #nav li li.sfhover ul, #nav li li li.sfhover ul {
        /* lists nested under hovered list items */
    left: auto;
}
```

Now in WordPress, our menu item's ul is within a div id called top_navlist, and the ul ID is referred to as navlist. There may or may not be lots of other unordered lists used in our site, so we want to be sure that we *only* affect uls and lis within that top_navlist ID.

We'll simply tweak the CSS a bit to move items to the left (unfortunately, this works best with horizontal Navs that are positioned from the left instead of the right) and make sure to add #navlist to each element in the Suckerfish CSS. Also, we already have a general #top_navlist and #intTop_navlist rule for the div, so we'll want to make sure that this only affects the ul within that div by making sure it's named #navlist. So, our navigation CSS styles now look something like the following:

```
/*////////// NAV //////////*/
#top_navlist {
  position: absolute;
  top: 260px;
  width: 897px;
  text-align:left;
}
#intTop_navlist {
  position: absolute;
  top: 173px;
  width: 897px;
  text-align:left;
}
#top_navlist h2, #intTop_navlist h2{
  display: none;
}
#navlist{
  padding: 10px 10px;
  margin-left: 0;
  border-bottom: 1px solid #ccc;
  font-family: Georgia, Times, serif;
```

```
    font-weight: bold;
}
#navlist li{
  list-style: none;
  margin: 0;
  display: inline;
}
#navlist li a{
  padding: 11px 30px;
  margin-left: 3px;
  border: none;
  border-left: 1px solid #ccc;
  background: #8BA8BA url(images/oo_mag_main_nav.jpg) no-repeat top
                                                             right;
  text-decoration: none;
  color: #253A59;
}
#navlist li a:hover{
  background-color: #9E9C76;
  background-position: right -37px;
  border-color: #C5BBA0;
  color: #784B2C;
  text-decoration: underline;
}
#navlist li.current_page_item a{
  border-bottom: 1px solid white;
  background-color: #fff;
  background-position: right -74px;
}
#navlist li a:visited { color: #253A59; }
/*suckerfish menu starts here*/
#navlist li ul { /* second-level lists */
  position: absolute;
  border: none;
  margin-top: 10px;
  margin-left: 70px;
  left: -999em; /* using left instead of display to hide menus
                   because display: none isn't read by screen
                   readers */
}
#navlist li ul li a {
  display: block;
  width: 150px;
  font-family: Georgia, Century Schoolbook, Times, serif;
  font-size: 12px;
  text-transform:none;
  font-variant: normal;
  font-weight:bold;
```

```
    border: 1px solid #666666;
    background-color: #ffffff;
    background-image: none;
  }
#navlist li ul li a:hover {
    background-color: #cccccc;
    text-decoration: none;
  }
#navlist li ul ul { /* third-and-above-level lists */
    margin: -1em 0 0 7em;
  }
#navlist li:hover ul ul, #nav li:hover ul ul ul, #nav li.sfhover ul
ul, #nav li.sfhover ul ul ul {
    left: -999em;
  }
#navlist li:hover ul, #nav li li:hover ul, #nav li li li:hover ul,
#nav li.sfhover ul, #nav li li.sfhover ul, #nav li li li.sfhover ul {
/* lists nested under hovered list items */
    left: auto;
  }
```

# Applying the DOM script to WordPress

The last bit is the JavaScript that ensures the hover works in IE6. I call it DOM scripting or the DOM script, but it's basically just a JavaScript that rewrites your markup (how your DOM is being perceived by IE6) on-the-fly. This drop-down effect relies on the CSS hover attribute. IE6 only recognizes the hover attribute if it is applied to the a (link) entity. IE7 has fixed this limitation and it works similarly for Firefox and other browsers. Dan and Patrick's script appends the additional .sfhover class to the li items in IE6 only.

You'll need to add this script to your index.php and/or header.php template pages, inside the header tags. The thing to remember here is that Dan and Patrick named their ul tag's ID as nav and that's what this script is looking for. Our ul tag's ID is named top_navlist, so by simply switching out document. getElementById("nav"); to document.getElementById("navlist");, you're good to roll in IE.

The full script in your header tags should look like the following (I prefer to tuck it into an include and place it in my home.php (or index.php) and header.php files with a JavaScript include.):

```
<script type='text/javascript'><!--//--><![CDATA[//><!--
sfHover = function() {
    var sfEls = document.getElementById("navlist").getElementsByTagNam
e("LI");
    for (var i=0; i<sfEls.length; i++) {
```

```
        sfEls[i].onmouseover=function() {
                this.className+=" sfhover";
        }
        sfEls[i].onmouseout=function() {
                this.className=this.className.replace(new RegExp("
                                        sfhover\\b"), "");
        }
    }
}
if (window.attachEvent) window.attachEvent("onload", sfHover);
//--><!]]></script>
```

For demonstration purposes, I've kept the CSS pretty bare boned and ugly; however, when we check this out in our browser, we now see the following:

It's working! Remember, with the preceding code, you can have drop-down menus that go three levels deep (Dan and Patrick's *HTML Dog* article shows you how to make it handle as many levels as you'd like).

**Control those dropdown levels!**

As cool as SuckerFish drop-downs are, refrain from going overboard on those levels! Cascading levels can become really tedious for a user to mouse through and can turn a site with a "busy feel" into a total mess. You'll find that, with a little care, you can easily organize your site's page content so that it only requires two levels. From there, if you *really need it*, you can add an occasional third level without creating too much user distraction.

# Allowing only selected pages to display

In our theme, we used the `wp_list_pages()` template tag to display our pages. You can amend the template tag with an `exclude` parameter that will hide the pages we don't want to see, including their subpages (for example, `wp_list_pages("exclude=9&title_li=" );`). You do have to know what the page's ID number is. (You can temporarily set your permalinks to "default" to see the page's ID number in the site's URL.) The pages themselves will still be available for viewing if you know their direct URL path. Read more about it at `http://codex.wordpress.org/Template_Tags/wp_list_pages#Exclude_Pages_from_List`.

# Hiding pages the easy way with pageMash

In Chapter 7, we looked at the pageMash plugin by Joel Starnes `http://wordpress.org/extend/plugins/pagemash/`. If you've installed this plugin, displaying and hiding pages is super easy! Simply select **hide** from the option next to your page. The page will still be available via its permalink URL, but will not display in your drop-down menu.

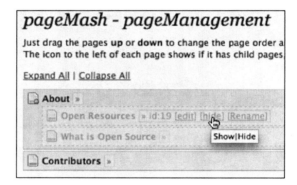

At this point, all that's left is fixing up the CSS to make it look exactly the way you want. There you go, semantic, SEO, and as accessible-as-possible dynamic menus in WordPress.

**Drop-down menu plugins**: Now you're probably already thinking, "Wait, this is WordPress; maybe there's a plugin" and you'd be right! By searching the "Extend" section of the `WordPress.org` site, you'll find that there are a handful of WordPress plugins that allow for drop-down menus under different conditions. Ryan Hellyer has written a plugin that uses the "Son-of-a-SuckerFish" method that we reviewed in detail earlier. You can review it at `http://wordpress.org/extend/plugins/ryans-suckerfish-wordpress-dropdown-menu/`.

# Adding Flash to your theme

Adobe Flash—it's come quite a long way since my first experience with it as a Macromedia product (version 2 in 1997). Yet still, it does not adhere to W3C standards, requires a plugin to view, and above all, is a pretty pricey proprietary product. So why is everyone so hot on using it? Love it or hate it, Flash is here to stay. It does have a few advantages that we'll take a quick look at.

The Flash player plugin does boast the highest saturation rate around (way above other media player plugins) and it now readily accommodates audio and video, as video sites such as You Tube take advantage of it. It's pretty easy to add and upgrade for all major browsers. The price may seem prohibitive at first, but after the initial purchase, additional upgrades are reasonably priced. Plus, many third-party software companies offer very cheap authoring tools that allow you to create animations and author content using the Flash player format. (In most cases, no one needs to know you're using the $50 version of Swish and not the $800 Flash CS3 to create your content.)

Above all, it can do so much more than just playing video and audio (like most plugins). You can create seriously rich and interactive content, even entire applications with it, and the best part is, no matter what you create with it, it is going to look and work *exactly* the same on all browsers and platforms. These are just a few of the reasons why so many developers chose to build content and applications for the Flash player.

Oh, and did I mention you can easily make awesome, visually slick, audio-filled stuff with it? Yeah, that's why your client wants you to put it in their site.

# Flash in your theme

A commonly requested use of Flash is usually in the form of a snazzy header within the theme of the site, the idea being that various relevant and/or random photographs or designs load into the header with some supercool animation (and possibly audio) every time a page loads or a section changes.

I'm going to assume if you're using anything that requires the Flash player, you're pretty comfortable with generating content for it. So, we're not going to focus on any Flash timeline tricks or ActionScripting. We'll simply cover getting your Flash content into your WordPress theme.

For the most part, you can simply take the HTML object embed code that Flash (or other third-party tools) will generate for you and paste it into the header area of your WordPress `index.php` or `header.php` template file.

# Handling users without Flash, older versions of Flash, and IE6 users

While the previous method is extremely clean and simple, it doesn't help all of your site's users in dealing with Flash. What about users who don't have Flash installed or have an older version that won't support your content? What about IE users who have the Active X restrain? You'll want your site and theme to gracefully handle users who do not have Flash (if you've used the overlay method, they'll simply see the CSS background image and probably not know anything is wrong!) or an older version of Flash that doesn't support the content you wish to display. This method lets you add in a line of text or a static image as an alternative, so people who don't have the plugin/correct version installed are either served up alternative content and they're none-the-wiser, or served up content that nicely explains that they need the plugin and directs them towards getting it. Most importantly, this method also nicely handles IE's ActiveX restrictions.

## Is the ActiveX restriction still around?

In 2006, the IE browser upped its security, so users had to validate content that shows up in the Flash player (or any player) via Microsoft's ActiveX controls). Your Flash content starts to play, but there's a "grey outline" around the player area which may or may not mess up your design. If your content is interactive, then people will need to click to activate it. This is annoying, but the main workaround involved "injecting" controls and players via JavaScript. Essentially, you need to include your Flash content via a JavaScript `include` file. As of April 2008, this restriction was reverted, but only if your user has updated their browser; chances are, if they intent on still using IE6 or 7, they haven't done this update.

Regardless of whether you are concerned about ActiveX restrictions, using JavaScript to help you instantiate your Flash will greatly add to the ease of embedding content. It will also make sure that users of all versions or who need to install Flash are handled either by directing them to the proper Flash installation and/or letting them see an alternative version of the content.

### swfObject

For a while, I used this standard `swfObject` method that was detailed in this great SitePoint article: `http://www.sitepoint.com/article/activex-activation-issue-ie`.

A similar, robust version of this JavaScript is located on Google Code's AJAX API `http://code.google.com/p/swfobject/wiki/hosted_library` (yes, the same Google Code CDN we discussed in Chapter 7). You can download the script (it's very small) or you can link directly to the `swfObject` AJAX API URL:

```
<script type="text/javascript"
 src="http://ajax.googleapis.com/ajax/libs/swfobject/2.2/swfobject.
js"></script>
```

Downloaded or linked to the Google Code CDN, be sure to place this below your `wp_head` or any `wp_enqueue_script` calls in your `<head>` tags in your `header.php` template file or other head template file.

# Adding a SWF to the template using swfObject

If you'd like to use the `swfObject.js` file and method, you can read the full documentation here: `http://code.google.com/p/swfobject/wiki/documentation`. But essentially, we're going to use the dynamic publishing option to include our SWF file.

1. Using the SWF file included in this book's code packet, create a new directory in your theme called `flash` and place the SWF file in it. Then, create a `div` with alternative content and a script tag that includes the following JavaScript:

```
<script type="text/javascript">
    swfobject.embedSWF("myContent.swf", "myContent", "300", "120",
"9.0.0");
</script>
. . .
    <div id="myContent">
      <p>Alternative content</p>
    </div>
. . .
```

2. Add this ID rule to your stylesheet (I placed it just below my `other` header and `intHeader` ID rules):

```
#flashHold{
  float: right;
  margin-top: 12px;
  margin-right: 47px;
}
```

As long as you take care to make sure the div is positioned correctly, the object embed code has the correct height and width of your Flash file, and you're not accidentally overwriting any parts of the theme that contain WordPress template tags or other valuable PHP code, you're good to go.

**What's the Satay method?**

It's a cleaner way to embed your Flash movies while still supporting web standards. Drew McLellan discusses its development in detail in his article: `http://www.alistapart.com/articles/flashsatay`. This method was fine on its own until IE6 decided to include its ActiveX security restriction. Nowadays, a modified embed method called the "nested-objects method": `http://www.alistapart.com/articles/flashembedcagematch/` is used with the swfObject JavaScript we just covered.

**Good developer's tip:**

Even if you loathe IE (as lots of us as developers tend to), it is an "industry standard" browser and you have to work with it. I've found the Microsoft's IE blog (`http://blogs.msdn.com/ie/`) extremely useful in keeping tabs on IE so that I can better develop CSS-based templates for it. While you're at it, go ahead and subscribe to the RSS feeds for Firefox (`http://developer.mozilla.org/devnews/`), Safari (`http://developer.apple.com/internet/safari/`), and your other favorite browsers. You'll be surprised at the insight you can glean, which can be extremely handy if you ever need to debug CSS or JavaScripts for one of those browsers.

# jQuery Flash plugin

In the past year, as I've found myself making more and more use of jQuery (we discussed in Chapter 7 that jQuery is part of WordPress), I've discovered and really liked Luke Lutman's jQuery Flash plugin. There is no CDN for this and it's not bundled with WordPress, so you'll need to download it and add it to your theme's js directory: `http://jquery.lukelutman.com/plugins/flash/`.

## Embedding Flash files using the jQuery Flash plugin

As we're leveraging jQuery already, I find Luke's Flash plugin a little easier to deal with.

1. Load the script under the wp_head.
2. Place a div of alternative content; just the div of alternative content and nothing else!

3. Write the jQuery script that will replace that content or show your alternative content for old/no Flash players.

4. Code goes here.

5. I think you see why I liked this so much more.

# Passing Flash a WordPress variable

So now you've popped a nice Flash header into your theme. Here's a quick trick to make it all the more impressive. If you'd like to keep track of what page, post, or category your WordPress user has clicked on and display a relevant image or animation in the header, you can pass your Flash SWF file a variable from WordPress using PHP.

I've made a small and simple Flash movie that will fit right over the top-right of my internal page's header. I'd like my Flash header to display some extra text when the viewer selects a different "column" (a.k.a. category). In this case, the animation will play and display **OpenSource Magazine: On The New Web** underneath the **open source** logo when the user selects the **On The New Web** category.

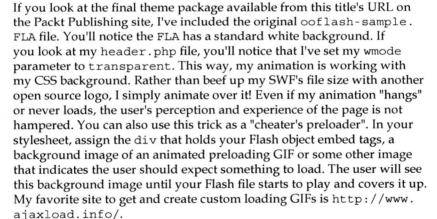

**More fun with CSS**

If you look at the final theme package available from this title's URL on the Packt Publishing site, I've included the original `ooflash-sample.FLA` file. You'll notice the `FLA` has a standard white background. If you look at my `header.php` file, you'll notice that I've set my `wmode` parameter to `transparent`. This way, my animation is working with my CSS background. Rather than beef up my SWF's file size with another open source logo, I simply animate over it! Even if my animation "hangs" or never loads, the user's perception and experience of the page is not hampered. You can also use this trick as a "cheater's preloader". In your stylesheet, assign the `div` that holds your Flash object embed tags, a background image of an animated preloading GIF or some other image that indicates the user should expect something to load. The user will see this background image until your Flash file starts to play and covers it up. My favorite site to get and create custom loading GIFs is `http://www.ajaxload.info/`.

In your Flash authoring program, set up a series of animations or images that will load or play based on a variable set in the root timeline called `catName`. You'll pass this variable to your `ActionScript`. In my `FLA` example, if the `catName` variable does not equal `On The New Web`, then the main animation will play, but if the variable returns `On The New Web`, then the visibility of the movie clip containing the words **OpenSource Magazine: On The New Web** will be set to "true".

Now, let's get our PHP variable into our SWF file. In your object embed code where your swfs are called, be sure to add the following code:

If you plan on using the Satay embed method, your object embed will look like this:

```
...
<script type="text/javascript">
var flashvars = {
  catName: "<?echo single_cat_title('');?>"
};
swfobject.embedSWF("<?php  bloginfo('template_directory');?>/
flash/ooflash-sample.swf", "flashHold", "338", "150",
"8.0.0","expressInstall.swf", flashvars);
</script>
...
```

If you'd like to use jQuery Flash, your jQuery will look like this:

```
...
<script type="text/javascript">
jQuery(document).ready(function(){
    jQuery('#flashHold').flash(
        {
            src: '<?php  bloginfo('template_directory');?>/flash/
ooflash-sample.swf',
            width: 338,
            height: 150,
            flashvars: { catName: '<?echo single_cat_title('');?>' }
        },
        { version: 8 }
    );
});
</script>
...
```

Be sure to place the full path to your SWF file in the `src` and `value` parameters for the embed tags or jQuery `src`. Store your Flash file inside your themes directory and link to it directly, that is, `src="<?php bloginfo('template_directory'); ?>/mythemename/flas');` template tag. This will ensure that your SWF file loads properly.

Using this method every time someone loads a page or clicks on a link on your site that is within the **On The New Web** category, PHP will render the template tag as `myswfname.swf?catName=On The New Web`, or whatever the `$single_cat_title("");` for that page is. So your Flash file's ActionScript is going to look for a variable called `catName` in `the_root` or `_level0`, and based on that value, do whatever you told it to do—call a function, go to a frame and animate; you can even name it.

For extra credit, you can play around with the other template tag variables such as `the_author_meta` or `the_date()`, for example, and load up special animations, images, or call functions based on them. Review the template tag options listed in Chapter 6 and experiment! There are a lot of possibilities for Flash control there!

## Adding sIFR text with the jQuery Flash plugin

I mentioned in Chapter 2 when designing this book's case study that you could use a method called sIFR to control font layouts. You can find out all about directly implementing the core method here: `http://www.mikeindustries.com/blog/sifr/`.

If you looked at Matt's page, you'll notice that, getting sIFR into your site, can take quite a few steps. However, as we've already taken the time to include Luke's jQuery Flash Plugin, it's even easier!

1.  Download Luke's font file. If you have Flash 8 or higher, you can open the file and select the **Dynamic Text** field on the stage, then using the **Properties** setting in Flash, assign any font in your system and make sure that the font is "embedded" in the dynamic text field.

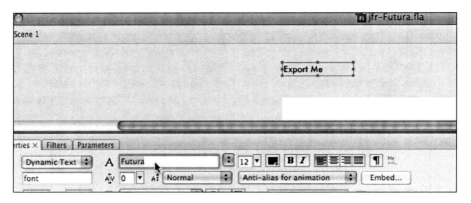

2.  Save and compile a SWF out to any name you'd like (I recommend placing the font's name in the file).

3.  Place this SWF in your `flash` directory in your theme's directory.

4.  Add the following jQuery Flash plugin code inside your `header.php` file's head tags (again, below your `wp_head()` tag). Remember, we're in No Conflict mode with jQuery, so be sure to change all variable instances of `$` into `jQuery` as discussed in Chapter 7:

```
. . .
<script type="text/javascript">
jQuery(document).ready(function(){
    jQuery('h2').flash(
        {
            src: '<?php bloginfo('template_directory'); ?>/flash/
jfr-Futura.swf',
            flashvars: {
                css: [
                    '* { color: #FFFFFF; }',
                    'a { color: #315a6c; text-decoration: none;
}',
                    'a:hover { text-decoration: underline; }'
                ].join(' ')
            }
        },
```

```
            { version: 7 },
            function(htmlOptions) {
                htmlOptions.flashvars.txt = this.innerHTML;
                this.innerHTML = '<div>'+this.innerHTML+'</div>';
                var $alt = jQuery(this.firstChild);
                htmlOptions.height = $alt.height();
                htmlOptions.width = $alt.width();
                $alt.addClass('alt');
                jQuery(this)
                    .addClass('flash-replaced')
                    .prepend(jQuery.fn.flash.transform(htmlOptions));
            }
        );
});
</script>
```

5. Make sure to add this CSS rule to your stylesheet as it hides the original text:

```
.flash-replaced .alt {
    display: block;
    height: 0;
    position: absolute;
    overflow: hidden;
    width: 0;
}
```

6. The resulting shot shows the **Futura** font in our site, replacing h2 headers. The headers are fully selectable and gracefully degrade back to whatever is in the stylesheet if Flash player 5 or newer is not available.

 The Flash file sizes the fonts based on your CSS size. You may need to adjust your font-size properties in your CSS sheet.

# Flash in a WordPress post or page

For Flash content that's going to go into a specific WordPress post or page, you'll need to be sure to switch over to the **HTML** view (or **Code** view in 2.3.x) and enter your object embed tag and `swfobject` register code or jQuery Flash plugin code into the post or page where you'd like it to appear within your content. In the next screenshot, I've added the direct embed object's embed tags for a You Tube video. (You Tube uses the Flash player for all their video content.)

## Adding You Tube video to a WordPress post

Your first option is pretty straightforward. Even if you've linked to the jQuery Flash plugin or `swfObject.js`, you can use the embed code that You Tube provides by selecting it from the right-hand side of the You Tube site.

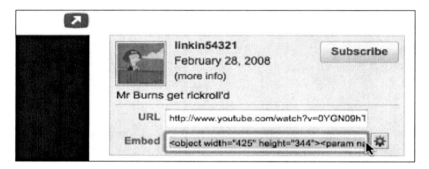

The markup looks something like this in the HTML view of your post:

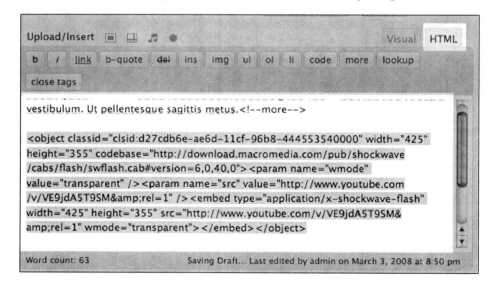

**As of version 2.5**: The **Code** view became the **HTML** view. As of WordPress 2.5 it is even easier to add media—images, video, and audio. Just select the appropriate media type from the left-hand side of the editor window.

If you're using an older version of WordPress, just be careful. The first time you enter custom HTML code into a post or page and hit **Save**, the post will be saved and will render your new code just fine. However, if you then edit that post, the custom code will look OK, as you edit it, but then, for some reason, it will be changed a little and might not display properly once you hit **Save**. (I believe it is because the WordPress editor attempts to "fix" any code it doesn't recognize.) WordPress 2.5 seems to fix this issue and I have no problems editing and re-editing posts with custom HTML code tags. (The editor works a lot better with the Safari browser too.)

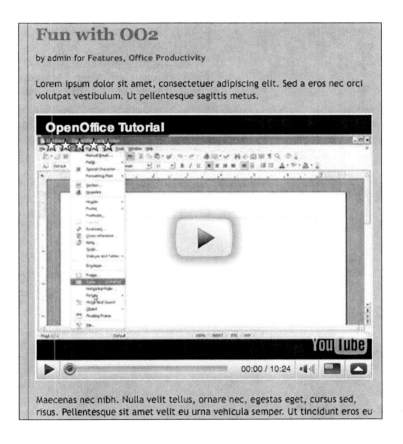

**Yes, of course there's a plugin**

This won't help you too much if you're planning on using Flash in your theme, but for Flash in your WordPress posts and pages, Jim Penaloza has written a great little plugin using the `swfObject` method. You can find out more about it here: `http://wordpress.org/extend/plugins/wp-swfobject/`.

**Want more Flash?**

If you want to add more interesting Flash to your site, there's a host of Flash-based WordPress plugins that allow you to easily embed Flash content and features into your WordPress posts and pages. Check out the plugins directory at `http://wordpress.org/extend/plugins/search.php?q=Flash`.

# Summary

In this chapter, we've looked at getting custom, dynamic drop-down Suckerfish menus implemented directly into your theme. We then moved on to placing Flash content into your theme as part of your theme's design, as well as getting it quickly and painlessly into your WordPress content using a variety of embed methods, most notably the jQuery Flash plugin. Up next—let's take a look at some final design tips for working with WordPress.

# 9
# Design Tips for Working with WordPress

Finally, we are into the last chapter of the title. For this last chapter, let's sum things up by giving you the following:

- A few final design tips and tricks
- Troubleshooting ideas to take with you into your future WordPress theme designs

As we've gone through this book, there are quite a few tips that have been given to you along the way. Here are the top four to remember:

- **Create and keep lists**: Keep all of the lists—namely check lists, color lists, font lists, image treatment lists, and so on—from your initial design phase handy. You'll find them to be useful and excellent inspiration for your designs to come.

- **Design for Firefox first and then fix for IE**: Firefox is more than a browser preference; it's a true web designer and developer's tool.

- **Validate your XHTML and CSS**: The more stable your markup and CSS, the less hacks and fixes you'll need to make.

- **Consider usability issues when implementing site enhancements**: Steve Krug is a cool guy. Moreover, good usability naturally lends itself to great design.

With that said, let's just go over a few last design techniques that any good designer wants in their arsenal these days.

# The cool factor essentials

Next, I'll go through what I feel are the most popular tricks used in website design today. Most of these design techniques are easily incorporated into WordPress, as they're handled 100% via CSS. A few items will require you to think and plan ahead, as you'll need to make sure the WordPress template code accommodates the effect. The best thing is, if you can implement these techniques into a WordPress template, you can implement them into any website.

First off, this book's case study has already looked at several "cool factor" techniques that are very popular in web design today. Among these techniques is using the CSS float property to create a three-column layout. And we've also covered styling an unordered list vertically and using the CSS hover property for our SuckerFish drop-down menus, which could be applied to text or used with images for a rollover effect without the use (or with minimal use) of JavaScript.

If you want to be able to do whatever you want in a site's design, get your head around these top five techniques that we'll go over in detail:

- **Backgrounds:** If you haven't already realized this by now, about 98% of the CSS that makes your WordPress template look great is dependent on how creative you get with the CSS background properties of your XHTML objects, classes, and id rules.

- **Lists:** You need to know how to style them horizontally and vertically as well as using background images.

- **Rounded corners:** We'll cover a couple of ways to tackle this. Again, it all centers around knowing the background property.

- **Text image replacement:** And yet again, like the rounded corner technique, the more you understand about the background property, the better.

- **Learn your image editor inside and out:** This is not a specific "web technique", but it is what will set you apart. Photoshop, Fireworks, GIMP, Illustrator, or Inkscape, whichever your editor of choice is, once you have a handle on controlling your layout with XHTML and CSS, the real factor that will make your WordPress themes pop off the screen is how good you are at creating all those graphics that get loaded in via the background property.

Let's go over each of these techniques in detail:

# Backgrounds

From your page header image background to data table spruce-ups, rounded corners, and fancy replaced text (as you'll find out about in a minute), knowing how to really control and manipulate background colors and images via CSS is the key. Check out `http://w3schools.com/CSS/CSS_background.asp` to learn the ins and outs of this CSS property.

You'll want to pay special attention to setting background images, controlling the vertical and horizontal repeat of these images, as well as controlling the positioning of the image. (This is great for using CSS sprite techniques for rollovers.) For a great article on using CSS sprites, check out `http://www.alistapart.com/articles/sprites/`.

The most common CSS shorthand of the background property that I often use is:

```
    . . .
      background: #fff url("images/imageName.jpg") no-repeat left top;
    . . .
```

The first item in the "pile" or "stack" is, of course, a hex color; you can then add an image URL. After that, you can set the horizontal "x" (repeat-x) or vertical "y" (repeat-y) of an image or set it to `no-repeat`. Finally, I like to set the position. The default position is `left top`. You can set it to right top, or left bottom, or right bottom, which is what you'll do with rounded corners. You can also set the exact pixel positioning (which works from the left and top), so 20px, 20px would mean 20 pixels in from the left and down from the top.

The next most useful property I often use is background-position:

```
    . . .
    background-position: 0px -20px;
    . . .
```

This applied to a class or id with an `a:hover` amendment would move the image loaded in with previous background shorthand back to the left by 20 pixels (because it goes from 20px to 0px) and up by a total of 40 pixels (because it moves from 20px to -20pixels for a total of 40 pixels up). This is key for using the CSS sprites technique for rollovers or just aiding in preloading images without JavaScript.

**CSS shorthand**

CSS shorthand has been mentioned a few times in this book. It allows you to use a more general property name and then pile or stack on the various properties for a CSS element, separating each with a space, without having to set up all the individual properties; in short, it allows you to set a background-color, a background image, a background position, and so on. Most elements of CSS do have a shorthand property name, especially if there are multiple variances of a property. Learning how to use these will greatly enhance your stylesheet's flow. However, be careful, as it's easy to mess up a property and not clearly be able to see where the syntax is wrong. IE requires the "piling" or "stacking" to be specific, whereas other browsers can recognize the properties no matter what order you place them in. Therefore, be sure to note the proper stacking order of shorthand properties. A good place to check your shorthand is in the correct order is to review the syntax of the specific property you're working with on the W3Schools site: `http://www.w3schools.com/css/css_syntax.asp`.

# Lists

In Chapters 2 and 3, we created a horizontally-styled list and then amended it to handle SuckerFish dropdowns. There are specific list properties that can help you control your lists to display vertically and horizontally. For an overview of all the list properties, check out `http://w3schools.com/CSS/css_list.asp`.

My most important list properties are controlling the liststyle:

```
list-style: none;
```

For lists, more than just properties, what you really need to know is how to structure CSS rules that will target the various list elements properly. For instance, consider the following rule:

```
.menu_sf ul{
```

This will target our main unordered list with that class assignment. On the other hand, the following rule:

```
.menu_sf li ul {
```

will allow us to target the styles of any nested unordered lists.

# See it in action

Most importantly, it just really helps to see and use good working sample list code often. Listamatic is a great place where you can see all sorts of list manipulation techniques. You can find it at http://css.maxdesign.com.au/listamatic/.

The Listamatic examples that I refer to most are:

- **For vertical lists**: A List Apart's Taming lists (http://css.maxdesign.com.au/listamatic/vertical10.htm) and Eric Meyer's Simple Separators, which you will notice have influenced the design of the main menu of this book's case study (http://css.maxdesign.com.au/listamatic/vertical06).
- **For horizontal lists**: Eric Meyer's tabbed navbar (http://css.maxdesign.com.au/listamatic/horizontal05.htm).

If you want to have infinitely scalable tabbed horizontal navs, you'll want to check out the "sliding door" technique from (of course) A List Apart: http://www.alistapart.com/articles/slidingdoors/.

# Rounded corners

Rounded corners have been pretty popular for the past few years, to the point that many sites have been accused of incorporating them just because they seemed "Web 2.0-ish". Fads aside, rounded corners occasionally just work well with a design (they're great for implying friendly-ish tones and/or retro styles), so you might as well know how to incorporate them into your WordPress theme.

## The classic—all four corners

Ideally, you'll wrap your WordPress template tag in enough div tags to be able to create a round cornered object that is flexible enough to scale horizontally and vertically. You can also use heading tags or probably any other XHTML tag that occurs in the element.

**Really understanding rounded corners in a table less design:**

If you haven't noticed by now, I'm a fan of A List Apart, so I'll leave it to these trusted experts to give you the complete lowdown on the details of making rounded-corner boxes with pure CSS: http://www.alistapart.com/articles/customcorners/.

Also, there are many rounded-corner generator sites that will do a lot of the work for you. If you're getting comfortable with CSS and XHTML markup, you'll be able to take the generated code from one of these sites and work it into your WordPresss style.css. RoundedCornr is my favorite: http://www.roundedcornr.com/.

To start with, just make four rounded-corner images named left-bot.gif, right-bot.gif, left-top.gif, and right-top.gif respectively (or generate them at RoundedCornr.com). Now, using a class name called .sidebarItem (you can name this class whatever you'd like), reference the images via background parameters in your CSS like the following:

```
...
.sidebarItem {
      background: #cccccc;
      background: url(../images/left-top.gif) no-repeat top left;
  /*be sure to set your
   preferred font requirements*/
}
.sidebarItem div {
      background: url(../images/right-top.gif)
                        no-repeat top right;
}
.sidebarItem div div {
background: url(../images/left-bot.gif) no-repeat bottom left;
}
.sidebarItem div div div {
background: url(roundedcornr_170953_br.png) no-repeat bottom
                                            right;
}
.sidebarItem div div div, .sidebarItem div div, .sidebarItem div,
.module{
width: 100%;
      height: 30px;
font-size: 1px;
}
.sidebarItem {
  margin: 0 30px;
}
...
```

The following is an example of the markup you should wrap your template tag(s) in:

```
  . . .
<div class='sidebarItem'> <!--//left-top.gif-->f
    <div> <!--//right-top.gif-->
     <div> <!--//left-bot.gif-->
            <div> <!--//right-bot.gif-->
                      <h3>Header</h3>
                   Content the Template Tag outputs goes in here
            </div>
       </div>
    </div>
    </div>
  . . .
```

Your end result should be something that looks like the following:

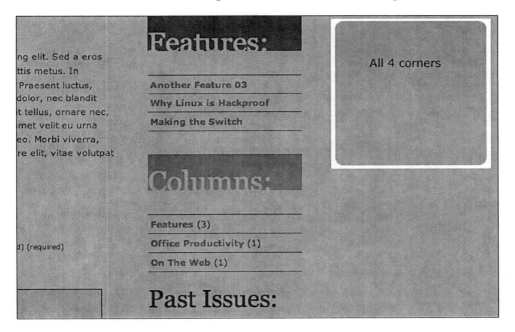

# The two-image cheat

I'll be honest; I'm on the cheater's band wagon when it comes to rounded corners. I often create locked-width designs, so I always know exactly how much room my columns can take up, and they only need to be able to expand vertically.

**More from A List Apart**

Again aListApart.com comes in with a great take on this two-image process, along with some great tips for creating the corners in your favorite graphic program: http://www.alistapart.com/articles/mountaintop/.

This rounded-corner fix works only for a set width with a variable height. This means how wide you make your graphic is as wide as your outer div should be. So, if you know the width of your columns and just need the height to expand, you can do this two-image cheat by making only a top image and an extended bottom image look like the following:

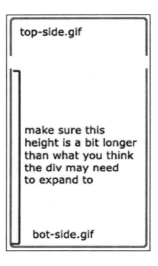

**Test this technique!**

In the previous graphic, I mention to make sure this height is a bit longer than what you think the div may need to expand to. Once you have it implemented, try it out in different browsers and set your browser's default type to different sizes. If someone has their browser set to very large type, this effect can be easily broken!

Next, reference the images in your CSS (note how much simpler the CSS becomes).

```
. . .
. sidebarItem {
      margin:0 0 10px 0;
      padding:0 0 10px 0;
      width: 150px;
      background:url(../images/bot-side.gif) bottom left
       no-repeat;
    /*be sure to set your
    preferred font requirements*/
}
.sidebarItem h3 {
      padding:8px 10px 6px 15px;
      margin-bottom:8px;
    /*be sure to set your
    preferred font requirements*/
      background:url(../images/top-side.gif) top left no-repeat;
}
. . .
```

You'll see the XHTML markup is now greatly simplified because I take advantage of my header tag as well.

```
. . .
<div class='sidebarItem'> <!--//bot-side.gif-->
    <h3>Header</h3><!--//top-side.gif-->
        Content the Template Tag outputs goes in here
</div>
. . .
```

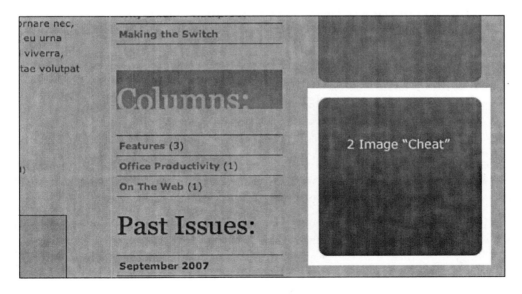

**Great for block quotes!**

I also use this technique to handle custom block quotes that are used inside static pages and posts (a great way to spice up pages so that they look like magazine pages). Again, the block quotes must be a set width, but then I only need to make sure my `<blockquote>` and `<h3>` tags are placed to have an effective style, with minimal (and semantic) markup. Just replace the `.sidebarItem{...` from the preceding code with `blockquote{...` (or make a special class to assign to your `<blockquote>` tag).

**The one-image cheat**

If you have the hang of the two-image cheat, then you can guess the one-image cheat. This method is not recommended for flexibility, but if you know the height and width will never change (say for including a single tweet feed that you know will never be more than 140 characters) and you're in a hurry, you can simply export a single rounded-box image to use in a specified `div`.

## CSS3—the new way to round corners

Those of you who are mostly interested in users surfing on Safari 3.1+ or Firefox 3.1+ are in for a few breaks. You can use the CSS 3 `border-radius` property to set up rounded corners on your `div` tags like the following:

```
.roundedCorner{
 width: 150px;
  background-color: #D9D8C6;
 -moz-border-radius: 10px;
 -webkit-border-radius: 105px;
 border: 1px solid #9E9C76;padding: 10px;
 }
```

Both Safari and Firefox seem to have their own property name. Firefox's property name starts with `-moz` while Safari's starts with `-webkit`; you'll just need to include them both to make sure each browser gets the property.

If any browser doesn't render these CSS3 properties, the `div` will gracefully degrade to a basic-styled `div` with a regular border. This is a great way to spruce up very basic designs for some users. Not great for IE users, but IE will get there, eventually.

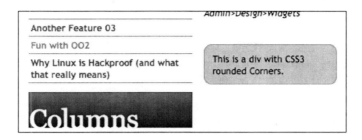

# Creative posting

In the next few sections, we're going to focus more on ideas than specific techniques. The good news is, because you're using the Firefox browser with the Web Developer Toolbar, you'll be able to easily "deconstruct" many of these site samples using the **CSS | View Style Information** and **CSS | View CSS** tools, and think of ways to creatively use them in your own themes.

HOWTOONS (`http://www.howtoons.com/`) is a great site for kids that teaches them interesting things in math, art, history, and science using fun comic illustrations. The site's blog features a great use of the Comic Sans font (we discussed in Chapter 2 how it's hard to make that font work well; here it's perfect), and the site's author has created a very unique post template.

If you explore this site with your Web Developer Toolbar, you'll see the author creates these posts using actual image tags inside the `.blogpost` class. It works, and it allows the author to easily and randomly assign bottom speech-bubble images with different cartoon scenes.

I'd like to point out that even though the author's technique works very well, using a variation of the "two-image cheat" listed previously will achieve the same effect. This would work best if you don't want to have randomly different post bottoms on each post. The point is, as you surf the Web, you'll find there are many ways to achieve the same effect. You'll need to decide which solutions work best for you and your theme.

## Breaking boundaries

The HOWTOONS site does something more than just make their posts creative. The speech-bubble bottoms of each post and the nice big background image that is positioned with `no-repeat` and `fixed` in the `bottom right`, achieve what I refer to as "boundary breaking".

Whether we realize it or not, we tend to create theme designs and page themes that adhere to a "grid" of some sort. This is not a bad thing. It makes for good design, easier use of the interface, and most importantly, easier content reading.

However, I tend to find we can become desensitized to many site designs, and thus it's interesting when a site's design displays clever ways of breaking out of the layout's grid.

Whenever I see boundary breaking done on other sites, it catches my eye and awakens it to really move around and take in the other details of the site's design that I might have otherwise ignored. As a result, I look for interesting ways to do this subtly within my own designs.

Within this book's case study, the OpenSource Magazine theme, I achieved this in the main and internal headers by extending it out past the **container2 div**. The graphic seems to swoop back to line up with the boundary of the **container2 div** for easy content reading, but the header extends past it, engaging the reader in a little design detail.

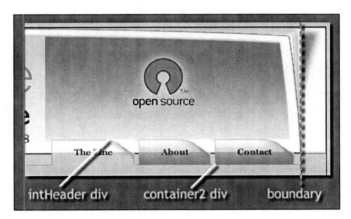

The designers at Arcsin.se have created this theme based on the book, *The Hobbit*: `http://templates.arcsin.se/demo/the-hobbit-wordpress-theme/`. His use of Bilbo's sword in the upper-left corner adds a nice layered dimension to the theme and interests your eyes in moving around, taking in all other nice details that Kashual took the time to put into it such as the detailed paisley corners, the "elfish" writing separating the posts, and so on.

Kaushal achieved this effect by splitting the sword and title graphic into two parts and then using an absolute-positioned `div` to lay the handle of the sword up against the part of the image contained inside the header `div`.

The left side of the image is opaque, so he had to pay very special attention, making sure the absolute positioning of the `div` not only aligned it with the rest of the header image but also overlaid the repeating background image perfectly.

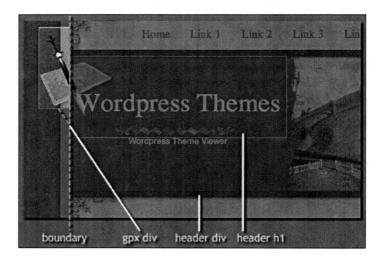

A minor drawback to the Hobbit theme is that on some browsers the delicate paisley background doesn't always overlay perfectly with the site's repeating background, even though the handle of the sword is always aligned perfectly with the `header h1` background image and, as a result, you're made aware of the image's edges against the background.

Rhodia Drive (`http://rhodiadrive.com/`) uses a similar technique to Kaushal's by using an absolute-positioned `div` to hold a CSS background image of an orange Rhodia notebook, which breaks the boundaries on the left side. Because the site's main background uses a subtle `repeat-x` gradient that has been set to `fixed`, the image uses a transparent PNG. This way, as you scroll the blog up, the background of the notebook reveals the site's true background gradient.

notepad div boundary

### Using transparent PNGs:

The great news is that IE7 and all newer browsers natively support transparent PNGs. For the few out there still clinging to IE6, there's a good IE6 fix that helps the browser to display transparent PNGs properly using a Microsoft filter that can be accessed via image, tags, and stylesheets.

The Rhodia Drive site makes use of alternative stylesheets using the `<!--[if IE6]>` solution discussed in Chapter 4, and an IE6 transparent PNG fix that you can find more about at `http://www.howtocreate.co.uk/alpha.html`.

**Want to really break the boundaries?**
Molly E. Holzschlag has an in-depth article that goes way beyond the occasional "overstepped line". With pure CSS, anything is possible and it's a great thought-provoking read: `http://www.alistapart.com/articles/outsidethegrid/`.

# Keeping tabs on current design trends

In addition to rounded corners, there are some fairly common graphic-interface techniques that seem to define those trendy "2.0" sites. These include the following:

- **Gradients and glows**: But remember, it's all about being subtle!
- **Reflections**: Again, just be subtle!
- **Vector images and creative drop-shadows**: Give your page a feeling of "space".

The following image collage depicts subtle reflection and shadows from `www.iomega.com`, vector flowers and subtle gradients from `verywildflowers.com`, and the glow effect from `http://psdtuts.com/`.

- **Thin, diagonally stripped background**: Could be for just header delineation, not necessarily the whole site's background!
- **Glass or "jelly" buttons and star-burst "stickers"**: You can get stripes from `arcsin.se` and sticker icons from `http://psdtuts.com/` (just use their search form to find "stickers").

- **Grunge-organic:** After emerging in the heyday of print design in the early 90s, it's quickly becoming the new "shiny, clean, and bright" of Web 2.0 sites. Paper-looking photos, X-File-ish folder/messy-desk layouts, decaying/misprinted fonts, natural edges, liberal (but again, subtle) doses of various spills, and drips-and-drops that we usually encounter in creative life.

  The following image collage depicts photo edge from `http://glassbury-court.com/coldspring/`, torn edges from `http://adventuretrekking.com`, and misprinted type with spills from `http://www.lataka.com/`.

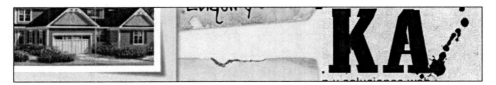

Design trends come and go. Even though the ones mentioned in the preceding list are popular today, they'll become "old hat" soon enough. Take note of and bookmark leading sites and blogs of designers, web programmers, and key contributors to the Web field. Visit these sites often. (The good ones update their interface at least once a year; most are constantly tweaking their interface adding new things little-by-little.) By keeping your finger on this design "pulse", you'll be able to recognize new trends as they start emerging. Think about how you can creatively leverage them into your own theme designs. You'll probably find yourself inventing your own unique looking interface that other people start adopting.

Learn the ins and outs of how to use your image-editing software. Right now, a large part of these design trends are graphics loaded in via CSS. To get those great trendy images into your theme, you'll need to understand CSS and, as I've already mentioned, you'll need to know how to effectively (and sometimes creatively) use the background property in your CSS rules.

**PSDTuts**

PSDTuts is a great site for picking up quick "how to" knowledge for current design techniques. The whole site is definitely worth a look through, but they have a special section for interfaces that covers how to create many design trends and visual effects using Adobe Photoshop:

`http://psdtuts.com/category/interface-tutorials/`.

**Stylegala and Smashing Magazine**

These are other good sources of keeping up on web design trends. Stylegala also has a great, clear, and concise CSS reference chart that I've found very useful from time to time:

`http://reference.sitepoint.com/css`

`http://smashingmagazine.com`

# Creative fonts

Now here's something that's a total pain and something all web designers have had to deal with. As we discussed in detail in Chapter 2, there are really only three, maybe five, truly safe fonts for the Web—fonts that you can be fairly sure that every PC and Mac (and maybe Linux) computer has natively installed. All other fonts tend to be off limits for web design. This is a shame, as typography is a huge element of great design.

In Chapter 7, we looked at the sIFR method that leverages JavaScript and Flash to display accessible custom fonts. While I'm now most happy with the sIFR method for custom fonts in a site, it's just not feasible for everyone, especially if you don't have access to the Flash IDE to embed your font in a `.fla` and compile to `.swf`. In the next few sections, we'll take a look at other W3C-compliant ways to get custom fonts into your WordPress theme.

# Graphic text

The most direct approach is to export selected text with your custom font as graphics and include the images into your layout.

The problem with using graphics instead of text is that it really messes with your site's semantics and SEO. Usually, it's the section headers that you want in the pretty font. However, if you use in-line image tags, your semantic markup gets thrown off and your SEO will fall because search engine bots really like to find those h1, h2, and h3 header tags to help them assess the real keywords in your page. Plus, if your style aesthetic changes, you have to not only change the theme but then update individual posts and pages with new images from within WordPress' Administration panel.

The solution is to use text in your header tags, yet display unique fonts as images, by setting up custom classes in your stylesheet that will "move" the text out of the way and insert your graphic font as a background image.

Again, as we mentioned in Chapter 4, search engine bots generally view your pages as though the stylesheet has been turned off. Therefore, the search engine bot and people using screen readers will keep flowing smoothly over pure text, while the rest of us get to see your sweet design and nice font selection. The bonus is that when the site design changes, all your images are handled via the CSS sheet, so you won't have to touch individual posts and static pages.

My WordPress theme makes use of Futura in the header. I'd love to use it for my section headers; however, the problem is that a lot of people don't have Futura on their computer. Even if my user has Futura on his/her machine, I think the font looks best when it's anti-aliased. While Mac users with Futura would then see it properly, PC users won't. I've created graphics of my headers using Futura and will set up my header tags with classes to move the XHTML text out of the way and use my new background images.

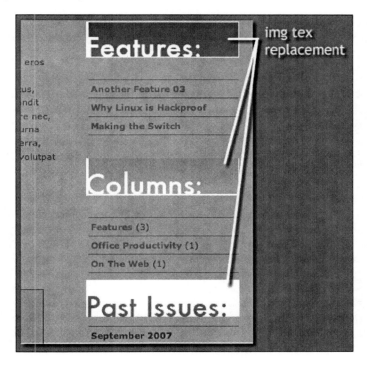

**The drawback:**

Try to keep track of the bandwidth your site needs to load. The more images and the bigger they are, of course the longer it will take to load. By switching my headers from XHTML text with a small, thin repeating background, to a full non-repeating image, I went from a 1k graphic to a 10k graphic. On the whole, especially in this day and age of broadband, it's no big deal, but it is still something to keep in mind as you try to assess what elements of your design will use pure XHTML and CSS and what will be images.

As an example, in your CSS page, set up the following class rules:

```
.textMove{ /*this is your standard for each header*/
     height: 23px;
     margin-top:10px;
     width: 145px;
     text-indent: -2000px;/*This pushes your text back so it's
invisible*/
}
.specificText{ /*specific header-text image*/
     background: url("../images/specificText.jpg") no-repeat left top;
}
```

Now, either in your theme's template pages or in posts and pages you've added via the Administration panel, apply the appropriate classes to the text headers that you would like replaced with graphics (again, if you're in the Administration panel, use the **Code** view).

```
<h2 class='textMove specificText">Section Header</h2>
```

**Assign more than one class rule to an XHTML markup object:**

As you can see in our earlier example, you can assign more than one class rule to a markup object. Simply separate each class rule with a space (not a comma), for example, `class="rule1 rule2"`. This comes in handy when you need to customize many elements, yet don't want to repeatedly copy similar properties across all of them (plus, you can easily change the main properties in just one spot instead of having to fix them all). In the case of graphic text headers, I like to make one rule that handles pushing the text out of the way and sets the height and margins for my header images; then, all my other class rules just handle the background image name, for example, `class='textMove graphicText"`. This trick works only with CSS class rules, not ID rules.

# Using PHP to make graphic headers easy

I like to simplify this process by using a simple PHP script with a local TrueType font to help me quickly generate my header graphics. I can then just include them into my CSS sheet, dynamically setting up the text that the header needs to say.

This technique is very useful if your site is going to be mainly controlled by a client, as they'll probably have to let you know every time they make a new header that needs to be a graphic loaded in via CSS. You'll be able to accommodate them on-the-fly (or even better, teach them how to do it), as opposed to having them wait for you to generate the graphic with Photoshop or Gimp and then implement the CSS.

**Heads up:** This PHP code requires the standard **ImageGD library** to be installed with your PHP configuration. This library has been on most shared/virtual hosting companies I've used; however, to be safe, contact your website host administrator to ensure the ImageGD library is installed.

You can place this script's file anywhere you like. I usually place it in my theme's image directory, `imgtxt.php`, as I will be referencing it as an image:

```
<?PHP
/*Basic JPG creator by Tessa Blakeley Silver
Free to use and change. No warranty.
Author assumes no liability, use at own risk.*/
header("Content-type: image/jpeg");
$xspan = $_REQUEST["xspan"];//if you want to adjust the width
$wrd = $_REQUEST["wrd"];//what the text is
if (!$xspan){//set a default width
        $xspan = 145;
}
$height = 20;//set a default height
$image = imagecreate($xspan, $height);
//Set your background color.
//set to what ever rgb color you want
if(!$bckCol){
    $bckCol = imagecolorallocate($image, 255, 255, 255);
}
//make text color, again set to what ever rgb color you want
if (!$txtCol){
    $txtCol = imagecolorallocate($image, 20, 50, 150);
}

    //fill background
```

```
imagefilledrectangle($image, 0, 0, $xspan, $height, $bckCol);
//set the font size on the 2nd parameter in
//set the server path (not the url path!) to the font location at
the 7th   parameter in:
imagettftext($image, 15, 0, 0, 16, $txtCol,    "home/user/sitename/
fonts/PLANE____.TTF", "$wrd");//add text
imagejpeg($image,"",80);//the last number sets the jpg compression
//free up the memory allocated for the image.
imagedestroy($image);
?>
```

This script works only with TrueType fonts. Upload the TrueType font and directory location you referenced in the script to the matching location on the server. Also, my script is very basic, with no drop-shadows or reflections. It only creates a JPG with a solid background color, TrueType font, font size, and solid font color. If you're comfortable with PHP, you can search the Web for PHP image scripts that allow you to do more with your text-image, that is, add gradient backgrounds or generate transparent PNGs or overlay other images on top of or behind your text.

From here on, you'll only need to reference this PHP script in your CSS, passing your text to it via a query string instead of the images you were generating:

```
.specificText {
  background: url("../images/imgtxt.php?xspan=300&wrd=
     This Is My New Text") no-repeat left top;
}
```

The `xspan` variable is optional; if you don't include it, the default in the script is set to 145 pixels wide. If your custom text will be longer than 145 pixels, you can set it to the pixel width you desire. (In the previous example, I have it set to 300. Be sure your width doesn't conflict with your `div` widths!)

The `wrd` variable is where you'll set your custom text. (Be aware that some characters may not come over, as the string will be `url` encoded.)

Each time you have a new graphic to generate, you can do it entirely via the theme's stylesheet. The following is a screenshot from my professional site that uses the PHP script in the previous example to generate header fonts:

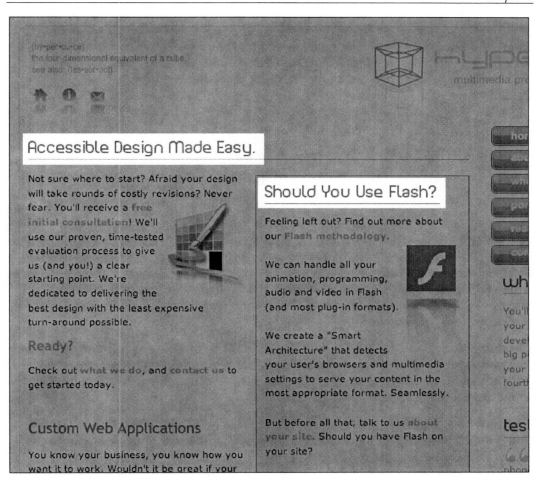

**Image replacement and sIFR plugins**

There are some good WordPress plugins that handle sIFR (we discussed the full technique in the section on Flash in Chapter 8): `http://wordpress.org/extend/plugins/wp-sifr/`.

These plugins also handle regular image replacement: `http://wordpress.org/extend/plugins/facelift-image-replacement/`.

# Custom fonts with CSS3

Safari and Firefox 3.1+ both support the `@font-face` rule that allows your stylesheet to point to a `.ttf` or `.otf` (open type font) on your server. You can then reference that font in your stylesheet using the normal `font-family` property like the following:

```
...
@font-face {
    font-family: CuprumFFU; src: url('Cuprum.otf');
}

h3 { font-family: CuprumFFU, sans-serif; }
...
```

Incidentally, IE has tried to implement this since version 5. The drawback is that they use the `.eot` format and it hasn't fully caught on. Safari and Firefox recognize the more prevalent `.ttf` and `.otf` file types with `@font-face`. However, the `.eot` format works too and also has a bonus associated with it—any font released with it was intended to be embedded in a site and thus you aren't infringing on anyone's font end-user-license agreement.

Another bonus to this method is, just like the sIFR method, it ensures people see the font you want them to see (so long as they're using a compliant browser) and it's fully accessible and functional. If someone wants to copy and paste a headline into a text file, they can!

The drawback to embedding fonts in your stylesheet using this method is that it is fraught with licensing and infringement issues. This is something we already ran into with the sIFR method in Chapter 8.

Font designers work very hard to come up with fonts and, just like illustrators and photographers, their creations are usually copyrighted and licensed for use by a purchaser for the specified use. This is an end-user agreement. The idea being that you, the end user, have the right to install the font on a single computer and create what you want with it. However, a person looking at your print design can admire your ingenious use of the font, but should not be able to easily see where it is on your computer (server so to speak) so as to download it and install it for themselves!

For this reason, if you choose to embed a font into your site, make sure you're using a font that is truly "open" and free to use (not *all* `.otf` fonts are, necessarily!) and that you won't be infringing on the designer's license by embedding it in your site where others could potentially download it.

**Good places to look for @font-face friendly fonts.**

I mentioned Font Squirrel already for sIFR fonts, but they have a handy sort by `@font-face` feature too: `http://www.fontsquirrel.com/fontface`.

The Webfonts site has a helpful page of fonts suitable for embedding: `http://www.webfonts.info/wiki/index.php?title=Fonts_available_for_%40font-face_embedding`.

# Good design isn't always visual—looking at SEO

At this point you've gone to the trouble of creating a semantic, user-friendly, and accessible XHTML theme, and one of the benefits of that structure is that it helps with SEO (Search Engine Optimization, if you haven't guessed by now). You might as well go all out and take time to set up a few more optimizations.

## Search engine friendly URLs

WordPress URLs by default are dynamic. This means they are a query string of the `index.php` page—for example, `http://mysite.com/?p=123`.

In the past, dynamic URLs were known to break search engine bots that either didn't know what to do when they hit a question mark or ampersand and/or started indexing entire sites as "duplicate content", which lowered page ranking because everything looked like it was coming from the same page (usually the `index.php` page).

This is no longer the case, at least not with the "big boy" search engines such as Google; but you never know who is searching for you, using what service.

Also, by changing the dynamic string URL to a more SEF (Search Engine Friendly) URL, it's a little harder for people to directly manipulate your URLs because they can't clearly see what variable they're changing once it's in a search engine friendly URL.

WordPress has this SEF URL feature built-in, but only if you're running PHP on Apache.

Go to **Administration | Settings | Permalinks (Administration | Options | Permalinks** in version 2.3.x) and simply switch the **Default** selection to either **Day and name**, **Numeric**, or **Custom Structure** based.

I like to select **Custom Structure** and tell my structure to be /%category%/
%postname%/. That way, my URLs will first reflect the category they are posted to,
and then the permalink title—your post's title with (-) dashes put in for spaces. If
your blog is going to be more date based, then one of the presets might be a better
option for you.

WordPress edits the .htaccess file in the installation's root directory
to get SEF URLs working. If WordPress doesn't have permission or can't
create/edit this file, the Administration panel will give you instructions
to manually copy the code into the .htaccess file. You'll need server
permission to do this. If you're unsure of how to do this, your best bet is
to contact your web hosting provider's support team.

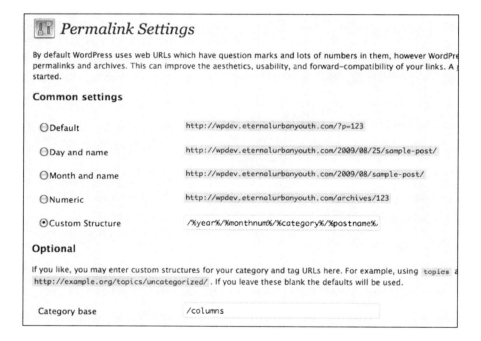

Search engine bots will think the forward slashes are directories, and will not freak
out about question marks and ampersands or assume that everything on your site is
really the same page.

**Forget the search engine friendly! What about people friendly URLs?**

WordPress is great at people friendly or comprehensive URLs. Comprehensive URLs are one of the great things about WordPress and a feature that places it above other comparable CMS and blog tools currently. (Even if you select "SEF" URL, it can still be a long URL of odd numbers, and incomprehensible variable names, separated by slashes.)

Sometimes, you're in situations where you just can't copy and paste your link. It's great to have lunch with your friend and be able to verbally give him/her the URL to your latest web-rant and know that he/she will easily remember `http://myurl.com/rants/newrant`. Also, clearly named URLs greatly boost your "link trust" (that's what I call it anyway). If the relevant link you've e-mailed people or posted in your blog, or that you have posted as a comment on someone else's blog, doesn't appear to clearly have any indication of what you promised is in it, people are much less likely to click on it (do you like clicking on strings of odd numbers and cryptic variable names?). And while the impact of keywords in URLs seems to be waning, there are SEO experts who still swear that your URLs should contain the top keywords in your document. If you haven't done so already, be sure to take advantage of this feature in WordPress.

# Keywords and descriptions

Most people just hardcode some general keyword and description meta tags into their theme's template files that best describe the overall gist of their WordPress site. However, if you want to aid in your content being indexed by search engines a little better and/or you use your WordPress site to cover a wide range of diverse information that an overall gist of keywords and a description just won't cover, you'll want to make metatags in your template files a bit more dynamic. There are several ways in which you can add keyword and description meta tags for individual posts and pages to your WordPress theme. You can use the available template tags within your theme's `header.php` or other header template pages to add content to your meta tags. Or you can install third-party plugins that will expand your administration page options and give you a little more control than what is produced by your post's content. In the next few sections, we'll look at doing it yourself as well as a few choice plugins to help you out.

# DYI meta tags

For most people (myself included), this method works well. In my `header.php` (or other header) template files, I set up my meta tags for keywords and descriptions. I then take advantage of the `single_cat_title()`, `single_post_title()`, and `the_exerpt()` template tags.

In my keywords meta tag, I include the `single_cat_title()` and then the `single_post_title()` tags like this:

```
...
    <meta name="keywords" content="<?echo single_cat_title("");?>,
<?echo    single_post_title("");?>" />
...
```

The previous modification will give my page the following runtime output:

```
...
<meta name="keywords" content="Office Productivity, Fun with OO2" />
...
```

This modification will be fairly comprehensive if you keep keywords in mind while writing your titles and assigning them to categories.

Setting up the description tag takes just a bit more as `the_exerpt()` tag works only within the loop. Therefore, you just need to make sure you set up a little mini loop for it to run in, like the following:

```
...
    <meta name='description" content="
    <? if(is_category() || is_archive()) {
        echo the_excerpt();
    } else {
      echo "This is my default description to use if a post or page
      doesn't have an excerpt";
    } ?>
    " />
...
```

The previous code will produce a description that looks like the following:

```
...
<meta name='description" content="This is the optional excerpt for
this article, Fun with OO2. I use the Optional Excerpt field to aid in
my description meta tags." />
...
```

## Meta tag plugins

If you're a serious blogger and really need more robust options for your meta tags, you might want to try one of the following two WordPress plugins:

- **All in One SEO Pack by uberdose 2.0.** (`http://wordpress.org/extend/plugins/all-in-one-seo-pack/` ):

  This plugin not only utilizes the `the_exerpt()` tag as we just did, but also allows you to set your own specific keywords and several other great options for handling robust meta tag information for each post.

- **Meta SEO Pack by Daniel Frużyński (**`http://wordpress.org/extend/plugins/meta-seo-pack/`**):**

  This plugin leverages several WordPress template tags and allows you to choose your preference of how they're used to generate specific `<title>` tags in your header and meta tags.

# Summary

We've reviewed the main tips you should have picked up from the previous chapters and covered some key tips for easily implementing today's coolest CSS tricks into your theme. We also saw a few final SEO tips that you'll probably run into once you really start putting content into your site or when you turn the site over to the content editors. I hope you've enjoyed this book and found it useful in aiding your WordPress theme creations.

# Index

## F

**Firebug** 137
**Firefox**
  about 118
  developing for 18
  need for 17
  testing with 118
**Firefox browser** 17
**Flash**
  ActiveX restriction 228
  ActiveX restriction, swfObject method 228
  adding, in theme 227
  advantages 227
  Flash swf file, passing variable from
    WordPress 231-233
  jQuery Flash plugin 230
  users, handling 228
**Flash player plugin**
  advantages 227
  Flash 227
  Flash swf file, passing variable from
    WordPress 231, 233
**fonts, design techniques**
  @font-face feature 263
  custom fonts, CSS3 used 262, 263
  drawbacks 258
  graphic text 256, 257
  PHP script, using 259-261
  XHTML markup object, one class rule 258
**fonts, text-typography**
  Arial and Helvetica 40
  cascading 41
  Century Gothic 40
  Century Schoolbook 41
  Comic Sans Serif 40
  Courier New 41
  default links 46, 47
  font stacks 42
  Georgia 41
  paragraphs 45
  pixels, need for 43
  proportion, maintaining 44, 45
  San-Serif Fonts 40
  Serif Fonts 41
  sIFR 43
  sizing 43-46

Times New Roman and Times 41
Trebuchet 40
Verdana 40

## G

**generated class styles**
  about 156
  body_class class styles 162
  class output, by media manager 157
  class output, by Sidebar widget 159
  class output, by wp_list_categories template
    tag 161
  class output, by wp_list_pages template tag
    160
  feature 156
  media manager used, image options 157
  post_class class styles 161
  search bar ID 156
**GNU GPL license** 146, 147
**Google Reader widget**
  about 211
  installing 211, 213
**graphic editor** 16
**graphic interface techniques**
  glass (jelly) button and star-burst stickers
    254
  gradients and glows 254
  grunge-organic 255
  grunge organic 255
  reflections 254
  thin, diagonally stripped background 254
  vector images and creative drop-shadows
    254
  vector images and creative drop shadows
    254

## H

**home page, WordPress theme**
  about 106
  custom home.php template file, creating
    106, 107
  second sidebar, creating 107
**hooks** 83
**HTML editor**
  features 15

**[PACKT]**
PUBLISHING

Thank you for buying
# WordPress 2.8 Theme Design

## Packt Open Source Project Royalties

When we sell a book written on an Open Source project, we pay a royalty directly to that project. Therefore by purchasing WordPress 2.8 Theme Design, Packt will have given some of the money received to the WordPress project.

In the long term, we see ourselves and you — customers and readers of our books — as part of the Open Source ecosystem, providing sustainable revenue for the projects we publish on. Our aim at Packt is to establish publishing royalties as an essential part of the service and support a business model that sustains Open Source.

If you're working with an Open Source project that you would like us to publish on, and subsequently pay royalties to, please get in touch with us.

## Writing for Packt

We welcome all inquiries from people who are interested in authoring. Book proposals should be sent to author@packtpub.com. If your book idea is still at an early stage and you would like to discuss it first before writing a formal book proposal, contact us; one of our commissioning editors will get in touch with you.

We're not just looking for published authors; if you have strong technical skills but no writing experience, our experienced editors can help you develop a writing career, or simply get some additional reward for your expertise.

## About Packt Publishing

Packt, pronounced 'packed', published its first book "Mastering phpMyAdmin for Effective MySQL Management" in April 2004 and subsequently continued to specialize in publishing highly focused books on specific technologies and solutions.

Our books and publications share the experiences of your fellow IT professionals in adapting and customizing today's systems, applications, and frameworks. Our solution-based books give you the knowledge and power to customize the software and technologies you're using to get the job done. Packt books are more specific and less general than the IT books you have seen in the past. Our unique business model allows us to bring you more focused information, giving you more of what you need to know, and less of what you don't.

Packt is a modern, yet unique publishing company, which focuses on producing quality, cutting-edge books for communities of developers, administrators, and newbies alike. For more information, please visit our website: www.PacktPub.com.

PUBLISHING

## WordPress 2.7 Complete

ISBN: 978-1-847196-56-9          Paperback: 296 pages

Create your own complete blog or web site from scratch with WordPress

1. Everything you need to set up your own feature-rich WordPress blog or web site

2. Clear and practical explanations of all aspects of WordPress

3. In-depth coverage of installation, themes, syndication, and podcasting

4. Explore WordPress as a fully functioning content management system

## WordPress 2.7 Cookbook

ISBN: 978-1-847197-38-2          Paperback: 275 pages

100 simple but incredibly useful recipes to take control of your WordPress blog layout, themes, widgets, plug-ins, security, and SEO

1. Take your WordPress blog to the next level with solutions to common WordPress problems that make your blog better, smarter, faster, and more secure

2. Enhance your SEO and make more money online by applying simple hacks

3. Fully tested and compatible with WordPress 2.7

4. Part of Packt's Cookbook series: Each recipe is a carefully organized sequence of instructions to complete the task as efficiently as possible

Please check **www.PacktPub.com** for information on our titles

Breinigsville, PA USA
21 January 2010
231106BV00003B/39/P